The Best
AMERICAN
ESSAYS
2005

GUEST EDITORS OF
THE BEST AMERICAN ESSAYS

1986 ELIZABETH HARDWICK
1987 GAY TALESE
1988 ANNIE DILLARD
1989 GEOFFREY WOLFF
1990 JUSTIN KAPLAN
1991 JOYCE CAROL OATES
1992 SUSAN SONTAG
1993 JOSEPH EPSTEIN
1994 TRACY KIDDER
1995 JAMAICA KINCAID
1996 GEOFFREY C. WARD
1997 IAN FRAZIER
1998 CYNTHIA OZICK
1999 EDWARD HOAGLAND
2000 ALAN LIGHTMAN
2001 KATHLEEN NORRIS
2002 STEPHEN JAY GOULD
2003 ANNE FADIMAN
2004 LOUIS MENAND
2005 SUSAN ORLEAN

The Best
AMERICAN
ESSAYS®
2005

Edited and with an Introduction
by SUSAN ORLEAN

Robert Atwan, Series Editor

HOUGHTON MIFFLIN COMPANY
BOSTON · NEW YORK 2005

ISSN 0888-3742
ISBN 0-618-35712-2
ISBN 0-618-35713-0 (pbk.)

Printed in the United States of America

QUM 10 9 8 7 6 5 4 3 2 1

Permission to come

Contents

Foreword

THIS IS THE TWENTIETH volume in *The Best American Essays* series. When I began work on the first book in 1985, the timing didn't look promising. Most major magazines were so heavily into journalism and commentary that they rarely welcomed the type of ruminative pieces that veteran editors — eschewing the word "essay" — habitually called "thumb sucking." Though they were being published, memoirs (then largely still a plural) hadn't yet captured the public attention as the singular "memoir" eventually would. Essays tended to be concealed here and there, for the most part in little magazines, and the essayists themselves seemed to be an apologetic breed.

With that in mind, I nervously contributed to the first book a foreword that began with E. B. White's disheartening comment, made some nine years earlier, that he was not "fooled about the place of the essayist in twentieth-century American letters." "The essayist," he said, "unlike the novelist, the poet, and the playwright, must be content in his self-imposed role of second-class citizen." I hoped that this was no longer true and that the series would showcase what I considered to be a long-neglected genre in the exciting process of being revitalized by an emerging group of younger writers and journalists.

Despite what looked like a rekindling of the form, my publishers at Ticknor & Fields (then an imprint of Houghton Mifflin) and I prudently agreed that "essay" remained an off-putting term, still too closely associated in most people's minds with the dreaded classroom assignment. (Perhaps it still is: a *New York Times* crossword clue for "essay" is "Blue book filler.") Essays would be a hard sell. So we decided to give the idea a two-year trial and afterward decide if an annual series was worth continuing. At the time, I couldn't be certain that there would even be a sufficient number of essays of literary merit published in periodicals each year to make the project viable. For a proposal, I sent in a description of intentions along with a sample of about ten recent essays; I had my fingers crossed that — as I promised — "there were plenty more where these came from."

Using my dot-matrix printer would look shoddy, so I typed out and mailed perhaps one hundred letters formally announcing the new series to magazine editors across the country. I received many encouraging words that boiled down to: "It's about time someone began paying attention to essays." But a number of editors also discouragingly added: "I rarely see any essays, though I wish I did." I also soon discovered that people had radically divergent ideas of what an essay was. A few editors of literary periodicals dutifully submitted academic articles and professional literary criticism — not the sparkling stuff I was eager to feature. When I received a paper from a dentist describing a new periodontal procedure, generously sprinkled with vivid photographs of diseased gums and accompanied with the comment "This is the best essay I ever wrote," I feared the worst.

Elizabeth Hardwick was courageous enough to assume the role of guest editor for the inaugural volume and to attempt the first introduction to the art of the essay. In so doing she established the distinctive literary tone of the series. Her final table of contents consisted of seventeen essays — the fewest of all the collections — but they strongly suggested that E. B. White's gloomy view of the essayist's literary status could be successfully challenged. One reason for this was that Hardwick, a novelist and essayist herself, included first-class essays by so many "first-class citizens": the poets Robert Fitzgerald and Joseph Brodsky (who the following year would win the Noble Prize in literature), and such well-known novelists as Joyce Carol Oates, Gore Vidal, Cynthia Ozick, Julian Barnes, and Donald Barthelme. Surely, E. B. White's distinction was hard to apply when so many talented poets and novelists clearly felt comfortable writing essays (and of course always had). Hardwick's collection, with a few notable exceptions (such as a remarkably perceptive essay on "Morality and Foreign Policy" by

George F. Kennan), was unmistakably literary. To help advance the essayist's level of citizenship in the republic of letters, Houghton Mifflin also issued an attractively boxed set that paired the essay volume with the publisher's venerable and highly respected short story series. To my mind, the shrink-wrapped package seemed to say to the world: See, essays are literature too.

We went into the do-or-die second year buoyed up not by outstanding sales but by the simple fact that we now felt confident that a sufficient number of literary essays were being published each year to justify a collection. And I felt I had helped boost the spirit of essayists. Upon the publication of the 1986 book, I received a letter from another one of its contributors, Stephen Jay Gould. "On behalf of all of us," he wrote, "who labor in the under-appreciated genre of the essay, I thank you for the first volume and for the promise of your continuing series."

I was delighted when Gay Talese agreed to guest-edit the second volume. American literary nonfiction had since midcentury followed two branching paths: down one path meandered the long-established personal, reflective, or intellectual essay. These could be eloquently familiar (E. B. White), socially urgent (James Baldwin), culturally and critically astute (Edmund Wilson and Elizabeth Hardwick), or passionately naturalist (Loren Eisley). This established strand of essay could take various forms, adopt a variety of voices, and nudge the edges of conventional nonfiction, but it was more or less an identifiable literary commodity. Many of these essays had become specimens of the genre, included again and again in college writing textbooks and anthologies. Once more "Once More to the Lake"!

By the 1960s, however, Tom Wolfe, John Sack, Terry Southern, Lillian Ross, Truman Capote, John McPhee, and Talese — among many others — pioneered a new mode of creative journalism that audaciously incorporated literary techniques from other genres into the standard magazine profile or feature article. Unlike the established essay, this branch of literary nonfiction was not easily identifiable and at first sparked a great deal of controversy: How much was accurate reporting? How much was fiction? Was it possible that journalism could also be *imaginative?* Was creative nonfiction — a term then coming into vogue — not so much a necessary literary designation as an oxymoron?

By the mid-eighties, as we launched the series, it had become impossible to ignore the cultural impact of literary journalism. To restrict *The Best American Essays* to the older, established (but still vital) genre would, I thought, seriously limit the books and prevent them from reflecting the ways in which narrative reporting had reinvigorated the essay. One could be guided by the slogans of two great poet-critics from the not too distant past: Matthew Arnold, "Journalism is literature in a hurry"; and Ezra Pound, "Literature is news that stays news." Like the Pop Art of the period, the New Journalism had succeeded in erasing many invidious artistic distinctions, and writers like Joan Didion had shown what the cross-pollination of nonfiction genres could lead to in the evolution of a new essay. Many of the New Journalists — Talese included — had not originally thought of their magazine features as essays, but the 1987 collection served as a clear indication that literary journalists had permanently entered the world of American letters. In the foreword to that volume I wrote: "The especially well-crafted journalism of the past two decades — though it may have dealt the final blow to the old 'familiar' essay — has in many ways given new life to the form, broadening the range of what an essay can be and do."

But something else was happening as well. And the next year Annie Dillard put it perfectly in the 1988 collection when she observed that the essay had "joined the modern world." Dillard's edition featured another strand of the American essay, a third path, one that emphasized the genre's imaginative possibilities. She noted a tendency among essayists to blur conventional prose genres by introducing such "bold contrivances" as fragmented narratives, symbolic imagery, and experimental structures. The 1988 collection highlighted a new American essay that could compete creatively with fiction and poetry: "The essay," Dillard wrote, "can do everything a poem can do, and everything a short story can do — everything but fake it."

As this brief history should make clear, the first three volumes laid the foundation of the series and helped define the range of essays that would annually be considered and featured. There are, of course, no precise labels for such fluid and malleable prose forms. But in volume after volume, readers have discovered essays that behave personally and familiarly, others that take a journalistic stance combining reportage with a sharp individual perspective and style, and still others that in their "impure forms" may appear indistinguishable from fiction, meditation, or lyric. Probably no other literary genre today is so diverse.

The essay's diversity can be taken as a sign of its growing vitality and popularity. But as I suggested earlier, in the first few years of the series I'd anxiously noted signs of what could only be interpreted as the essay's decline. In 1990, the *New York Times* ran a review of an essay collection headlined "A Book with the Nerve to Use 'Essays' in Its Title." The book under review was Wilfred Sheed's *Essays in Disguise.* If the term were that culturally taboo, I wondered, how could we realistically be planning a book every year with that word appearing explicitly in its title? So it was especially gratifying to watch this year's NCAA men's basketball finals. As I settled in front of the TV to enjoy the annual sport spectacular along with millions of other Americans, I was amazed to learn that at halftime viewers would be treated to an "essay" by sportscaster Dick Enberg. There was no disguise. The E-word had finally made prime time.

The Best American Essays features a selection of the year's outstanding essays, essays of literary achievement that show an awareness of craft and forcefulness of thought. Hundreds of essays are gathered annually from a wide variety of national and regional publications. These essays are then screened, and approximately one hundred are turned over to a distinguished guest editor, who may add a few personal discoveries and who makes the final selections. The list of notable essays appearing in the back of the book is drawn from a final comprehensive list that includes not only all of the essays submitted to the guest editor but also many that were not submitted.

To qualify for the volume, the essay must be a work of respectable literary quality, intended as a fully developed, independent essay on a subject of general interest (not specialized scholarship), originally written in English (or translated by the author) for publication in an American periodical during the calendar year. Today's essay is a highly flexible and shifting form, however, so these criteria are not carved in stone.

Magazines editors who want to be sure their contributors will be considered each year should submit issues or subscriptions to: Robert Atwan, Series Editor, The Best American Essays, P.O. Box

220, Readville, MA 02137. Writers, editors, and readers can also contact me by writing to: Robert Atwan, Director, Blue Hills Writing Institute, Curry College, 1071 Blue Hill Avenue, Milton, MA 02186-2395. You can also visit www.curry.edu and look for the writing institute under "Continuing Education." If you use the Curry College address, please be sure to indicate "Attention: Best American Essays" on the envelope. Writers and editors are welcome to submit published essays from any American periodical for consideration; unpublished work does not qualify for the series and cannot be reviewed or evaluated. Please note: all submissions must be directly from the publication and not in manuscript or printout format.

For this edition, I'd like to acknowledge a friend and colleague, David A. Fedo (vice president and dean of the faculty of Curry College), for his kind encouragement and support over the past ten years. David was especially helpful in setting up the Blue Hills Writing Institute, where each August the "Life Writing" program features notable authors — such as Rebecca McLanahan, Sven Birkerts, Kyoko Mori, and Danielle Ofri — whose essays have appeared in this series. I'd also like to thank several people I work with directly at Houghton Mifflin and who help make this annual collection possible — Deanne Urmy, Ryan Mann, and Larry Cooper. It was a distinct pleasure working this year with Susan Orlean, a writer who weaves together the art of the essay and the craft of reporting so skillfully that no seams ever show. This volume of twenty-five remarkable essays reflects what we are accustomed to find throughout her writing: an abiding honesty, curiosity, humor, and civility.

R.A.

Introduction

NOT LONG AGO, I went to New Hampshire to watch some dogsled races, and during a break in the action I wandered into a hobby shop on the main drag of the town. It was a dusty old store, dim and crowded, the shelves loaded with the usual array of hobby gear — Popsicle sticks, model railroad switches, beads and buttons and toxic glue. I have no use for Popsicle sticks once the Popsicles are eaten, and no wish to build miniature railroads or embellish the surfaces of the objects in my home, so it seemed there was nothing in the store for me. But as I was about to leave, a large box behind the cash register caught my eye. It was, according to the label, the amazing Skilcraft Visible Cow, an anatomically accurate model kit featuring "highly detailed parts representing the structures of the skeleton and vital organs." The picture on the label showed a big cow — a Guernsey, perhaps? or maybe a Milking Shorthorn? — made of some sort of clear glossy plastic. The exterior of the Visible Cow was invisible. The visible part of it was its innards — the major bones, the most popular organs, the spine, the ribs, the tongue. It was a marvelous construction, a complete inversion of the usual order of things: everything you usually expect to see of a cow was see-through, and everything you usually can't make out was there, plain as day. The insides of the cow were held together by its transparent shell, which gave order and structure to the jumble of guts and skeleton and plumbing. I purchased the Visible Cow, and putting it together (which, according to the label, will allow me to "Study Anatomy As You Build Your Visible Cow Model") is on my long-term To Do list. In the meantime, I keep the box in my office so I can look at it every day.

Which brings me, more directly than it might seem, to the subject of essays. Anytime I read an essay, write an essay, or, as is the case here, sort through and select the very best of a year's essays, I find myself wondering what an essay *is* — what makes up the essential parts and structure of the form. Is it a written inquiry? A meditation? A memoir? Does it concern the outside world or just probe the writer's interior world? Can it be funny? Does it have answers or does it just raise questions? Does it argue a point or is it a cool, impartial view of the world? Does it have a prescribed tone or is it absolutely individual — a conversation between the writer and reader, as idiosyncratic as any conversation might ever be?

As near as I can figure, an essay can be most of the above — it can be a query, a reminiscence, a persuasive tract, an exploration; it can look inward or outward; it can crack a lot of jokes. What it need not be is objective. An essay can certainly present facts and advocate a position, but that seems quite different from objectivity, whereby a writer just delivers information, adding nothing in the process. Instead, essays take their tone and momentum from the explicit presence of the writer in them and the distinctiveness of each writer's perspective. That makes essays definitely subjective — not in the skewed, unfair sense of subjectivity, but in the sense that essays are conversations, and they should have all the nuances and attitude that any conversation has. I'm sure that's why newspapers so rarely generate great essays: even in the essay-allowed zone of a newspaper, the heavy breath of Objective Newspaper Reporting is always blowing down the writer's neck. And certainly there is no prescribed tone that is "correct" for essays. Sometimes it seems that they have a sameness of manner, a kind of earnest, hand-wringing solemnity. Is this necessary? I don't think so. Many of the essays that intrigued me this year were funny, or unusually structured, or tonally adventurous — in other words, not typical in sound or shape. What mattered was that they conveyed the writer's journey, and did it intelligently, gracefully, honestly, and with whatever voice or shape fit best.

So essays can range in content, tone, structure, and approach. It's a loose construct. I happen to love essays that take a small notion and find the universe inside it. As Emerson advised, "Put the argument into a concrete shape, into an image, some hard phrase, round and solid as a ball, which they can see and handle and carry home with them, and the cause is half won." An essay spun out of ideas only feels too wifty to me; one that's all observation doesn't seem to have enough soul. What moves me most is an essay in which the writer turns something over and over in his or her head, and in examining it finds a bit of truth about human nature and life and the experience of inhabiting this planet. To follow as a writer examines the nature of long-term love through the experience of removing a boil on his back, or comes to understand her sexuality by questioning the history of her mother's cooking — two of the pieces I've chosen to include here — is to read a wonderful essay and to appreciate the elasticity of the form. In many ways, it's the most intimate of reading experiences, in which the reader is invited to follow along as the writer works through a thought or excavates a memory. The writer can be explicit, in the first person, or just implicit, as the person behind the words, but he or she is absolutely, powerfully present. It's as if, for those few thousand words, we are invited deep inside someone's mind.

Which brings me, after some rumination, back to my Visible Cow. I know it's ultimately impossible and probably unnecessary to define what an essay is, but I think the Visible Cow offers an interesting and tangible analogue. What holds an essay together — the cowhide, so to speak — should be nearly invisible. The structure should be organic, revealing only the very natural way a smart person's mind works through a topic, making connections and conclusions as they occur. And an essay can contain many thoughts and observations (those organs! those bones!) that might not seem to fit together, but in the end lead to a satisfying whole — a cow.

And if you'll allow me to torture this poor cow — the Visible one and now all the real, live cows on the planet — for one more moment: just as each cow is individual, each of these essays is, too, though they are identifiably part of the same species. I realized only after the fact that I'd chosen to include a number of essays that deal with the same subject — cooking, for instance. What's notable is that they deal with their subject so differently that they stand as a perfect example of how singular an essay is, and how they reflect the thinking and emotions of the writer, rather than merely recording a subject. That is what makes reading essays so marvelous. Nothing is ever more singular than our efforts to tell each other the story of ourselves, of what it's like to be who we are, to think the things we think, to live the lives we live.

Susan Orlean

The Best
AMERICAN
ESSAYS
2005

ROGER ANGELL

La Vie en Rose

FROM THE NEW YORKER

A SATURDAY EVENING IN MAY, 1949, and I am taking a moonlight leak in the garden at Ditchley. Hedges and statuary cast
elegant shadows nearby, but I've had a bit of wine and it probably doesn't occur to me that this is one of the better alfresco loos
I have visited — the Italianate garden installed by Sir Geoffrey
Jellicoe in 1935, as a culminating grace note to the celebrated
Georgian pile of Ditchley Park, in Oxfordshire, designed by James
Gibbs and built in 1722. Ditchley, with a deer park and a village
within its borders, is headed inexorably for the English Heritage
Register but for the moment remains the country home of my old
friend Marietta FitzGerald and her delightful, fairly recent second
husband, Ronald Tree, who is standing a few feet to my left here,
in identical posture, his chin in the air as he breathes in traces of
boxwood and early primrose. Beyond him, also aiming, is Major
Metcalfe, a neighbor of Ronnie's and another dinner guest of his
on this evening. He is the same Major Metcalfe who proved such a
staunch friend to the Prince of Wales at Fort Belvedere during the
difficult abdication days in 1936, and who stood up as best man
the following year, when the prince, reborn as the Duke of Wind-
sor, married Wallis Warfield Simpson in Monts, France. Major Edward Dudley Metcalfe, MVO, MC, I mean, who at any moment,
surely, will invite me to call him Fruity, the way everybody else does.
He and I are in black tie, and the moonlight lies magically on his
satin lapels, just as it does on mine. Ronnie is wearing a beige velvet smoking, perfectly OK for a country host, I guess, but he looks
less dashing or narrow, less right, than Fruity and I do. Good old

Fruity. Soon we three will amble back up the terrace steps, toward the tall lighted doors and the sounds of conversation and rattled dice within. My wife, Evelyn, ravishing in her silk top and shimmery gray skirt, will look up from the backgammon table, where she has taken on Ronnie's first son, Michael (he's in his late twenties), and has just realized that she's in over her head. "How much is eleven pounds?" she whispers urgently. It's around forty-five dollars, I figure quickly — big bucks, to us — but of course none of this is for keeps. Only it is, we find.

Memory stops here. Nothing more can be made of that ancient weekend. Evelyn and I were impostors — not members of the bon ton but a visiting, unembarrassed American couple, still in their twenties, on a lucky six-week dive into England and France, mostly paid for by the magazine *Holiday*, where I was an editor and writer. I was scouting the Continent for writers and picture ideas, or some such scam. We had married in 1942, were separated by the war, and when it was over swiftly acquired New York jobs and friends, an apartment in the upper reaches of Riverside Drive, a two-tone Ford Tudor, a bulldog, and, sixteen months before this, a baby daughter, now in the hands of an affectionate grandmother. The works. But, given this chance, we grabbed it, booked passage on the slowpoke liner *De Grasse* — the only French Line vessel as yet restored to the Atlantic run after the war — and after six entrancing days and nights debarked and did the tourist thing. Westminster Abbey, the bombed-out City, St. Paul's. Green Park in the spring sunshine. The British Museum. Oxford and the Trees. Paris. The Orangerie and the Cimetière Père-Lachaise. Our rented Citroën Onze — with its chevron-striped grille, crooked-arm gearshift, low power, and sneaky reverse gear — would carry us faithfully along the uncrowded two-lane routes to the south. What was the French word we needed for "windshield wiper," after ours gave out during a thunderstorm outside Le Puy? Why, *essuie-glace*, of course. Who could forget that? There was a funeral going on at the cathedral in Chartres when we arrived, the soaring gray columns enfolded in black at their base. The next noon, on Ascension Day, we walked into Bourges Cathedral to blazing candlelight and mauve sunlit shafts above, just in time for a raft of first Communions. "Be joyful, *mes enfants*," said the white-hatted bishop to the three-deep rows of pink-cheeked, well-combed nine-year-olds. "You are being accepted into the one true Church, here in the most beautiful structure in the world." Why, yes — where do we go to sign up?

We were lucky, but this was long ago and one wants more than a pee on the grass or the *tong* of a funeral bell, behind the altar at Chartres, to bring it clear. But only anecdote continues to work. Late at night aboard the *De Grasse,* Evelyn is dancing with our friend Tom Hollyman, a *Holiday* photographer, and Jean Hollyman with a young purser. At our tiny table, with its crowded champagne glasses and triangular white CGT ashtrays, I am in deep converse with a fellow passenger, Alfonso Bedoya, the Mexican movie actor who was such a hit last year as the bandito chief in *The Treasure of the Sierra Madre.* (Encounters like this happened all the time on the Atlantic run just then. The dearth of shipping — the *De Grasse* herself had recently been raised from the bottom of the Gironde estuary, where the Gerimans scuttled her — made for a travelers' bottleneck, where celebrities and the rest of us squashed cheerfully together for a few days at a time.) Here, sometimes in French, sometimes in Spanish, Bedoya is discussing monetary or agricultural issues — I'm not always sure which, though I nod in agreement — in emerging Latin America. Part of me is listening to him and another part following the ship's five-piece dance band as it shifts shamelessly from "La Seine" to "J'Attendrai," but in truth I am only waiting for my new friend to flash his enormous teeth and cry, "Badges, badges — I don't have to show you any steenking badges!"

In London, I know, we caught Laurence Olivier as Chorus and Vivien Leigh as an anguished Antigone at the New Theatre, but not a word or gesture of it comes back now. Instead, I see us sitting down to dinner at the Café Brevaux in Paris, with *The New Yorker*'s Janet Flanner, where another guest of hers, Tennessee Williams, seizes Evelyn's hand and presses it to his forehead. "What do you think?" he asks, and Evelyn, shaking her head sadly, supplies the right answer. "I think you're really getting sick," she says. Looking for a second opinion, he produces a thermometer from an inner pocket, shakes it down, and takes his temperature behind a menu. "Go home, Tenn," says Flanner in her field marshal's contralto, but he stays on and does away with a white-asparagus salad, his veal Marengo and *fonds d'artichauts à la crème,* and, a brave though gravely ill playwright, remains as well for a *mousseline au chocolat* and the cheese platter and coffee and a tiny Armagnac and then, why not, one more.

Southward in our Citroën, we came out of the mountains at Alès and on from there to Les Baux (no one else turns up for lunch at the fabled Baumanière) and Arles and Nîmes (there's a bloodless Provençal bullfight in the blazing-hot Roman amphitheater) and Tarascon and, with the sea now shining off to our right, Saint-Tropez and Antibes. Arrived at our destination, we're at breakfast on the terrace of the modest Hôtel Metropole, in Beaulieu-sur-Mer, when we are startled by the unmistakable sounds of a Boeing 377 starting its four propellers — *WHEE-EEE-eee-ouzzzze* — and warming for takeoff — *RhhhOUUMMMM!* — from a room on the second floor. It is the S. J. Perelman family — Sid and Laura and twelve-year-old Abby and ten-year-old Adam — or, more accurately, the pair of caged mynah birds they brought along from Singapore to this wildly accidental meeting, here by the lapping Mediterranean. The Perelmans had been in the Far East for three months and, with many stops along the way (giving the mynahs a chance to tune up their act), were by degrees heading home.

Perelman, already a Mount Rushmore eminence on the landscape of American humor, was more a friend of my mother and stepfather's than mine, but, anxious for company as tourists are, we two families palled up: ate and drank and swam and talked together and, jamming all six of us into the Citroën, drove up the corniches and then back down from Menton, mousing around (as Sid put it) among the white villages, with their withered trees, dusty pétanque courts, and alleylike streets, half empty in this off-season. Mornings, Abby serenaded our breakfasts from above, practicing on her well-traveled cello. Sid, natty and with his gagman's jaw always fractionally agape, followed every conversation with terrifying attention. He and the tall, dark-eyed Laura liked it here and arranged to rent a villa in Èze for an extra week or two. When we looked the place over one morning, the kids went rocketing off down a steep path to the shore while Perelman conferred with the owner and a rental agent. There was a discussion of some sort between the two locals, and Sid, his eyeglasses glittering, offered free translation: "*Hélas,* these hectares themselves find encumbered."

That afternoon, we went to Monte Carlo in two cars, and, while Laura took Abby and Adam off somewhere, ventured into the

Société Anonyme des Bains de Mer et du Cercle des Étrangers de Monaco for a spot of gaming. The long rooms were not stuffed with slot machines and customers in shorts, as they are said to be now, but did not exactly come up to expectation. A bare two tables were in business in the curtained, fusty Public Gaming Rooms, with others shrouded in tattered baize. The handful of players, bending over their skimpy stacks of thirty-franc chips, appeared to include some local widows, making a late-afternoon stop-off before the evening rates and lighting came on. But the quiet commands from the formally garbed croupiers were straight out of E. Phillips Oppenheim, and the suave Sid now faltered a moment before a vacant seat. "Do you know how to do this?" he whispered. "Sure," I said and slipped in. I lost two early bets on Rouge and another on Passe, got eleven chips back for my one on a Transversale Pleine, and, encouraged, plunked down four on number 26 — the traditional spot for an opening 37-to-1 long shot. Around went the little ball, to the croupier's *"Mesdames, messieurs, faites vos jeux. Les jeux sont faits — rien ne va plus!,"* then slowed and bounced — ricketytackety tipitty-tup — and nestled sweetly into my slot. There was a gasp — it came from me — and piles of oblong chips, triangular chips, and variously tinted round chips slid smoothly to my part of the green. "Jesus, what did you do!" Perelman cried, but I was no longer of his party. Seizing a casual stack of counters from the top of the pile, I tossed it toward the man at the middle of the table — I really did this — who raked it into a slot next to the wheel. *"Merci, monsieur,"* came the murmured response (with little bows) from the band of croupiers. *"La maison vous remercie."* I smiled, extracted a Sobranie from my silver case, and accepted a light from the white-gloved countess at my shoulder.

I had won perhaps fifty dollars and, staying on, added a lucky ten or fifteen more before we arose. Perelman, betting his kids' birthdays, then his hotel room number subtracted by the number of letters in his name, worked like a trooper and wound up seven or eight bucks to the good. "Never again, Étienne," he said as we walked out into the late sunlight. "You must swear to stop me." Not till the next day did I give him a break and confess that my expertise and gambling manners had all come out of the *Encyclopædia Britannica,* consulted back home before my departure, which had a terrific "Roulette" entry in the RAY–SAR volume. I took notes.

Our last stop — Evelyn and I had to start back — came the next afternoon, when we pressed a call on W. Somerset Maugham at his Villa Mauresque, next door on Cap Ferrat. Perelman, a fabled reader, told me he had once written the grand old man of British letters to express admiration for his effortless style, and won a similar mash note in return. Now they had a date. In the Perelman wheels this time, I think, we noticed Maugham's adopted Moorish symbol — for good fortune, I think — here worked into an iron arch at his entranceway. The same sign appeared on the covers of *Of Human Bondage* and *The Moon and Sixpence* and *Cakes and Ale* and the rest, which the world had snapped up in staggering numbers over the previous decades. A flood of bestsellers and long-running West End plays had earned him this comely retreat, in a part of the world that even then looked lightly on his private life. Here, twisting and turning around corners, up hill and down dale, we followed the raked driveway onward through stunning groves of palm and pine and splashy bougainvillea. "The royalties! The royalties!" cried Sid in pure admiration and purer envy, as we drew up at last at the flowering stone steps and spreading red-tiled roofs of the shrine.

Maugham appeared, a frail gent of seventy-five, slightly bent in his soft shirt, pleated summery trousers, and suede pumps. With his skimpy, slicked-back hair and heavily lidded eyes, he suggested a Galápagos tortoise, wise and of immense age. He shook hands with us each, repeating our names, and told Abby and Adam to make themselves at home. Indoors, tea was produced and Maugham's cheerful partner, Alan Searle, introduced. Two house guests, the tall poet C. Day-Lewis and a slim, long-necked woman in gray, floated in and silently took places in the vast low living room. All went well except the conversation, which soon became a trickle, unhelped by Maugham's famous and extraordinarily demanding stammer and my sudden realization that the woman next to me, Day-Lewis's companion, was the novelist Rosamond Lehmann, whose *Dusty Answer* and *The Weather in the Streets* I had sighed over while in college. Silences fell, broken by thumpings and running feet above, from Abby and Adam. "They're in my st-study, I believe," Maugham said, smiling, as Sid bolted from the room. Dadly noises arose from the stairs. We picked up a bit after a round of Maugham Specials, a grenadine concoction prepared by Searle. Sipping mine, I saw Evelyn gesture with her eyes toward the window over Maugham's shoulder, and shifting my gaze, caught sight of a paper airplane as it sailed slowly down from above and impaled itself in a jacaranda.

Ever the host, Maugham pulled over his footstool and sat down again, one leg tucked beneath him. "Tell me, Mr. Angell," he said, "have you ever worn a s-s-sarong?" I had to ask him to repeat the word and then said no, not yet. "Oh, but you m-must!" he cried, wrinkling his wrinkles with kindness. "V-very *cool* — but they do f-f-fall off!"

On the way back, Perelman lit into his progeny. "This was a big, big disappointment," he said. "I don't see how we can take you anywhere." Silence. "Listen," he resumed in a different voice, "what was it like up there?"

These tales and name-droppings grow dim with repeating, and hearing them once again, in the fashion with which we stare into the too small black-and-white snapshots in a family album, we look into their corners and distant porches or mysterious windows in search of something more — times of day, a day of the week, other names and other tones of voice, beyond recall. What in the world did Evelyn and I talk about — beyond our adored but absent baby, I mean — all those weeks and miles? How did we survive the shriveling boredom of long days on the road, through landscapes relentlessly renewed and snatched away but never entered. Conversation saved us, but I can't bring back a word now. What books were we reading, which crisis were the French and British papers and the Paris *Tribune* full of each day? What fears or sadness woke us up at night, either or both of us, and made it hard to sleep again? With effort, if I wait not too eagerly, I can sometimes bring back her voice. She was happy on this trip, and could prove it. She had been a diabetic since the age of six, but here in France, while eating two exceptional meals every day, all over the map, and drinking down the splendid wines, she was able to cut down her daily insulin — a stab in the thigh, mornings and evenings — to her lowest levels in a lifetime. We divorced in the sixties and she died — can it be? — almost seven years ago.

On the *De Grasse* again, homeward bound, we were old hands. We told our new friends the Sidney Simons — he was a painter and sculptor coming back from a spell in France — which deck chairs

were out of the wind and which dinner service to sign up for (the
deuxième, except on cabaret nights, so you could leave earlier and
grab a better table by the floor). In our cabin, Evelyn told me that
she had wept a bit in the taxi on the way to our train to Cherbourg,
but couldn't tell if it was from leaving Paris or missing Callie. I said
we could do this again, maybe next year, and make it a shorter trip.
We never did. Life and work and a second daughter intervened,
and there was the money problem and the kids' summers to think
about, and almost before we knew it the *De Grasse* and every other
Atlantic passenger vessel were gone, swept clean away by the airlin-
ers' seven hours to Orly, and by Eurail Pass and Junior Year
Abroad, and by the hundreds of thousands of kids and travelers
and shifting populations from all over the world who filled the fabled capitals and charming roads and did away with our postwar afternoon, leaving only these moments.

On the *De Grasse* the night of the Captain's Gala, a day and a half
before New York, Evelyn and I are in close embrace, dancing to
the Jerome Kern chestnut "You're Devastating." Our dancing has
picked up, and we know how to let the slow lift of the floor tip us
together, and to wait for the sensual tilt and counterflow of the de-
parting wave. The bandleader, Tony Prothes, gives us a little nod as
we swing by. He remembers us from the trip over, I've decided, but
of course he's good at this. Like our cabin steward and the second
sommelier and the barman Charles — Jules? Gérard? — he goes
back to the *Normandie,* before the war. Half an hour later — or is
this on another crossing, years later? — I am sitting at a cabaret table next to Mme. Hervé Alphand, the wife of the French ambassa-
dor, whom I met at a cocktail party earlier in the evening. Tall and
olive-skinned — I think she is Greek by origin — she will become
one of the great Washington hostesses. She is wearing an amazing
evening gown, and when I say something about it she suddenly
spreads the skirt's thick folds so they cover my knees and those of
the man on her opposite side. The three of us are under the multicolored skirt, which lies in glistening heaps, holding us together.
"Mainbocher," she says, smiling. "It's *élégante,* don't you think? It
brings pleasure."

ANDREA BARRETT

The Sea of Information

FROM THE KENYON REVIEW

I'VE ALWAYS THOUGHT of myself as a writer more than usually dependent on news from the outside world. My imagination is nourished by old books, old bones, fossils, feathers, paintings, photographs, museums of every kind and size, microscopes and telescopes, plants and birds; I like to learn things, and I thought — I still do think, although my ideas have darkened — that all this information feeds my fiction.

It wasn't so strange, then, to find myself excited by the slim gray book stamped "Property of the City of New York" and titled *What You Should Know about TUBERCULOSIS,* which fell into my hands sometime during 1999. Inside it I found photographs of children deformed by tuberculosis of the spine; of a young man perched on a tenement roof, gazing at the tattered tent and cot in which he is "taking the cure at home, in summer"; of a young woman on a similar roof, bundled in mittens and a thick coat, smiling as she sweeps the snow from around her tent while curing "on the roof in winter." Copies of this book, I learned, had been passed out to public high school students in New York City between 1910 and 1920, a place and a period I knew almost nothing about. Still, I found myself wondering what it might have been like to be one of the students studying the book and preparing to answer the test questions at the end. Pausing, maybe, over a clumsy drawing of a tree being attacked by an ax; noticing that the trunk was labeled "Tuberculosis" and the many branches bore such names as "incapacitated workers," "thousands dependent on charity," and "hunchbacks," while the tangled roots included "poverty," "child labor," and "careless consumptives."

Perhaps that student might have flipped between the Tuberculosis Tree and the map of a nearby neighborhood, the blocks bounded by the Bowery, East Houston, Canal, East Broadway, and Columbia. Within that area, every building sheltering a known case of tuberculosis was marked by a black dot. There were a great number of dots; some blocks were almost entirely black, and anyone living there would have known tuberculosis intimately. Everywhere people suffered while visitors, often unwelcome, descended upon them. Doctors, charity workers, public-health officials. Visiting nurses, trained by a 1915 handbook to think that

> in the first place, tuberculosis is largely a disease of the poor — of those on or below the poverty line. We must further realize that there are two sorts of poor people — not only those financially handicapped and so unable to control their environment, but those who are mentally and morally poor, and lack intelligence, will power, and self-control. The poor, from whatever cause, form a class whose environment is difficult to alter. And we must further realize that these patients are surrounded in their homes by people of their own kind — their families and friends — who are also poor. It is this fact which makes the task so difficult, and makes the prevention and cure of a preventable and curable disease a matter of utmost complexity.[1]

The *sound* of that language — the officious, pushy, condescending *sound* of that — along with the eerie photographs and the remarkable drawing of the Tuberculosis Tree, made me want to write a novel. The feeling was as sudden, as intense, and as irrational as falling in love.

Who can say why we're drawn to one person, or one subject? All I knew was that I was, and that the impulse was powerful. The novel would be set, I thought, in a public sanatorium; I imagined a sort of working-class American version of Thomas Mann's *The Magic Mountain,* which is set at a fancy private sanatorium in the Alps in the years just before the First World War erupted throughout Europe. Mine would start a little later — but before the American entry into the war, I thought; I didn't want to have to deal with the war, which seemed like a whole other subject — and would explore not the lives of the rich and idle but those of the working poor. A friend to whom I tried to describe it jokingly called it "The Magic Molehill."

*

Several things happened to that impulse, though, along the way.

One is that I used a description of that little gray book, and the world from which it had come, as part of a proposal, by means of which I hoped to gain a fellowship at the New York Public Library. There I planned to research the novel, and to begin writing it in congenial surroundings. A library seemed like the perfect temporary home for me. Over the past decade or so I've written about subjects as diverse as China during the Cultural Revolution, the evolutionary biologist Alfred Russel Wallace in the Malay Archipelago, the monk and botanist Gregor Mendel and his experiments with peas, nineteenth-century Arctic exploration, surveying and mapmaking in the 1860s, and the development of paleontology in nineteenth-century America. I've studied early conceptions of the formation of dew and rain, the founding of the utopian colony of New Harmony, and the manufacture of the glass eyes used by taxidermists to simulate life in stuffed game.

Ridiculous, I know. But by now, despite that, I've learned to follow where the spark of interest leads me. Often I'm drawn toward the past, and toward material involving natural history and the sciences; I can't explain that either, except to say that for me this material seems full of potential, charged and fresh and inspiring. Sometimes the stories *lead* me to the research: halfway into a sentence I may realize I don't have any idea whether a character climbing in the Karakorum range in the 1850s would be wearing hobnailed boots or metal crampons, and then it's time to study the history of mountaineering. Sometimes, as with the little gray book, I bump into things by accident, and they in turn either lead to stories or bend stories already in progress into a different shape. But always, libraries have been my most dependable resource for this material. At the enormous library in New York, I imagined I'd find all sorts of secret treasures, as indeed I did. But I also found myself strangely lost and in unknown territory.

Because I was granted that fellowship, my husband and I moved to New York City for a year. During that July and August I walked around the Lower East Side, looking at tenement buildings marked on the map in the gray book. In the Williamsburg section of Brooklyn, where we were living, I walked around the waterfront and inspected the shattered docks from which a largely immigrant population had stepped onto ferries headed for Manhattan. I walked around an old sugar refinery, hardly changed from the early twentieth century and still belching steam, in which I decided I'd have one of my characters work. I read Walt Whitman's "Crossing Brooklyn Ferry," and I flipped through old maps of the neighborhood, and I looked forward to the start of the fellowship itself, to the nine months during which I'd occupy a little office, grouped with fourteen other offices around a common area where I and my fellow Fellows might gather to share ideas.

We were a mixed group, I knew: four fiction writers, one poet, the remainder historians, biographers, and critics, studying everything from Ben Franklin's attitudes toward slavery to Russian iconography to the social history of an extended African-American family. I knew that the scholars were also excited by books and maps and unusual facts, although I had little sense, then, of the different ways in which we'd actually use the materials we found. We'd have access, I knew, to virtually any source we could imagine; fill out a call slip and it would appear. This part I imagined as heavenly, and that turned out to be true. But what also turned out to be true was that the first day of our fellowship was September 10, 2001. We had our pictures taken, we met the staff, we got ID cards, and had a tour. The next day, we were told, would be our first real introduction to the library's resources.

That morning I woke early, gathered my papers together, dressed, and then walked our dog to the dog-sitters' place in an old garage beside the East River, directly across from lower Manhattan. On my way back to pick up my briefcase and head for the subway, I heard a thump and turned to see smoke and flames pouring out of one of the towers that had dominated our view since we'd moved there. Later, from the roof of our building, I saw the towers burn and fall.

This isn't meant to be an exploration of the effects of September 11, and so I won't include any more details about the next few weeks except to say that, unlike so many others, my husband and I were extraordinarily fortunate. Neither of us was hurt, nor were family members, nor close friends. We were bystanders, nothing more. But even for us, as for everyone, everything was different after that day.

Like many writers, I found myself unable to write in the aftermath of the attacks — not just fiction, but anything. What was the point? I thought at first, and for a long time after. But of course there's always a point: reading and writing are two of the ways we make sense of our mysterious, sometimes terrible, world. There were reasons why, all through the autumn months, the Main Reading Room at the library was packed with people reading newspapers and books, searching for material on-line, talking to each other and to the librarians. Eventually I took my cue from those people pouring in off the street. It was through reading, which grew into a more directed kind of research, that I first began to try to grapple with what had happened.

I wrote, haltingly, an autobiographical essay about witnessing the attacks as a new New Yorker, but although there was some relief in trying to get a sketch of those weeks down on paper, I couldn't get at the heart of things; the experience was still too raw, and some of it was still going on. Anthrax was floating through the mails; subway trains were mysteriously stopped, rerouted, evacuated; buildings where I went to meet friends would be suddenly sealed, surrounded by armed men and flashing lights. The newspapers were filled with rumors and fresh horrors, with heart-wrenching photographs and rhetorical excess and calls for war. I found myself driven not toward these renderings of what surrounded me but away, toward other times and places in which similar events — events that felt analogous — had taken place. More and more I found myself delving not into what I'd once thought was the central subject matter of my novel, but into what had been going on around my characters in their sanatorium, which was World War I.

If novelists think, perhaps this is *how* we think: through a frenzy of metaphor-making and analogy-building, an accretion of meaningful images juxtaposed in ways that seem to us fruitful, although to someone else they might seem baffling. On different days (or sometimes on the same day, when I was feeling particularly lost), I read about the history of Brooklyn in the early twentieth century; the process of sugar refining; immigration policy; the histories of nursing, dispensaries, and public health; what it was like to live in Russian Poland at the end of the nineteenth century and the beginning of the twentieth; the Russian Revolution; the experience of Americans who enlisted with Canadian or British regiments during the early years of the Great War; the American response to the war before entering it; the military draft and how it was imple-

mented; the uses of such chemical and biological weapons as gas
and anthrax, both of which were used for the first time then; and
the polio epidemic that started in Brooklyn during the summer of
1916.

I read with a kind of terrible fascination about a night in the
middle of that same summer, when what had once been a munitions dump on Black Tom Island, warehouses and boxcars filled
with shells and powder made here and waiting to be shipped to
France, detonated in an explosion so massive that windows blew
out across lower Manhattan and New Jersey, the ground shook in
Brooklyn, and the island itself disappeared. German spies were
blamed for that; German Americans were blamed for having sheltered the spies. The waves of anti-German prejudice that followed
helped shift American sentiment from neutrality toward participa-
tion in the war.

Why was I reading all this? Why do all this work, especially when
I wasn't writing and didn't know if, when I started again, I'd find a
way to use any of it? And especially when I might more usefully
have been out in the world, helping someone, fixing something:
cleaning up the rubble or raising money or aiding the families of
the dead. Instead I read, which is what I do. I read like that — I
have always read like that — because it's the only way I know to
deeply inhabit a world other than the limited one of my own experience. It's the way I sink into the hearts and minds of invented
characters, who incarnate themselves in the odd intersections of
apparently disparate fields, and who then, if I'm lucky, manage to
understand and articulate what I cannot. Reading, which gives me
access to lives I haven't lived, am not living, probably won't live, is
how I find my way to writing: in this case, how I found my way *back*
to writing.

And yet — for the first time in my life, I was surrounded by actual scholars as I read, who swam through a sea of information and
marshaled facts in ways that were unfamiliar to me. As I listened to
them talk about their own researches into history and culture and
the intersections between what they were studying and what was
going on around us that fall and winter, I was forced to think about
how very differently scholars on the one hand, and poets and novelists on the other, approach their material. We not only do research differently, we do it in a different spirit, for a different purpose; and then we turn the results to different ends. My colleagues

spoke about discovering new sources, about rummaging around in original sources, sometimes in several languages; about finding evidence and, from that evidence, constructing and testing hypotheses and then building chains of argument. Their process reminded me of science, seemed almost like a *kind* of science.

Because I'm so drawn to scientific material, I'm sometimes also drawn to its methods. But although I found my colleagues' approach both admirable and fascinating, I got lost when I attempted to emulate it. I've never been able to write unless I take a different, more wandering path. While brilliant fiction has been written by people who work rationally, write outlines, plan beforehand where they are going, and are able to think their way through the structure of a novel or a story, I've always had to feel my way more blindly and intuitively. There are excellent novels that *do* make arguments, and are as essentially polemical as a work of nonfiction: Dickens's *Hard Times* comes to mind. But these aren't the novels, for whatever reasons, that I most love; nor are they what I attempt to write. Usually what I'm trying to build isn't an argument, isn't overtly didactic, doesn't state its premises clearly, often doesn't operate linearly, and can't be reduced to a clear statement.

It took being in the company of this group of scholars to teach me that when I did what, up until then, I had always *thought* of as "research," I was only skimming the surface. I know a little about a lot of things, but the only thing I really know well is storytelling, in all its forms — and that's the end my so-called research serves. Although most of my fiction is set in the past and employs the materials of history, I'm not trying to discover new facts or develop new hypotheses or in some sense prove "how it was." I'm trying to shape a narrative that allows a reader to *feel* what it was like to be a particular person, or set of persons, caught in a particular situation at a particular place and time. When I looked at the sugar factory in Williamsburg and dug up early photographs of it or articles about how sugar was processed there, I was looking for those details that would allow me to imagine *one person* working in and moving through that space; I was imagining it as background. A social historian, looking at the same material, might ask what wages were, what the ethnicity of the workers was, where those workers lived, who got paid what for what hours. Facts from which inferences could be drawn. I was looking for something else.

I wanted what would help me not to tell but to *show.* If I could convey what I wanted to convey by a set of logically ordered and clear statements, I'd do that. But a good novel or story or poem tries to convey a different kind of knowledge and to operate on the reader in a different way, through the emotions and the senses. Facts can help *evoke* emotion, especially those that transmit texture, tonality, and sensual detail. But facts can't drive a piece. Research, no matter how compelling, may give me the bones of a fiction but never the breath and the blood. It's a wonderful, sometimes immensely useful tool that helps give me something to write about. But without the transforming force of the imagination, the result is only information.

In 1936, when a different war was looming on the horizon, Walter Benjamin wrote this:

> Every morning brings us the news of the globe, and yet we are poor in noteworthy stories. This is because no event any longer comes to us without already being shot through with explanation. In other words, by now almost nothing that happens benefits storytelling; almost everything benefits information. Actually, it is half the art of storytelling to keep a story free from explanation as one reproduces it . . . The value of information does not survive the moment in which it was new. It lives only at that moment; it has to surrender to it completely and explain itself to it without losing any time.[2]

Information, information. I was drowning in it, one stream pouring in from the daily news of the world, the other bubbling up from the library stacks, while all around me people used it to build explanations for the present and the past. Every day I'd learn something more about the world, the war, tuberculosis, public health, propaganda. And every day I felt farther away from the writing itself. It was as if, to hark back again to *Hard Times*, I had turned while my attention had drifted into the student in Professor Gradgrind's class who, when asked to define a horse, responded:

> "Quadruped. Graminivorous. Forty teeth, namely twenty-four grinders, four eye-teeth, and twelve incisive. Sheds coat in the spring; in marshy countries, sheds hoofs, too. Hoofs hard, but requiring to be shod with iron. Age known by marks in the mouth."[3]

Caught up in learning about the equivalent of grinders and eye-teeth, I'd forgotten that while facts may be *in* a text — sometimes delectably — they can't *be* the text itself. Slowly I began to relearn something I'd once grasped but had lost sight of: that emotion — that central element of fiction — derives not from information or explanation, nor from a logical arrangement of facts, but specifically from powerful images and from the qualities of language: diction, rhythm, form, structure, association, metaphor. And sometimes I also had glimmers of another thing I'd once known: how effectively information can be used to wall off emotion. How the gathering of information can take the place of actual understanding. I had built, as I am only now realizing, quite a substantial wall. As if any wall could block out those two towers.

As I went longer and longer without writing fiction, the novel I wanted to write — at that point still purely hypothetical — began to seem as if it should encompass not only the sanatorium experience but also the experience of a country on the verge of entering a war. When I did finally start writing in the autumn of 2002, around the anniversary of September 11, what I began was no longer the novel I'd first imagined. Still, I thought this had to do with a change in the *kind* of information I needed — less about tuberculosis, more about the war. More recently I've come to see that the change is of a different sort.

There's no single, central character anymore, no one prism through which everything is refracted. Instead there are a tangle of characters talking to and through and around one another, struggling to make sense of both what's happened to them personally and what's going on in the larger world: not just the distant war but the burgeoning implements and technologies of war, the changes in politics and society. Does that sound a bit like a group of people gathered in a library during and after a crisis, talking their way through the events of the day? Perhaps it does. A war, like an epidemic, happens to everyone; as autobiography, no matter how vigorously squelched, has a way of pulsing beneath the surface of one's work.

In this version of the novel, a character named Leo Marburg is among a handful of patients who, in a state sanatorium in the Adirondacks, amid a swirl of conversations about the war abroad and the contributions made to it here — chemical weapons, x-ray machines, munitions, eager volunteers — cause something to happen. It's pointless to say more about Leo or how I think the plot might unfold. Partly that's because I don't *know* yet — I can guess, and I can plan, but the experience of writing previous books suggests that I'll be wrong, and that I'll be surprised at every turn. Partly it's because plot summaries are boring. If the novel's working, I shouldn't be able to reduce it to an outline, and I shouldn't be able to articulate what it's really about. All I can say is that, partly through the experience of living in New York during that difficult year, the world of these characters keeps enlarging and the series of intersecting circles keeps widening.

The more I learned about the First World War, the more I saw how much it had in common with what was known at the time as the "War Against Tuberculosis": the material contained in the little gray book. Those wars overlap exactly in time — but also, more important, in their uses of propaganda and corrupted public language. The militaristic and yet at the same time euphemistic language of the War Against Tuberculosis is very like that found in the documents used to whip up American support for entry into the war. The *sound* of that language interests me a good deal — it's a sound that's becoming familiar again. And it was sound — the rhythm and tone of a particular narrative voice, its diction and pacing and music — that helped me begin the actual writing. What I had experienced changed the novel; the new information I gathered was necessary to it; neither experience nor information was sufficient. What I needed was a resonant metaphoric framework, and a voice.

In the handful of pages I wrote before I had any real sense of where the novel was headed, there's hardly a single complete sentence, never mind a coherent paragraph. But even from those I could get a sense of structure, intent, and a kind of verbal patterning, despite the fact that most of the nouns — the facts — were still missing. Actual phrases and sentences are mingled with lumpy directions to myself, enclosed within parentheses — and these, not a chain of reasoning, led me on. This is how the first gesture sounded on the day I sketched it out:

"That summer, everything seemed to be crumbling (*disintegrating, catching fire, happening . . .*) all at once. (*see the NYC newspapers. Focus down a window of time — roughly the last week or two weeks of June 1916. Impending war with Mexico, news of the war overseas, all the local accidents and labor disputes, incidents of German sabotage*). A ship blew up, a train was (. . .); in France (*insert some event from the war here*), while a (. . .) was (. . .) in New York Harbor. A (. . . *insert two other trivial events here, from Brooklyn newspaper*).

"In Brooklyn (. . *x* . .) children had been paralyzed by polio on June (. . *y* . .), and another (. . *x* . .) on June (. . *z* . .). By the end of the month, (. . . *summarize the panic of the epidemic here; the children being turned back by police on Long Island, the families being rousted from their apartments, etc.*) In Greenpoint and Williamsburg, (. . . *more examples here. Then end this opening beat, which has narrowed from Europe and all over the States, to New York Harbor, to Brooklyn, and down to Leo's neighborhood, with this*):

"At the sugar refinery where Leo Marburg worked, three men had been dismissed on suspicion of sabotage after a fire broke out in the warehouse. Leo, now working more hours than usual, was exhausted. Two of his landlady's children were sick; his own head ached and the nagging cough he'd had since winter kept him up even when the children weren't crying and the ambulances weren't roaming the streets with their sirens shrieking. Each day he went in to work and (*summarize his routine duties here*).

"One Wednesday, early in July . . ."

Essentially that's an information-free passage; truly, writing can be ridiculous. And yet despite the obvious problems and omissions, there's something — a kind of feeling, a structure, a tone — gesturing there. That something springs not from experience or information but from their synthesis and growth in my imagination.

Each time I try to do this, I relearn the lesson that I can't, during the process of writing, relegate imagination to an inferior place. I can't let research, my ally and comfort for so long, push its way to the head of the line. The work never comes alive until I give up the idea that I know what I'm writing about, and allow myself to be led — by the life that goes on outside us, in the world, and also by the fertile life going on in secret, inside our heads — into new and strange territory. Any text, I learn each time, is a tissue of the imagination in which facts, if we choose to embed them, rest safely encysted.

By now, of course, that first, exploratory passage has disappeared, replaced by something that sounds almost shockingly different. But that too is part of the journey of the imagination, which the dictionary defines as "the act or power of forming a mental image of something not present to the senses or never before wholly perceived in reality." A useful reminder that the imagination is founded in, flourishes on, *images:* pictures fortified by sight, touch, taste, sound, and passionate emotion. One image leads me to the next, and the next; the next requires the revision of all that has come before, and on it goes.

So what is it, then, that I'm trying to say? I went to New York with an idea for a book, which was inspired by another book; the world changed while I was there, and so did I; the book I meant to write changed as well. Do I mean to say that writers should look within, or look without? That they should write from experience, or from research, or from imagination?

Yes, I would say. Not either/or, but all those things. Writing is mysterious, and it's supposed to be. Craft guides a writer at every step, as does knowledge of earlier work; we accomplish little without those foundations. Research can help, if it feeds the imagination and generates ideas; a plan is also a wonderful thing, if a writer's imagination works that way. Groping blindly, following glimmers of structure and sound, is far from the only way; other writers work differently to good effect, and any path that gets you there is a good path in the end. But one true thing among all these paths is the need to tap a deep vein of connection between our own uncontrollable interior preoccupations and what we're most concerned about in the world around us. We write in response to that world; we write in response to what we read and learn; and in the end we write out of our deepest selves, the live, breathing, bleeding place where the pictures form, and where it all begins.

Notes

1. Ellen N. LaMotte, *The Tuberculosis Nurse: Her Functions and Qualifications* (New York: G. P. Putnam's Sons, 1915). Reprinted in *From Consumption to Tuberculosis: A Documentary History,* edited by Barbara Rosenkrantz (New York: Garland Publishers, 1994), 442.

2. Walter Benjamin, "The Storyteller," in *Illuminations* (New York: Schocken Books, 1969), 89–90.

3. Charles Dickens, *Hard Times* (1854) (New York: Holt, Rinehart and Winston, 1961), 4.

PAUL CRENSHAW

Storm Country

)M SOUTHERN HUMANITIES REVIEW

RMS CAME in the spring, we went underground.
kansas, not far from the Oklahoma line, and all
lio gave reports of thunderstorms marching
own prairie, my father would alternate be-
lio and watching the sky, the radio braying
tning. My mother opened windows, wor-
My brother and I got out candles, a
went out. Outside, the air was heavy
ees listlessly hanging as the storm
e on the radio told of a line of se-
ogee, moving east at thirty-five
s and hail, lightning, the possi-
go outside and stand in the
nd at some point, usually
r the purple hills, or even
looked like it was seen
off the radio.
out through the be-
or a hot night lit up
e darkness seemed
a hostile wind,
s and branches
air. My father
head as we
ndfather's
storm cel-

ler
ded
the
n the
wall.
ly four
e lamp,
ide, the
y grand-
and only
ght, if the
middle of
e cellar, my
closing our
ces above the
is safe.
m of the stairs,
to watch my fa-
step inside the
of coming down,
ground level for
ettes and the rain
ad been opened to
d toward a cloud off
ent into a tornado.
when it might be safe

lar. When they saw us coming up the road they rushed to the truck, taking my brother and me, ushering my mother inside, out of the wind and rain. My father would stay outside, accept a cup of coffee and a cigarette, join the other men in keeping an eye on the developing storm.

The cellar was built away from the house, a small structure of cinderblocks about the size of an outhouse. The door stood upright, opening on a sharp descent of concrete steps that were always crossed by spiderwebs that would wrap around my face as I hurried down. A small window was cut into the cinderblocks just above ground level, so you could walk a few steps down the stair and still see what was forming in the air outside.

Inside, the cellar smelled of damp and earth. While my fath and uncles and grandfather watched the storm, my mother her my brother and me down the stairs where, in a little room a bottom, my grandmother and aunts and cousins sat quietly i light of a kerosene lamp, their shadows thrown large on th Their eyes were dark and silent. In the room there were on cots with damp quilts and a small table holding the kerosen a twelve-volt flashlight, some candles, and the Bible. Out storm was gathering strength, and to quiet the children, m mother would tell stories or sing songs in a deep voice occasionally would her eyes flicker to the door. Late at n storm was a long one, or if we'd been woken up in th the night and torn from our beds to be taken to th brother and I would fall asleep in our mother's lap eyes to the movement of shadows on the wall, soft vo sound of the wind and rain outside telling us all w

Sometimes I'd stand near the door at the botto peeking through the crack and craning my head u ther. When the rain and wind hit, the men woul door. They'd stay on the stairs, though, instead watching the storm through the window cut a that purpose. They smelled of coffee and ciga that sometimes blew in the little window if it h hear the storm better. Sometimes they nodde over the hills that might uncoil at any mor They scanned the skies, judging the weather to return home.

Throughout the evening the radio would give reports, telling where tornadoes had touched down and where power lines had fallen and where golfball-sized hail had been seen. Sometimes the radio reported that the storms were losing intensity, or that they had all moved through and passed on, and sometimes we slept in the cellar, waking up in the morning to the smell of moldy quilts and kerosene, climbing the stairs to emerge into a bright world after the storms had passed, the spring grass glistening with the rain from the night and all around leaves and branches and debris from the storm littering the ground. We'd climb in the truck and drive around, surveying the damage. Sometimes trees would be blocking the road, or an old barn would have fallen from the wind. Sometimes there'd be hail covering the ground as if it had snowed, and as the day warmed, the hail would steam as it evaporated, a low mist hanging over the fields.

Other times there would be no sign that any storm had ever come through but for a light rain that patterned the dirt, but when we got home and watched the news we would learn that the next town over had been hit, that people were dead and homes were destroyed, that anyone wishing to donate food or clothing or blood could call this number on the screen. On these days I'd walk out under the clear sky, trying to recall the night in the cellar, the way it smelled and felt and tasted, the way the storm looked when it passed, at what point the men decided it was over. After the storms I always felt unmoored and adrift, as if something had passed that I didn't quite understand.

In March in Arkansas the Gulf Stream sucks up moisture from the Gulf of Mexico to collide with cold air from up north, lingering remnants of winter meeting the warmth of spring. The clash of opposite air masses sends lines of tornadoes spinning out over the prairies of Kansas and Oklahoma and Texas, into the hills of Arkansas. In the late afternoon, they color the day like an old sepia photograph as they roll in, shading the light. At night, you can see funnel clouds in the flashes of lightning, or low-hanging spikes from which — my father would tell me as I got older — tornadoes could spawn.

Long before storm-chasing became an excursion for the rich or fool-hearted, my father and grandfather watched tornadoes from the stairs of our cellar, judging when they might drop, how big they might be, if we were in danger. They judged clouds as some men judge the stock market, wondering if it might rise or fall, as all through spring and into summer the storms in Tornado Alley rolled up out of the west, advancing in lines extending from thirty miles south of Broken Bow, Oklahoma, to fifteen miles north of De Queen, Arkansas. I learned the counties of Arkansas — Logan and Sequoia and Crawford and Sebastian and Scott, Franklin and Johnson and Washington and Pope and Polk — through radio reports of tornado warnings or sightings, my geography formed of radio static in lightning, late nights in a storm cellar. I learned to judge the movement of storms across a TV screen, how a storm moving north-northeast through Scott County might end up in my own Logan, or how long it might take a tornado in Sebastian County to reach my house if it was moving at thirty-five miles an hour. I learned to recognize at a glance my own county and the counties surrounding it, because when tornado watches or warnings were issued, in the bottom right part of the TV screen would be a map of Arkansas with certain counties flashing red. On these nights I lay awake in bed, red bands of heavy storms moving across computer-drawn counties in my mind, reciting the path of storms: LeFlore, Sebastian, Crawford, Logan, knowing that at some time in the night I would be awakened, either by my father or the storm outside. I would be wrapped in a blanket, hurried through the rain and into the truck and up the hill, to the flickering kerosene images of aunts and cousins, sleepy-eyed like myself, their shadows large on the wall, as outside the storm raged on.

My grandfather could tell by the way leaves hung on the trees if it would rain that day or not — an old-time meteorologist who watched the seasons and the sky simply because they were there.

"See there?" he said once. We were standing outside the cellar as the first storms began to fire up in the heat of late afternoon. Low green clouds hung silent in the distance, and I have since learned that when clouds turn green, one should take cover. A point hung from the clouds, a barb that looked ominous as the clouds passed on and we watched them go, and always after I have looked for low barbs hanging from dark green clouds, for silent formations that might spawn destruction. He knew, standing on the cellar stairs watching through the little window, when a tornado might drop from the clouds. He knew the feel of the air, the presence that announces a heavy storm.

Sometimes it will stop raining when the funnel falls. Sometimes the wind stops and the trees go still and the air settles on you as everything goes quiet. Then, faint at first as the storm gathers speed, you can hear the force as it spins itself into existence, touching earth, whirling out into the day or night. It sounds like rusted sirens, howling dogs, the call of a freight train on a long trip across the plains somewhere in the western night, pushing speed and sound before it, lonely and forlorn on its midnight ride.

I've seen tornadoes drop from a clear blue sky. I've seen barns and houses and fields wiped out, cattle thrown for a distance to lie in the rain bawling with broken legs. Once I watched as a three- or four-hundred-pound cut of sheet metal floated across the highway, touched down once, then lifted off again, light as air. I've seen towns wrecked by tornadoes in November, houses swept away, all that was left of a church the roof lying on the ground, unscathed but for a few shingles missing at one corner. One time I was almost struck by a bullet of hail the size of my fist. It crashed through the window and landed on our living room floor. We all looked at it for a moment. My mother tried to protect the curtains as the rain came in, but my father herded us toward the cellar up the hill at my grandfather's house.

I know the sound of storms, the low growl of thunder that means storms in the distance, the loud quick clap that means storms overhead. I've blinked in the afterglow of forked lightning, watched flash lightning light the hills as night turns into day. I've seen the remains of exploded houses, nothing left of the house but kindling, from when the tornado drops and the air pressure changes and the air inside the house has to get out.

I've seen storms come with no warning, boiling up out of a western sky rimmed with the red rays of the last sun, lightning flickering in the twilight, the air gone heavy and still. I've seen them sweep through with hardly a ripple but the wind in your hair, passing to other places and other times. I've huddled in hallways and bathtubs and cellars listening to tornadoes pass overhead, and when I see on television the remnants of a town destroyed by the force of storms, I always offer, however briefly, a thanks that it was not my people or my town.

*

The first tornado I can remember was when I was eight. The storm came in the afternoon, as many storms do. It was early in March — a month that, as the saying goes in Arkansas, enters like a lion, leaves like a lion. My father was watching a basketball game on TV when the sound disappeared, followed by the steady beep that meant an announcement was coming. Thunderstorms are moving through the area, the announcement ran at the bottom of the screen. Tornadoes possible. Take shelter. When the announcement disappeared, the state of Arkansas appeared on the screen, the western counties lit like radiation. My father went out to study the sky and came back in at a run.

"Let's go," he said.

The trees were dancing as we ran to the truck, leaves and small branches swirling in the wind and falling all around. At the road up the hill to my grandfather's house a dust devil danced before my father ran his truck through it, dispersing the dust. A line of rain moved toward us through the fields. The clouds in the distance were green.

By the time we reached the top of the hill the wind was rocking the truck and the first drops of rain were hitting the hood, big and loud and hard. The curtain of rain reached us, going from a few drops to a downpour in an instant. The wind ripped the truck door from my father's hand. My grandfather ran out from the cellar door, where he'd been watching for us, waiting. He took my brother, my father took me. We couldn't see the cellar in the rain. Thunder rumbled the hills, and lightning stabbed down, sharp and quick, splitting the rain, everything quiet for an instant before the thunder struck.

We splashed through the rain and into the cellar. I was wet, plastered to my father's chest. My mother took us down the stairs. My father and grandfather stood peering through the window at the rain. The day had gone dark.

Downstairs, my grandmother was telling stories to my two younger cousins, who were flinching in the sharp crashes of each thunder. The room smelled of kerosene, of earth and wind and rain. My skin was wet, hair cold, as my mother wrapped me in a quilt. In the brief silences between thunderclaps, we could hear the rain and my father and grandfather on the stairs. I peered through the door and heard my father say, "There it is."

He turned and saw me standing at the bottom of the stairs and motioned me up. The rain had slowed and was falling lightly now; the wind settled down in the trees. I stood on the steps with my father as he pointed into the distance, where a dark funnel coiled downward from the black clouds, like smoke, or wind taking shape and color. At the base of the tornado, dust and debris hovered, circling slowly, and I heard the sound of storm for the first time. It grew out of air, out of wind. It seemed as silent as noise can be, a faint howling that reached us over the rain, almost peaceful from a distance. But then it would hit a line of trees or a fence, shooting trees and fence posts and barbed wire into the air. It crossed over a pond, and water turned it almost white for an instant. It hit an old barn like a fist, smashing boards and metal, slinging the debris about.

We watched, not speaking, as the tornado moved over the empty fields in the distance, leaving a swath of devastation in its wake. After a time it folded itself back into the underbelly of the clouds, rising silently, dispersing like smoke in the wind, the sound gone and the air still once again.

"It's over," my father said, but I could still see in my mind the black funnel dropping from the clouds, twisting across the landscape, throwing trees and dirt and anything in its path, tearing tracts of land as it went on its way. Before me was the result, the path of the tornado, cut through the hills. And, for no reason it seemed, it faded away, gone as surely as it had come.

We stood there for a long time after it was over, silent, watching the clouds roll on through, speeding swiftly toward night. After a time — an hour or three or four — the clouds peeled back, revealing bright stars flung across the sky.

My father and my grandfather had watched other tornadoes before, just like that one, had seen them and knew what they could do. I had thought that they were standing guard through the night, watching until it was safe for us to come out, putting themselves between us and the danger that lurked outside. But as we turned and went down the stairs together, I realized they watched from the window to see the terrible beauty of the storm rolling across the hills, hail falling from the sky, streaks of lightning in the jagged edges of the storm, the twisting funnel of clouds that held such power.

BRIAN DOYLE

Joyas Voladoras

FROM THE AMERICAN SCHOLAR

CONSIDER THE HUMMINGBIRD for a long moment. A hummingbird's heart beats ten times a second. A hummingbird's heart is the size of a pencil eraser. A hummingbird's heart is a lot of the hummingbird. *Joyas voladoras*, flying jewels, the first white explorers in the Americas called them, and the white men had never seen such creatures, for hummingbirds came into the world only in the Americas, nowhere else in the universe, more than three hundred species of them whirring and zooming and nectaring in hummer time zones nine times removed from ours, their hearts hammering faster than we could clearly hear if we pressed our elephantine ears to their infinitesimal chests.

Each one visits a thousand flowers a day. They can dive at sixty miles an hour. They can fly backward. They can fly more than five hundred miles without pausing to rest. But when they rest they come close to death: on frigid nights, or when they are starving, they retreat into torpor, their metabolic rate slowing to a fifteenth of their normal sleep rate, their hearts sludging nearly to a halt, barely beating, and if they are not soon warmed, if they do not soon find that which is sweet, their hearts grow cold, and they cease to be. Consider for a moment those hummingbirds who did not open their eyes again today, this very day, in the Americas: bearded helmetcrests and booted racket-tails, violet-tailed sylphs and violet-capped woodnymphs, crimson topazes and purple-crowned fairies, red-tailed comets and amethyst woodstars, rainbow-bearded thornbills and glittering-bellied emeralds, velvet-purple coronets and golden-bellied star-frontlets, fiery-tailed awlbills and Andean hillstars, spatuletails and pufflegs, each the most amazing thing you have never seen, each thunderous wild heart the size of an infant's fingernail, each mad heart silent, a brilliant music stilled.

Hummingbirds, like all flying birds but more so, have incredible enormous immense ferocious metabolisms. To drive those metabolisms they have racecar hearts that eat oxygen at an eye-popping rate. Their hearts are built of thinner, leaner fibers than ours. Their arteries are stiffer and more taut. They have more mitochondria in their heart muscles — anything to gulp more oxygen. Their hearts are stripped to the skin for the war against gravity and inertia, the mad search for food, the insane idea of flight. The price of their ambition is a life closer to death; they suffer more heart attacks and aneurysms and ruptures than any other living creature. It's expensive to fly. You burn out. You fry the machine. You melt the engine. Every creature on earth has approximately two billion heartbeats to spend in a lifetime. You can spend them slowly, like a tortoise, and live to be two hundred years old, or you can spend them fast, like a hummingbird, and live to be two years old.

The biggest heart in the world is inside the blue whale. It weighs more than seven tons. It's as big as a room. It *is* a room, with four chambers. A child could walk around in it, head high, bending only to step through the valves. The valves are as big as the swinging doors in a saloon. This house of a heart drives a creature a hundred feet long. When this creature is born it is twenty feet long and weighs four tons. It is waaaaay bigger than your car. It drinks a hundred gallons of milk from its mama every day and gains two hundred pounds a day, and when it is seven or eight years old it endures an unimaginable puberty and then it essentially disappears from human ken, for next to nothing is known of the mating habits, travel patterns, diet, social life, language, social structure, diseases, spirituality, wars, stories, despairs, and arts of the blue whale. There are perhaps ten thousand blue whales in the world, living in every ocean on earth, and of the largest mammal who ever lived we know nearly nothing. But we know this: the animals with the largest hearts in the world generally travel in pairs, and their penetrating moaning cries, their piercing yearning tongue, can be heard underwater for miles and miles.

Mammals and birds have hearts with four chambers. Reptiles and turtles have hearts with three chambers. Fish have hearts with two chambers. Insects and mollusks have hearts with one chamber. Worms have hearts with one chamber, although they may have as many as eleven single-chambered hearts. Unicellular bacteria have no hearts at all; but even they have fluid eternally in motion, washing from one side of the cell to the other, swirling and whirling. No living being is without interior liquid motion. We all churn inside.

So much held in a heart in a lifetime. So much held in a heart in a day, an hour, a moment. We are utterly open with no one, in the end — not mother and father, not wife or husband, not lover, not child, not friend. We open windows to each but we live alone in the house of the heart. Perhaps we must. Perhaps we could not bear to be so naked, for fear of a constantly harrowed heart. When young we think there will come one person who will savor and sustain us always; when we are older we know this is the dream of a child, that all hearts finally are bruised and scarred, scored and torn, repaired by time and will, patched by force of character, yet fragile and rickety forevermore, no matter how ferocious the defense and how many bricks you bring to the wall. You can brick up your heart as stout and tight and hard and cold and impregnable as you possibly can and down it comes in an instant, felled by a woman's second glance, a child's apple breath, the shatter of glass in the road, the words "I have something to tell you," a cat with a broken spine dragging itself into the forest to die, the brush of your mother's papery ancient hand in the thicket of your hair, the memory of your father's voice early in the morning echoing from the kitchen where he is making pancakes for his children.

KITTY BURNS FLOREY

Sister Bernadette's Barking Dog

FROM HARPER'S MAGAZINE

DIAGRAMMING SENTENCES is one of those lost skills, like darning socks or playing the sackbut, that no one seems to miss. Invented, or at least codified, in an 1877 text called *Higher Lessons in English*, by Alonzo Reed and Brainerd Kellogg, it swept through American public schools like the measles, and was embraced by teachers as the way to reform students who were engaged in "the cold-blooded murder of the English tongue" (to take Henry Higgins slightly out of context). By promoting the beautifully logical rules of syntax, diagramming would root out evils like "it's me" and "I ain't got none," until everyone wrote like Ralph Waldo Emerson, or at least James Fenimore Cooper.

In my own youth, many years after 1877, diagramming was still serious business. I learned it in the sixth grade from Sister Bernadette. I can still see her: a tiny nun with a sharp pink nose, confidently drawing a dead-straight horizontal line like a highway across the blackboard, flourishing her chalk in the air at the end of it, her veil flipping out behind her as she turned back to the class. "We begin," she said, "with a straight line." And then, in her firm and saintly script, she put words on the line, a noun and a verb — probably something like *dog barked*. Between the words she drew a short vertical slash, bisecting the line. Then she made a road that forked off at an angle — a short country lane under the word *dog* — and on it she wrote *The*.

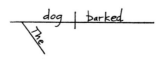

That was it: subject, predicate, and the little modifying article that civilized the sentence — all of it made into a picture that was every bit as clear and informative as an actual portrait of a beagle in mid-woof. The thrilling part was that this was a picture not of the animal but of the words that stood for the animal and its noises. It was a representation of something both concrete and abstract. The diagram was a bit like art, a bit like mathematics. It was much more than words uttered or words written: it was a picture of language.

I was hooked. So, it seems, were many of my contemporaries. Among the myths that have attached themselves to memories of being educated in the fifties is the notion that activities like diagramming sentences (along with memorizing poems and adding long columns of figures without a calculator) were pointless and monotonous. I thought diagramming was fun, and most of my friends who were subjected to it look back with varying degrees of delight. Some of us were better at it than others, but it was considered a kind of treat, a game that broke up the school day. You took a sentence, threw it against the wall, picked up the pieces, and put them together again, slotting each word into its pigeonhole. When you got it right, you made order and sense out of what we used all the time and took for granted: sentences.

Gertrude Stein, of all people, was a great fan of diagramming. "I really do not know that anything has ever been more exciting than diagramming sentences," she wrote in the early 1930s. "I like the feeling the everlasting feeling of sentences as they diagram themselves."

In my experience they didn't exactly diagram themselves; they had to be coaxed, if not wrestled. But — the feeling the everlasting feeling: if Gertrude Stein wasn't just riffing on the words, the love-song sound of them, she must have meant the glorious definiteness of the process. I remember loving the look of the sentences, short or long, once they were tidied into diagrams — the curious maplike shapes they made, the way the words settled primly along their horizontals like houses on a road, the way some roads were culs-de-sac and some were long meandering interstates with many exit ramps and scenic lookouts. And the clarity of it all, the ease with which — once they were laid open, their secrets exposed — those sentences could be comprehended.

On a more trivial level, part of the fun was being summoned to the blackboard to show off. There you stood, chalk in hand, while, with a glint in her eye, Sister Bernadette read off an especially tricky sentence. Compact, fastidious handwriting was an asset. A good spatial sense helped you arrange things so that the diagram didn't end up with the words jammed together against the edge of the blackboard like commuters in a subway car. The trick was to think fast, write fast, and not get rattled if you failed in the attempt.

As we became more proficient, the tasks got harder. There was great appeal in the Shaker-like simplicity of sentences like *The dog chased a rabbit* (subject, predicate, direct object), with their plain, no-nonsense diagrams:

But there were also lovable subtleties, like the way the line that set off a predicate adjective slanted back like a signpost toward the subject it modified:

Or the thorny rosebush created by diagramming a prepositional phrase modifying another prepositional phrase:

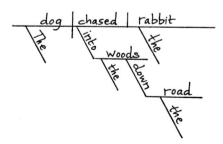

Or the elegant absence of the preposition when using an indirect object, indicated by a short road with no house on it:

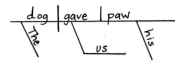

The missing preposition — in this case *to* — could also be placed
on that road in parentheses, but this always seemed to me a clumsy
solution, right up there with explaining a pun. In a related situation, however, the void where the subject of an imperative sentence would go was better filled, to my mind, with the graphic and
slightly menacing parenthesized pronoun, as in:

Questions were a special case. For diagramming, they had to be
turned inside out, the way a sock has to be eased onto a foot: *What
is the dog doing?* transformed into the more dramatic *The dog is doing what?*

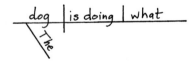

Mostly we diagrammed sentences out of a grammar book, but
sometimes we were assigned the task of making up our own, taking
pleasure in coming up with wild Proustian wanderings that — kick-
ing and screaming — had to be corralled, harnessed, and made to
trot into the barn in neat rows.

Part of the fun of diagramming sentences was that it didn't matter what they said. The dog could bark, chew gum, play chess — in
the world of diagramming, sentences weren't about meaning so
much as they were about subject, predicate, object, and their various dependents or modifiers. If they were diagrammed properly,
they always illustrated correct syntax, no matter how silly their content. We hung those sentences out like a wash until we understood

every piece of them. We could see for ourselves the difference between *who* and *whom*. We knew what an adverb was, and we knew where in a sentence it went, and why it went there. We were aware of dangling modifiers because we could see them, quite literally, dangle.

Today, diagramming is not exactly dead, but for many years it has been in sharp decline. This is partly because diagramming sentences seems to double the task of the student, who has to learn a whole new set of rules — where does that pesky line go, and which way does it slant? — in order to illustrate a set of rules that, in fact, has been learned pretty thoroughly simply by immersion in the language from birth. It's only the subtleties that are difficult — *who* versus *whom,* adjective versus adverb, *it's I* versus *it's me* — and most of those come from the mostly doomed attempt, in the early days of English grammar, to stuff English into the well-made boxes of Latin and Greek, which is something like forcing a struggling cat into the carrier for a trip to the vet.

Another problem is that teachers — and certainly students — have become more willing to accept the idea that the sentences that can be popped into a diagram aren't always sentences anyone wants to write. One writer friend of mine says that she disliked diagramming because it meant "forcing sentences into conformity." And indeed language can be more supple and interesting than the patterns that perfect syntax forces on it. An attempt to diagram a sentence by James Joyce, or one by Henry James (whose style H. G. Wells compared so memorably to "a magnificent but painful hippopotamus resolved at any cost . . . upon picking up a pea"), will quickly demonstrate the limitations of Sister Bernadette's methods. Diagramming may have taught us to write more correctly — and maybe even to think more logically — but I don't think anyone would claim that it taught us to write well. And besides, any writer knows that the best way to learn to write good sentences is not to diagram them but to read them.

Still, like pocket watches and Gilbert and Sullivan operas, diagramming persists, alternately reviled and championed by linguists and grammarians. It can be found in university linguistics courses and on the Web sites of a few diehard enthusiasts. There are teachers' guides, should any teacher want one; it's taught in ESL courses and in progressive private schools. There's a video, *English Grammar: The Art of Diagramming Sentences,* that features a very 1950s-looking teacher named Miss Lamb working at a blackboard. There's even a computer program, apparently, that diagrams.

Sometimes, on a slow subway or a boring car trip, I mentally diagram a sentence, just as I occasionally try to remember the declension of *hic, haec, hoc* or the words to the second verse of "The Star-Spangled Banner." I have no illusions that diagramming sentences in my youth did anything for me, practically speaking. But in an occasional fit of nostalgia, I like to bring back those golden afternoons when

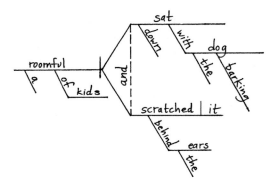

JONATHAN FRANZEN

The Comfort Zone

FROM THE NEW YORKER

IN MAY 1970, a few nights after the Kent State shootings, my father and my brother Tom, who was nineteen, started fighting. They weren't fighting about the Vietnam War, which both of them opposed. The fight was probably about a lot of different things at once. But the immediate issue was Tom's summer job. He was a good artist, with a meticulous nature, and my father had encouraged him (you could even say forced him) to choose a college from a short list of schools with strong programs in architecture. Tom had deliberately chosen the most distant of these schools, Rice University, and he had just returned from his second year in Houston, where his adventures in late-sixties youth culture were pushing him toward majoring in film studies, not architecture. My father, however, had found him a plum summer job with Sverdrup & Parcel, the big engineering firm in St. Louis, whose senior partner, General Leif Sverdrup, had been an Army Corps of Engineers hero in the Philippines. It couldn't have been easy for my father, who was shy and morbidly principled, to pull the requisite strings at Sverdrup. But the office gestalt was hawkish and buzz-cut and generally inimical to bell-bottomed, lefty film-studies majors; and Tom didn't want to be there.

Up in the bedroom that he and I shared, the windows were open and the air had the stuffy wooden-house smell that came out every spring. I preferred the make-believe no-smell of air conditioning, but my mother, whose subjective experience of temperature was notably consistent with low gas and electric bills, claimed to be a devotee of "fresh air," and the windows often stayed open until Memorial Day.

On my night table was the *Peanuts Treasury*, a large, thick hard-cover compilation of daily and Sunday funnies by Charles M. Schulz. My mother had given it to me the previous Christmas, and I'd been rereading it at bedtime ever since. Like most of the nation's ten-year-olds, I had an intense, private relationship with Snoopy, the cartoon beagle. He was a solitary not-animal animal who lived among larger creatures of a different species, which was more or less my feeling in my own house. My brothers, who are nine and twelve years older than I, were less like siblings than like an extra, fun pair of quasi-parents. Although I had friends and was a Cub Scout in good standing, I spent a lot of time alone with talking animals. I was an obsessive rereader of A. A. Milne and the Narnia and Doctor Dolittle novels, and my involvement with my collection of stuffed animals was on the verge of becoming age-inappropriate. It was another point of kinship with Snoopy that he, too, liked animal games. He impersonated tigers and vultures and mountain lions, sharks, sea monsters, pythons, cows, piranhas, penguins, and vampire bats. He was the perfect sunny egoist, starring in his ridiculous fantasies and basking in everyone's attention. In a cartoon strip full of children, the dog was the character I recognized as a child.

Tom and my father had been talking in the living room when I went up to bed. Now, at some late and even stuffier hour, after I'd put aside the *Peanuts Treasury* and fallen asleep, Tom burst into our bedroom. He was shouting with harsh sarcasm. "You'll get over it! You'll forget about me! It'll be so much easier! You'll get over it!"

My father was offstage somewhere, making large abstract sounds. My mother was right behind Tom, sobbing at his shoulder, begging him to stop, to stop. He was pulling open dresser drawers, repacking bags he'd only recently unpacked. "You think you want me here," he said, "but you'll get over it."

What about me? my mother pleaded. *What about Jon?*

"You'll get over it!"

I was a small and fundamentally ridiculous person. Even if I'd dared sit up in bed, what could I have said? "Excuse me, I'm trying to sleep"? I lay still and followed the action through my eyelashes. There were further dramatic comings and goings, through some of which I may in fact have slept. Finally I heard Tom's feet pounding down the stairs and my mother's terrible cries, now nearly shrieks, receding after him: "Tom! Tom! Tom! Please! Tom!" And then the front door slammed.

Things like this had never happened in our house. The worst fight I'd ever witnessed was between Tom and our older brother, Bob, on the subject of Frank Zappa, whose music Tom admired and Bob one day dismissed with such patronizing disdain that Tom began to sneer at Bob's own favorite group, the Supremes, which led to bitter hostilities. But a scene of real wailing and doors slamming in the night was completely off the map. When I woke up the next morning, the memory of it already felt decades-old and semi-dreamlike and unmentionable.

My father had left for work, and my mother served me breakfast without comment. The food on the table, the jingles on the radio, and the walk to school all were unremarkable; and yet everything about the day was soaked in dread. At school that week, in Miss Niblack's class, we were rehearsing our fifth-grade play. The script, which I'd written, had a large number of bit parts and one very generous role that I'd created with my own memorization abilities in mind. The action took place on a boat, involved a taciturn villain named Mr. Scuba, and lacked the most rudimentary comedy, point, or moral. Not even I, who got to do most of the talking, enjoyed being in it. Its badness — my responsibility for its badness — became part of the day's general dread.

There was something dreadful about springtime itself, the way plants and animals lost control, the *Lord of the Flies* buzzing, the heat indoors. After school, instead of staying outside to play, I followed my dread home and cornered my mother in our dining room. I asked her about my upcoming class performance. Would Dad be in town for it? What about Bob? Would he be home from college yet? And what about Tom? Would Tom be there too? This was quite plausibly an innocent line of questioning — I was a small glutton for attention, forever turning conversations to the subject of myself — and, for a while, my mother gave me plausibly innocent answers. Then she slumped into a chair, put her face in her hands, and began to weep.

"Didn't you hear anything last night?" she said.

"No."

"You didn't hear Tom and Dad shouting? You didn't hear doors slamming?"

"No!"

She gathered me in her arms, which was probably the main thing I'd been dreading. I stood there stiffly while she hugged me. "Tom and Dad had a terrible fight," she said. "After you went to bed. They had a terrible fight, and Tom got his things and left the house, and we don't know where he went."

"Oh."

"I thought we'd hear from him today, but he hasn't called, and I'm frantic, not knowing where he is. I'm just frantic!"

I squirmed a little in her grip.

"But this has nothing to do with you," she said. "It's between him and Dad and has nothing to do with you. I'm sure Tom's sorry he won't be here to see your play. Or maybe, who knows, he'll be back by Friday and he will see it."

"OK."

"But I don't want you telling anyone he's gone until we know where he is. Will you agree not to tell anyone?"

"OK," I said, breaking free of her. "Can we turn the air conditioning on?"

I was unaware of it, but an epidemic had broken out across the country. Late adolescents in suburbs like ours had suddenly gone berserk, running away to other cities to have sex and not attend college, ingesting every substance they could get their hands on, not just clashing with their parents but rejecting and annihilating everything about them. For a while, the parents were so frightened and so mystified and so ashamed that each family, especially mine, quarantined itself and suffered in isolation.

When I went upstairs, my bedroom felt like an overwarm sickroom. The clearest remaining vestige of Tom was the *Don't Look Back* poster that he'd taped to a flank of his dresser where Bob Dylan's psychedelic hair style wouldn't always be catching my mother's censorious eye. Tom's bed, neatly made, was the bed of a kid carried off by an epidemic.

In that unsettled season, as the so-called generation gap was rending the cultural landscape, Charles Schulz's work was almost uniquely beloved. Fifty-five million Americans had seen *A Charlie Brown Christmas* the previous December, for a Nielsen share of better than fifty percent. The musical *You're a Good Man, Charlie*

Brown was in its second sold-out year on Broadway. The astronauts of *Apollo X*, in their dress rehearsal for the first lunar landing, had christened their orbiter and landing vehicle *Charlie Brown* and *Snoopy*. Newspapers carrying *Peanuts* reached more than 150 million readers, *Peanuts* collections were all over the bestseller lists, and if my own friends were any indication, there was hardly a kid's bedroom in America without a *Peanuts* wastebasket or *Peanuts* bedsheets or a *Peanuts* gift book. Schulz, by a luxurious margin, was the most famous living artist on the planet.

To the countercultural mind, a begoggled beagle piloting a doghouse and getting shot down by the Red Baron was akin to Yossarian paddling a dinghy to Sweden. The strip's square panels were the only square thing about it. Wouldn't the country be better off listening to Linus Van Pelt than Robert McNamara? This was the era of flower children, not flower adults. But the strip appealed to older Americans as well. It was unfailingly inoffensive (Snoopy never lifted a leg) and was set in a safe, attractive suburb where the kids, except for Pigpen, whose image Ron McKernan of the Grateful Dead pointedly embraced, were clean and well spoken and conservatively dressed. Hippies and astronauts, the Pentagon and the antiwar movement, the rejecting kids and the rejected grownups were all of one mind here.

An exception was my own household. As far as I know, my father never in his life read a comic strip, and my mother's interest in the funnies was limited to a single-panel feature called *The Girls*, whose generic middle-aged matrons, with their weight problems and stinginess and poor driving skills and weakness for department-store bargains, she found just endlessly amusing.

I didn't buy comic books, or even *Mad* magazine, but I worshiped at the altars of Warner Bros. cartoons and the funnies section of the *St. Louis Post-Dispatch*. I read the section's black-and-white page first, skipping the dramatic features like *Steve Roper* and *Juliet Jones* and glancing at *Li'l Abner* only to satisfy myself that it was still trashy and repellent. On the full-color back page I read the strips strictly in reverse order of preference, doing my best to be amused by Dagwood Bumstead's midnight snacks and struggling to ignore the fact that Tiger and Punkinhead were the kind of messy, unreflective kids I disliked in real life, before treating myself to my favorite strip, *B.C.* The strip, by Johnny Hart, was caveman humor. Hart wrung hundreds of gags from the friendship between a flightless bird and a long-suffering tortoise who was constantly attempting unturtlish feats of agility and flexibility. Debts were always paid in clams; dinner was always roast leg of something. When I was done with *B.C.,* I was done with the paper.

The comics in St. Louis's other paper, the *Globe-Democrat,* which my parents didn't take, seemed bleak and foreign to me. *Broom Hilda* and *Animal Crackers* and *The Family Circus* were off-putting in the manner of the kid whose partially visible underpants, which had the name CUTTAIR hand-markered on the waistband, I'd stared at throughout my family's tour of the Canadian parliament. Although *The Family Circus* was resolutely unfunny, its panels clearly were based on some actual family's life and were aimed at an audience that recognized this life, which compelled me to posit an entire subspecies of humanity that found *The Family Circus* hilarious.

I knew very well, of course, why the *Globe-Democrat*'s funnies were so lame: the paper that carried *Peanuts* didn't *need* any other good strips. Indeed, I would have swapped the entire *Post-Dispatch* for a daily dose of Schulz. Only *Peanuts,* the strip we didn't get, dealt with stuff that really mattered. I didn't for a minute believe that the children in *Peanuts* were really children — they were so much more emphatic and cartoonishly *real* than anybody in my own neighborhood — but I nevertheless took their stories to be dispatches from a universe of childhood that was somehow more substantial and convincing than my own. Instead of playing kickball and foursquare, the way my friends and I did, the kids in *Peanuts* had real baseball teams, real football equipment, real fistfights. Their interactions with Snoopy were far richer than the chasings and bitings that constituted my own relationships with neighborhood dogs. Minor but incredible disasters, often involving new vocabulary words, befell them daily. Lucy was "blackballed from the Bluebirds." She knocked Charlie Brown's croquet ball so far that he had to call the other players from a phone booth. She gave Charlie Brown a signed document in which she swore not to pull the football away when he tried to kick it, but the "peculiar thing about this document," as she observed in the final frame, was that "it was never notarized." When Lucy smashed the bust of Beethoven on Schroeder's toy piano, it struck me as odd and funny that

Schroeder had a closet full of identical replacement busts, but I accepted it as humanly possible, because Schulz had drawn it.

To the *Peanuts Treasury* I soon added two other equally strong hardcover collections, *Peanuts Revisited* and *Peanuts Classics.* A well-meaning relative once also gave me a copy of Robert Short's national bestseller, *The Gospel According to Peanuts,* but it couldn't have interested me less. *Peanuts* wasn't a portal to the Gospel. It was my gospel.

Chapter 1, verses 1–4, of what I knew about disillusionment: Charlie Brown passes the house of the Little Red-Haired Girl, the object of his eternal fruitless longing. He sits down with Snoopy and says, "I wish I had two ponies." He imagines offering one of the ponies to the Little Red-Haired Girl, riding out into the countryside with her, and sitting down with her beneath a tree. Suddenly, he's scowling at Snoopy and asking, "Why aren't you two ponies?" Snoopy, rolling his eyes, thinks, "I knew we'd get around to that."

Or Chapter 1, verses 26–32, of what I knew about the mysteries of etiquette: Linus is showing off his new wristwatch to everyone in the neighborhood. "New watch!" he says proudly to Snoopy, who, after a hesitation, licks it. Linus's hair stands on end. "YOU LICKED MY WATCH!" he cries. "It'll rust! It'll turn green! He's ruined it!" Snoopy is left looking mildly puzzled and thinking, "I thought it would have been impolite not to taste it."

Or Chapter 2, verses 6–12, of what I knew about fiction: Linus is annoying Lucy, wheedling and pleading with her to read him a story. To shut him up, she grabs a book, randomly opens it, and says, "A man was born, he lived and he died. The End!" She tosses the book aside, and Linus picks it up reverently. "What a fascinating account," he says. "It almost makes you wish you had known the fellow."

The perfect silliness of stuff like this, the koanlike inscrutability, entranced me even when I was ten. But many of the more elaborate sequences, especially the ones about Charlie Brown's humiliation and loneliness, made only a generic impression on me. In a classroom spelling bee that Charlie Brown has been looking forward to, the first word he's asked to spell is "maze." With a complacent smile, he produces "M-A-Y-S." The class screams with laughter. He returns to his seat and presses his face into his desktop, and when his teacher asks him what's wrong, he yells at her and ends up in the principal's office. *Peanuts* was steeped in Schulz's awareness that for every winner in a competition there has to be a loser, if not twenty losers, or two thousand, but I personally enjoyed winning and couldn't see why so much fuss was made about the losers.

In the spring of 1970, Miss Niblack's class was studying homonyms to prepare for what she called the Homonym Spelldown. I did some desultory homonym drilling with my mother, rattling off "sleigh" for "slay" and "slough" for "slew" the way other kids roped softballs into center field. To me, the only halfway interesting question about the Spelldown was who was going to come in second. A new kid had joined our class that year, a shrimpy black-haired striver, Chris Toczko, who had it in his head that he and I were academic rivals. I was a nice enough little boy as long as you didn't compete on my turf. Toczko was annoyingly unaware that I, not he, by natural right, was the best student in the class. On the day of the Spelldown, he actually taunted me. He said he'd done a lot of studying and he was going to beat me! I looked down at the little irritant and did not know what to say. I evidently mattered a lot more to him than he did to me.

For the Spelldown, we all stood by the blackboard, Miss Niblack calling out one half of a pair of homonyms and my classmates sitting down as soon as they had failed. Toczko was pale and trembling, but he knew his homonyms. He was the last kid standing, besides me, when Miss Niblack called out the word "liar." Toczko trembled and essayed, "L . . . I . . . ." And I could see that I had beaten him. I waited impatiently while, with considerable anguish, he extracted two more letters from his marrow: "E . . . R?"

"I'm sorry, Chris, that's not a word," Miss Niblack said.

With a sharp laugh of triumph, not even waiting for Toczko to sit down, I stepped forward and sang out, "L-Y-R-E! *Lyre.* It's a stringed instrument."

I hadn't really doubted that I would win, but Toczko had got to me with his taunting, and my blood was up. I was the last person in class to realize that Toczko was having a meltdown. His face turned red and he began to cry, insisting angrily that "lier" *was* a word, it *was* a word.

I didn't care if it was a word or not. I knew my rights. Toczko's tears disturbed and disappointed me, as I made quite clear by fetching the classroom dictionary and showing him that "lier" wasn't in it. This was how both Toczko and I ended up in the principal's office.

I'd never been sent down before. I was interested to learn that the principal, Mr. Barnett, had a *Webster's International Unabridged* in his office. Toczko, who barely outweighed the dictionary, used two hands to open it and to roll back the pages to the "L" words. I stood at his shoulder and saw where his tiny, trembling index finger was pointing: *lier, n., one that lies (as in ambush)*. Mr. Barnett immediately declared us cowinners of the Spelldown — a compromise that didn't seem quite fair to me, since I would surely have murdered Toczko if we'd gone another round. But his outburst had spooked me, and I decided it might be OK, for once, to let somebody else win.

A few months after the Homonym Spelldown, just after summer vacation started, Toczko ran out into Grant Road and was killed by a car. What little I knew then about the world's badness I knew mainly from a camping trip, some years earlier, when I'd dropped a frog into a campfire and watched it shrivel and roll down the flat side of a log. My memory of that shriveling and rolling was sui generis, distinct from my other memories. It was like a nagging, sick-making atom of rebuke in me. I felt similarly rebuked now when my mother, who knew nothing of Toczko's rivalry with me, told me that he was dead. She was weeping as she'd wept over Tom's disappearance some weeks earlier. She sat me down and made me write a letter of condolence to Toczko's mother. I was very much unaccustomed to considering the interior states of people other than myself, but it was impossible not to consider Mrs. Toczko's. Though I never met her, in the ensuing weeks I pictured her suffering so incessantly and vividly that I could almost see her: a tiny, trim, dark-haired woman who cried the way her son did.

"Everything I do makes me feel guilty," says Charlie Brown. He's at the beach, and he has just thrown a pebble into the water, and Linus has commented, "Nice going . . . It took that stone four thousand years to get to shore, and now you've thrown it back."

I felt guilty about Toczko. I felt guilty about the little frog. I felt guilty about shunning my mother's hugs when she seemed to need them most. I felt guilty about the washcloths at the bottom of the stack in the linen closet, the older, thinner washcloths that we seldom used. I felt guilty for preferring my best shooter marbles, a solid red agate and a solid yellow agate, my king and my queen, to marbles farther down my rigid marble hierarchy. I felt guilty about the board games that I didn't like to play — Uncle Wiggily, U.S. Presidential Elections, Game of the States — and sometimes, when my friends weren't around, I opened the boxes and examined the pieces in the hope of making the games feel less forgotten. I felt guilty about neglecting the stiff-limbed, scratchy-pelted Mr. Bear, who had no voice and didn't mix well with my other stuffed animals. To avoid feeling guilty about them, too, I slept with one of them per night, according to a strict weekly schedule.

We laugh at dachshunds for humping our legs, but our own species is even more self-centered in its imaginings. There's no object so Other that it can't be anthropomorphized and shanghaied into conversation with us. Some objects are more amenable than others, however. The trouble with Mr. Bear was that he was more realistically bearlike than the other animals. He had a distinct, stern, feral persona; unlike our faceless washcloths, he was assertively Other. It was no wonder I couldn't speak through him. An old shoe is easier to invest with comic personality than is, say, a photograph of Cary Grant. The blanker the slate, the more easily we can fill it with our own image.

Our visual cortexes are wired to quickly recognize faces and then quickly subtract massive amounts of detail from them, zeroing in on their essential message: Is this person happy? angry? fearful? Individual faces may vary greatly, but a smirk on one is a lot like a smirk on another. Smirks are conceptual, not pictorial. Our brains are like cartoonists — and cartoonists are like our brains, simplifying and exaggerating, subordinating facial detail to abstract comic concepts.

Scott McCloud, in his cartoon treatise *Understanding Comics,* argues that the image you have of yourself when you're conversing is very different from your image of the person you're conversing with. Your interlocutor may produce universal smiles and universal frowns, and they may help you to identify with him emotionally, but he also has a particular nose and particular skin and particular hair that continually remind you that he's an Other. The image you have of your own face, by contrast, is highly cartoonish. When you feel yourself smile, you imagine a cartoon of smiling, not the complete skin-and-nose-and-hair package. It's precisely the simplicity and universality of cartoon faces, the absence of Otherly particulars, that invite us to love them as we love ourselves. The most widely loved (and profitable) faces in the modern world tend to be exceptionally basic and abstract cartoons: Mickey Mouse, the Simpsons, Tintin, and, simplest of all — barely more than a circle, two dots, and a horizontal line — Charlie Brown.

Schulz only ever wanted to be a cartoonist. He was born in St. Paul in 1922, the only child of a German father and a mother of Norwegian extraction. As an infant, he was nicknamed Sparky, after a horse in the then popular comic strip *Barney Google*. His father, who, like Charlie Brown's father, was a barber, bought six different newspapers on the weekend and read all the era's comics with his son. Schulz skipped a grade in elementary school and was the least mature kid in every class after that. Much of the existing Schulzian literature dwells on the Charlie Brownish traumas in his early life: his skinniness and pimples, his unpopularity with girls at school, the inexplicable rejection of a batch of his drawings by his high school yearbook, and, some years later, the rejection of his marriage proposal by the real-life Little Red-Haired Girl, Donna Mae Johnson. Schulz himself spoke of his youth in a tone close to anger. "It took me a long time to become a human being," he told NEMO magazine in 1987.

> I was regarded by many as kind of sissyfied, which I resented because I really was not a sissy. I was not a tough guy, but . . . I was good at any sport where you threw things, or hit them, or caught them, or something like that. I hated things like swimming and tumbling and those kinds of things, so I was really not a sissy. [But] the coaches were so intolerant and there was no program for all of us. So I never regarded myself as being much and I never regarded myself as being good looking and I never had a date in high school, because I thought, who'd want to date me? So I didn't bother.

Schulz "didn't bother" going to art school, either — it would only have discouraged him, he said, to be around people who could draw better than he could. You could see a lack of confidence here. You could also see a kid who knew how to protect himself.

On the eve of Schulz's induction into the army, his mother died of cancer. She was forty-eight and had suffered greatly, and Schulz later described the loss as an emotional catastrophe from which he almost did not recover. During basic training, he was depressed, withdrawn, and grieving. In the long run, though, the army was good for him. He went into the service, he recalled later, as "a nothing person" and came out as a staff sergeant in charge of a machine-gun squadron. "I thought, By golly, if that isn't a man, I don't know what is," he said. "And I felt good about myself and that lasted about eight minutes, and then I went back to where I am now." After the war, Schulz returned to his childhood neighborhood, lived with his father, became intensely involved in a Christian youth group, and learned to draw kids. For the rest of his life, he virtually never drew adults. He avoided adult vices — didn't drink, didn't smoke, didn't swear — and, in his work, he spent more and more time in the imagined yards and sandlots of his childhood. But the world of *Peanuts* remained a deeply motherless place. Charlie Brown's dog may (or may not) cheer him up after a day of failures; his mother never does.

Although Schulz had been a social victim as a child, he'd also had the undivided attention of two loving parents. All his life, he was a prickly Minnesotan mixture of disabling inhibition and rugged self-confidence. In high school, after another student illustrated an essay with a watercolor drawing, Schulz was surprised when a teacher asked him why he hadn't done some illustrations himself. He didn't think it was fair to get academic credit for a talent that most kids didn't have. He never thought it was fair to draw caricatures. ("If somebody has a big nose," he said, "I'm sure that they regret the fact they have a big nose and who am I to point it out in gross caricature?") In later decades, when he had enormous bargaining power, he was reluctant to demand a larger or more flexible layout for *Peanuts,* because he didn't think it was fair to the papers that had been his loyal customers. His resentment of the name *Peanuts,* which his editors had given the strip in 1950, was still fresh in the eighties, when he was one of the ten highest-paid entertainers in America (behind Bill Cosby, ahead of Michael Jackson). "They didn't know when I walked in there that here was a fanatic," he told *NEMO.* "Here was a kid totally dedicated to what he was going to do. And to label then something that was going to be a life's work with a name like *Peanuts* was really insulting." To the suggestion that thirty-seven years might have softened the insult, Schulz said, "No, no. I hold a grudge, boy."

I never heard my father tell a joke. Sometimes he reminisced about a business colleague who ordered a "Scotch and Coke" and a "flander" fillet in a Dallas diner in July, and he could smile at his own embarrassments, his impolitic remarks at the office and his foolish mistakes on home-improvement projects, but there wasn't a silly bone in his body. He responded to other people's jokes with a wince or a grimace. As a boy, I told him a story I'd made up about a trash-hauling company cited for "fragrant violations." He shook his head, stone-faced, and said, "Not plausible."

In another archetypal *Peanuts* strip, Violet and Patty are abusing Charlie Brown in vicious stereo: "GO ON HOME! WE DON'T WANT YOU AROUND HERE!" As he trudges away with his eyes on the ground, Violet remarks, "It's a strange thing about Charlie Brown. You almost never see him laugh."

My father only ever wanted not to be a child anymore. His parents were a pair of nineteenth-century Scandinavians caught up in a Hobbesian struggle to prevail in the swamps of north-central Minnesota. His popular, charismatic older brother drowned in a hunting accident when he was still a young man. His nutty and pretty and spoiled younger sister had an only daughter who died in a one-car accident when she was twenty-two. My father's parents also died in a one-car accident, but only after regaling him with prohibitions, demands, and criticisms for fifty years. He never said a harsh word about them. He never said a nice word, either.

The few childhood stories he told were about his dog, Spider, and his gang of friends in the invitingly named little town, Palisade, that his father and uncles had constructed among the swamps. The local high school was eight miles from Palisade. To attend, my father lived in a boarding house for a year and later commuted in his father's Model A. He was a social cipher, invisible after school. The most popular girl in his class, Romelle Erickson, was expected to be the valedictorian, and the school's "social crowd" was "shocked," my father told me many times, when it turned out that "the country boy," "Earl Who," had claimed the title.

When he registered at the University of Minnesota, in 1933, his father went with him and announced, at the head of the registration line, "He's going to be a civil engineer." For the rest of his life, my father was restless. He was studying philosophy at night school when he met my mother, and it took her four years to persuade him to have children. In his thirties, he agonized about whether to study medicine; in his forties, he was offered a partnership in a contracting firm which he almost dared to accept; in his fifties and sixties, he admonished me not to waste my life working for a corporation. In the end, though, he spent fifty years doing exactly what his father had told him to do.

My mother called him "oversensitive." She meant that it was easy to hurt his feelings, but the sensitivity was physical as well. When he was young, a doctor gave him a pinprick test that showed him to be allergic to "almost everything," including wheat, milk, and tomatoes. A different doctor, whose office was at the top of five long flights of stairs, greeted him with a blood-pressure test and immediately declared him unfit to fight the Nazis. Or so my father told me, with a shrugging gesture and an odd smile (as if to say, "What could I do?"), when I asked him why he hadn't been in the war. Even as a teenager, I sensed that his social awkwardness and sensitivities had been aggravated by not serving. He came from a family of pacifist Swedes, however, and was very happy not to be a soldier. He was happy that my brothers had college deferments and good luck with the lottery. Among his patriotic colleagues and the war-vet husbands of my mother's friends, he was such an outlier on the subject of Vietnam that he didn't dare talk about it. At home, in private, he aggressively declared that, if Tom had drawn a bad number, he personally would have driven him to Canada.

Tom was a second son in the mold of my father. He got poison ivy so bad it was like measles. He had a mid-October birthday and was perennially the youngest kid in his classes. On his only date in high school, he was so nervous that he forgot his baseball tickets and left the car idling in the street while he ran back inside; the car rolled down the hill, punched through an asphalt curb, and cleared two levels of a terraced garden before coming to rest on a neighbor's front lawn.

To me, it simply added to Tom's mystique that the car was not only still drivable but entirely undamaged. Neither he nor Bob could do any wrong in my eyes. They were expert whistlers and chess players, phenomenal wielders of tools and pencils, sole suppliers of whatever anecdotes and cultural data I was able to impress my friends with. In the margins of Tom's school copy of *A Portrait of the Artist*, he drew a two-hundred-page riffle-animation of a stick-figure pole-vaulter clearing a hurdle, landing on his head, and being carted away on a stretcher by stick-figure EMS personnel; this seemed to me a masterwork of filmic art and science. But my father had told Tom: "You'd make a good architect, here are three schools to choose from." He said: "You're going to work for Sverdrup."

Tom was gone for five days before we heard from him. His call came on a Sunday after church. We were sitting on the screen porch, and my mother ran the length of the house to answer the phone. She sounded so ecstatic with relief I felt embarrassed for her. Tom had hitchhiked back to Houston and was doing deep-fry at a Church's Fried Chicken, hoping to save enough money to join his best friend in Colorado. My mother kept asking him when he might come home, assuring him that he was welcome and that he wouldn't have to work at Sverdrup; but there was something toxic about us now which Tom obviously wanted nothing to do with.

Charles Schulz was the best comic-strip artist who ever lived. When *Peanuts* debuted, in October 1950 (the same month Tom was born), the funny pages were full of musty holdovers from the thirties and forties. Even with the strip's strongest precursors, George Herriman's *Krazy Kat* and Elzie Segar's *Popeye*, you were aware of the severe constraints under which newspaper comics operated. The faces of Herriman's characters were too small to display more than rudimentary emotion, and so the burden of humor and sympathy came to rest on Herriman's language; his work read more like comic fable than like funny drawing. Popeye's face was proportionately larger than Krazy Kat's, but he was such a florid caricature that much of Segar's expressive budget was spent on nondiscretionary items, like Popeye's distended jaw and oversized nose; these were good jokes, but the same jokes every time. The very first *Peanuts* strip, by contrast, was all white space and big funny faces. It invited you right in. The minor character Shermy was speaking in neat letters and clear diction: "Here comes ol' Charlie Brown!

Good ol' Charlie Brown . . . Yes, sir! Good ol' Charlie Brown . . .
How I hate him!"

This first strip and the 759 that immediately followed it have recently been published, complete and fully indexed, in a handsome
volume from Fantagraphics Books. (This is the first in a series of
twenty-five uniform volumes that will reproduce Schulz's entire
daily oeuvre.) Even in Schulz's relatively primitive early work, you
can appreciate what a breakthrough he made in drawing characters with large, visually uncluttered heads. Long limbs and big
landscapes and fully articulated facial features — adult life, in
short — were unaffordable luxuries. By dispensing with them, and
by jumping from a funnies world of five or ten facial expressions
into a world of fifty or a hundred, Schulz introduced a new infor-
mational dimension to the newspaper strip.

Although he later became famous for putting words like "depressed" and "inner tensions" and "emotional outlets" in the
mouths of little kids, only a tiny percentage of his strips were actually drawn in the mock-psychological vein. His most important
innovations were visual — he was all about *drawing funny* — and
for most of my life as a fan I was curiously unconscious of this fact.
In my imagination, *Peanuts* was a narrative, a collection of locales
and scenes and sequences. And, certainly, some comic strips do fit
this description. Mike Doonesbury, for example, can be translated
into words with minimal loss of information. Garry Trudeau is essentially a social novelist, his topical satire and intricate family dy-
namics and elaborate camera angles all serving to divert attention
from the monotony of his comic expression. But Linus Van Pelt
consists, first and foremost, of pen strokes. You'll never really understand him without seeing his hair stand on end. Translation
into words inevitably diminishes Linus. As a cartoon, he's already a
perfectly efficient vector of comic intention.

The purpose of a comic strip, Schulz liked to say, was to sell
newspapers and to make people laugh. Although the formulation
may look self-deprecating at first glance, in fact it is an oath of loy-
alty. When I. B. Singer, in his Nobel address, declared that the novelist's first responsibility is to be a storyteller, he didn't say "mere
storyteller," and Schulz didn't say "merely make people laugh." He
was loyal to the reader who wanted something funny from the
funny pages. Just about anything — protesting against world hun-

ger, getting a laugh out of words like "nooky," dispensing wisdom, dying — is easier than real comedy.

Schulz never stopped trying to be funny. Around 1970, though, he began to drift away from aggressive humor and into melancholy reverie. There came tedious meanderings in Snoopyland with the unhilarious bird Woodstock and the unamusing beagle Spike. Certain leaden devices, such as Marcie's insistence on calling Peppermint Patty "sir," were heavily recycled. By the late eighties, the strip had grown so quiet that younger friends of mine seemed baffled by my fandom. It didn't help that later *Peanuts* anthologies loyally reprinted so many Spike and Marcie strips. The volumes that properly showcased Schulz's genius, the three hardcover collections from the sixties, had gone out of print. There were a few critical appreciations, most notably by Umberto Eco, who argued for Schulz's literary greatness in an essay written in the sixties and reprinted in the eighties (when Eco got famous). But the praise of a "low" genre by an old semiotic soldier in the culture wars couldn't help carrying an odor of provocation.

Still more harmful to Schulz's reputation were his own kitschy spinoffs. Even in the sixties, you had to fight through cloying Warm Puppy paraphernalia to reach the comedy; the cuteness levels in latter-day *Peanuts* TV specials tied my toes in knots. What first made *Peanuts Peanuts* was cruelty and failure, and yet every *Peanuts* greeting card and tchotchke and blimp had to feature somebody's sweet, crumpled smile. (You should go out and buy the new Fantagraphics book just to reward the publisher for putting a scowling Charlie Brown on the cover.) Everything about the billion-dollar *Peanuts* industry, which Schulz himself helped create, argued against him as an artist to be taken seriously. Far more than Disney, whose studios were churning out kitsch from the start, Schulz came to seem an icon of art's corruption by commerce, which sooner or later paints a smiling sales face on everything it touches. The fan who wants to see an artist sees a merchant instead. Why isn't he two ponies?

It's hard to repudiate a comic strip, however, when your memories of it are more vivid than your memories of your own life. When Charlie Brown went off to summer camp, I went along in my imagination. I heard him trying to make conversation with the fellow camper who sat on his bunk and refused to say anything but "Shut up and leave me alone." I watched when he finally came home again and shouted to Lucy "I'm back!" and Lucy gave him a bored look and said, "Have you been away?"

I went to camp myself, in the summer of 1970. But, aside from an alarming personal-hygiene situation that seemed to have resulted from my peeing in some poison ivy, and which, for several days, I was convinced was either a fatal tumor or puberty, my camp experience paled beside Charlie Brown's. The best part of it was coming home and seeing Bob's new yellow Karmann Ghia waiting for me at the YMCA.

Tom was also home by then. He'd managed to make his way to his friend's house in Colorado, but the friend's parents weren't happy about harboring somebody else's runaway son, and so they'd sent Tom back to St. Louis. Officially, I was very excited that he was back. In truth, I was embarrassed to be around him. I was afraid that if I referred to his sickness and our quarantine I might trigger a relapse. I wanted to live in a *Peanuts* world where rage was funny and insecurity was lovable. The littlest kid in my *Peanuts* books, Sally Brown, grew older for a while and then hit a glass ceiling. I wanted everyone in my family to get along and nothing to change; but suddenly, after Tom ran away, it was as if the five of us looked around, asked why we should be spending time together, and failed to come up with many good answers.

For the first time, in the months that followed, my parents' conflicts became audible. My father came home on cool nights to complain about the house's "chill." My mother countered that the house wasn't cold if you were *doing housework all day*. My father marched into the dining room to adjust the thermostat and dramatically point to its "Comfort Zone," a pale blue arc between 72 and 78 degrees. My mother said that she was *so hot*. And I decided, as always, not to voice my suspicion that the Comfort Zone referred to air conditioning in the summer rather than heat in the winter. My father set the temperature at 72 and retreated to the den, which was situated directly above the furnace. There was a lull, and then big explosions. No matter what corner of the house I hid myself in, I could hear my father bellowing, "LEAVE THE GOD-DAMNED THERMOSTAT ALONE!"

"Earl, I didn't touch it!"

"You did! Again!"

"I didn't think I even moved it, I just *looked* at it, I didn't mean to change it."

"Again! You monkeyed with it again! I had it set where I wanted it. And you moved it down to seventy!"

"Well, if I did somehow change it, I'm sure I didn't mean to. You'd be hot, too, if you worked all day in the kitchen."

"All I ask at the end of a long day at work is that the temperature be set in the Comfort Zone."

"Earl, it is so hot in the kitchen. You don't know, because you're never *in* here, but it is *so* hot."

"The *low end* of the Comfort Zone! Not even the middle! The low end! It is not too much to ask!"

I wonder why "cartoonish" remains such a pejorative. It took me half my life to achieve seeing my parents as cartoons. And to become more perfectly a cartoon myself: what a victory that would be.

My father eventually applied technology to the problem of temperature. He bought a space heater to put behind his chair in the dining room, where he was bothered in winter by drafts from the bay window. Like so many of his appliance purchases, the heater was a pathetically cheap little thing, a wattage hog with a stertorous fan and a grinning orange mouth which dimmed the lights and drowned out conversation and produced a burning smell every time it cycled on. When I was in high school, he bought a quieter, more expensive model. One evening, my mother and I started reminiscing about the old model, caricaturing my father's temperature sensitivities, doing cartoons of the little heater's faults, the smoke and the buzzing, and my father got mad and left the table. He thought we were ganging up on him. He thought I was being cruel, and I was, but I was also forgiving him.

IAN FRAZIER

If Memory Doesn't Serve

FROM THE ATLANTIC MONTHLY

AMONG THE CRUELEST tricks life plays is the way it puts the complicated part at the end, when the brain is declining into simplicity, and the simple part at the beginning, when the brain is fresh and has memory power to spare. As a boy I had only a few things to keep track of. There was one place, the small town where I lived; two pro sports, baseball and football; three TV channels; four sequential seasons, as yet unmixed by global warming; five kids in my neighborhood to play with; and so on. In no category did the number of entries go much above a dozen or two. I didn't meet people and have to remember their names, because everybody I ran into I already knew. With my extra, leftover memory I preserved pointless conversations, nonsense phrases my brother made up, remarks by adults they later claimed they hadn't said, and incidental data such as the farthest point up our street from which it was possible to run and still catch the school bus.

Since then my memory has been required to hold gigantically much more, the bulk of it so dull. Feats of adult remembering often conform to the "negative Disneyland" rule of grown-up pleasures: that is, it is fun, of a sort, suddenly to remember where you left the registration stickers for your car, but only in comparison to the trip to the Department of Motor Vehicles you would have to make if you didn't. I sometimes nearly crumble in self-pity at the mnemonic brain-busters life hands me. An example: a few years ago the friends my young son usually played with were Joshua, Rhys, and Julian. No memory problems there — each interesting and lively boy easily matched with his name in my mind. The mothers of the boys, however, were (respectively) Georgeanne, Geraldine, and Gabrielle. To a person whose days of high-detail remembering are gone, those are essentially the same name. When greeting someone, it is not enough to know that her name begins with a G. I held this unfair complicatedness against each of them and acted put-upon and odd around them.

Does anyone remember the name of Russ Nixon, catcher for the Cleveland Indians in 1958? Once I spent lonely hours trying to remember it, and when morning came and I could call a friend who knew, I understood what had happened. My friend spoke and the name emerged, good as new, from the later Nixon overlays that had hidden it. The brain has only so many slots, and by the time you reach fifty they have become cluttered and full. I'm sure most of us have a small place in our brains containing the following four items:

1. H. G. Wells
2. George Orwell
3. Orson Welles
4. Orson Bean

They cluster together through some unknown law of the synapses. The first two are easy to confuse because both are thirties-era, English, and science-fictiony (*The Time Machine, Nineteen Eighty-four*). The second and third blend because George Orwell and Orson Welles, as names, sound like made-up, roman-à-clef versions of each other. Also, Welles did a famous hoax radio broadcast of Wells's *War of the Worlds,* a confusing event in itself. And then you have Orson Bean, who is in there probably just to round out the conjugation, or through one of those comic mishaps he used to get into in his roles as an actor. Sometimes when I have a spare moment I take each name out, consider it, link it to the proper person, recall each one's face and biography, and then put all the names back in place in my mind. I believe this is a basically healthy exercise, like flossing.

Then, if I'm feeling like it, or if I'm still lying awake, I run through a few more calisthenics to keep myself sharp. AA is not the same as Triple A — a fact I learn and relearn at car-rental counters when I ask for an AA discount. Michael Moore, the activist author and documentary filmmaker, once made a movie called *Roger and*

Me, partly about Roger Smith, then the president of General Motors. Consequently, it is quite natural to slip up and refer to Michael Moore as Roger Moore. The two are different, however; Roger Moore is a suave-seeming English movie actor who used to play James Bond, a couple of James Bonds ago. And speaking of that, I am me, and not James Bond's creator, Ian Fleming, the late English intelligence officer and author of spy thrillers. Twice now while I've been on book tours the person introducing me to the audience at a reading has said, "And now, please join me in welcoming Ian Fleming." After the second time I took to carrying a copy of *Goldfinger,* just to be ready, but so far it hasn't happened again.

Jamie Bassett was my son's third-grade teacher; Diana Tackett was my daughter's second-grade teacher. Kathy York was my daughter's third-grade teacher; Drury Thorp was my son's second-grade teacher. (Drury Thorp is related to the humorist Robert Benchley, who still has his own slot in my mind.) Ashanti is not the same as Beyoncé; the former is a popular singer who recently appeared on the cover of a New York newspaper carrying a handbag printed with a greatly enlarged photograph of her own face; the latter is a popular singer who has won several Grammy Awards and who performed the national anthem at the 2004 Super Bowl — the Janet Jackson one. Russell Means and Dennis Banks were both leaders of the American Indian Movement back in the seventies; I am prone to refer to either or both as Russell Banks, who is neither, but a well-known novelist. Victor Klemperer, the German writer, kept a detailed two-volume journal of his days in Dresden during World War II, and has been called "the great diarist of the Holocaust"; Werner Klemperer is the American television and movie actor who played Colonel Klink on the TV series *Hogan's Heroes.* (Remarkably, Werner and Victor were cousins.)

Suddenly a nagging thought occurs to me: there is Ashanti, and there is Beyoncé . . . but wasn't there a third in that category? Yes. There was another like them — another young, model-beautiful black woman singer usually referred to by a single name. She has recently disappeared over the music-scene horizon. Her big hit song was "The Boy Is Mine." She sang it as a duet with somebody. I saw the video of it many times. In it she did a lot of vogueing, hand gestures, framing her face with her fingers, and so forth. I used to do a lip-sync imitation of her, using the same gestures but ending with one of my own, which was to lift my baseball cap above my head twice with both hands. I showed my imitation often to my teenage daughter and her friends, embarrassing her. What was that singer's name? It was . . . Brandy! Thank you, memory. Ashanti, Beyoncé, and Brandy.

Jamie Bassett, Diana Tackett; Drury Thorp, Kathy York. The names of elementary school teachers have a strange power to evoke the past. Ashanti, Beyoncé, Brandy. I am slightly afraid there's yet another in that category I've forgotten about, but I won't worry over it now. Russell Means (AIM), Russell Banks (novelist), Dennis Banks (AIM). Victor Klemperer, diarist of the Holocaust; Werner Klemperer, actor who played Colonel Klink. When I have all the names straight, maybe I will get to sleep.

F. Scott Fitzgerald, whom I confuse with nobody, once said that the measure of a first-rate intellect is its ability to hold two contradictory ideas at the same time. I believe this may be one of those profound sayings that fall apart if you examine them closely. Holding two contradictory ideas simultaneously is a stunt that millions of minds pull off every day. A fifth of the people on the planet believe that their spouse is both the most wonderful person alive and the biggest disaster that ever happened to them; many of the inhabitants, sophisticated or not, of New York and Los Angeles will affirm in a single conversation that theirs is both the best and the worst city in the world. In fact, holding contradictory ideas simultaneously is a snap, because they are so distinct, and thus unlikely to interpenetrate dizzyingly with each other and swap themselves around.

A better gauge of mental subtlety, it seems to me, is whether you can retain ideas that are very similar but also different. For example, can you simultaneously think of, while noting the differences between, the dancer/actresses Rita Moreno and Chita Rivera? If you can accomplish that, try upping the ante by adding the actresses Carmen Miranda and Ida Lupino. Now see if you can hold all four in your mind simultaneously. The world of TV and movies offers many such tests. It takes all my mind's agility to hold at once the actresses Sarah Jessica Parker and Jennifer Aniston. The first step is not to think about Sarah Michelle Gellar or Sally Jessy Ra-

phael, because that will only confuse things. Sarah Jessica Parker
and Jennifer Aniston are both young, blond, beautiful, and wise-
cracking but vulnerable. Both were in successful TV series that just
ended. The first is married to Matthew Broderick, the second to
Brad Pitt. Sarah has wavy hair; Jennifer's is straight. Thinking of
one somehow makes it almost impossible to think of the other.
Both are in the news a lot, which allows more chances to practice.

Then there are Charles Durning and Brian Dennehy (Wilford
Brimley being the confusing third in that category); Fernando
Lamas and Ricardo Montalban (José Ferrer, ditto); Norman Fell
and Jack Klugman; Van Heflin and Red Buttons; Swoosie Kurtz
and Stockard Channing; Wally Cox and Don Knotts . . . My only advice about untangling the whole Lee Majors/William Shatner/
Chad Everett/Robert Wagner/Robert Conrad/William Conrad
nexus is: don't go there. As actors from old TV series recede in
time, memory conflates them into a single ur–TV star. Recently
I've found that even the movie stars Robert De Niro and Al Pacino
are starting to blur together in my mind.

The other day, while cleaning the house, I pointed to the dustpan in the corner of the living room and asked my daughter,
"Could you please bring me the spatula?" She asked, "You mean
the dustpan?" I replied — taking a page from her book — "Whatever." A dustpan and a spatula really are a lot alike. Why use a
separate word for each object? "Dustpan" is drab and colorless,
whereas "spatula" is a poetic-sounding creation that just rolls off
the tongue. Also, "spatula" has a venerable history as a comic key-
word, like "rutabaga" and "Buick" and "schnauzer." So why not call
both objects "spatula"? That's the decision I've made. "Spatula"
might not be quite accurate when applied to a dustpan, but for
most practical purposes it's close enough. As you get older, you
don't want to waste time on tiny details.

On the other hand, you don't want to become so carried away
with "spatula" that you repeat it over and over to yourself as you lie
in bed late at night. It's a perfect example of the kind of word that,
if repeated often enough, will make you insane.

If despair is a sin (and it is — it's an aspect of the deadly sin of
sloth), the virtuous person must resist it, and all tendencies likely
to lead to it. Torturing the mind with minutiae is one of those. Originally, I seem to recall, America took pride in its plainspoken re-

jection of all the pomp and foofaraw of corrupt, overcomplicated Europe. Now America is complication itself. Look down the table at the public library where people plug in their laptops, and see the heaped-up entanglements of cables and wires. Try to read the pamphlet in six-point type that your new phone carrier sends you when you change long-distance service. Go to the supermarket to buy an ordinary item for your spouse. The other day at the A&P I noticed a man lost in thought in front of a bank of different kinds of brownie mix. Then he took out his cell phone and made a call: "Hi, babe . . . You wanted Triple Chunk? Okay . . . I thought you said Triple *Fudge* Chunk." At some point the brain, in order to avoid despair, begins to shut down.

My son, who is eleven, has a memory like wet cement. Occurrences leave impressions on it and are there to stay — clear, manifest, close at hand. Like apparently all children today, he has an effortless affinity with gadgetry that exhausts me just to look at it. I call him when I want some advanced appliance turned off or on. Even more useful is his ability to replay data he has observed. Ask him what we were talking about before we started talking about what we're talking about now, and he knows. He always retrieves the thread of a conversation in a manner that's matter-of-fact or bored.

For me, however, the feeling at these moments is a vast and happy relief. When you've been trying to remember something and you suddenly remember it, the mental pleasure is keen. Not remembering eats at you, but remembering soothes and resoothes. I imagine that feeling might be what heaven is like. You pop through to the other side, and suddenly every question you have wondered about for years and then given up on is answered. The fate of an object lost in childhood, the names of people met only once at a cocktail party, the difference between William Conrad and Robert Conrad — every answer coming to you in a limpid rush of enlightenment, as if you'd known it all along.

MARK GREIF

Against Exercise

FROM N+1

WERE "In the Penal Colony" to be written today, Kafka could only be speaking of an exercise machine. Instead of the sentence to be tattooed on its victims, the machine would inscribe lines of numbers. So many calories, so many miles, so many watts, so many laps.

Modern exercise makes you acknowledge the machine operating inside yourself. Nothing can make you believe we harbor nostalgia for factory work but a modern gym. The lever of the die press no longer commands us at work. But with the gym we import vestiges of the leftover equipment of industry into our leisure. We leave the office, and put the conveyor belt under our feet, and run as if chased by devils. We willingly submit our legs to the mangle, and put our stiffening arms to the press.

It is crucial that the machines are simple. The inclined planes, pins, levers, pulleys, locks, winches, racks, and belts of the Nautilus and aerobic machines put earlier stages of technical progress at our disposal in miniature. The elements are visible and intelligible for our use but not dangerous to us. Displaced, neutralized, they are traces of a necessity that no longer need be met with forethought or ingenuity. A farmer once used a pulley, cable, and bar to lift his roofbeam; you now use the same means to work your lats.

Today, when we assume our brains are computers, the image of a machine-man, whether Descartes's or La Mettrie's, has an old and venerable quality, like a yellowed poster on the infirmary wall. Blood pressure is hydraulics, strength is mechanics, nutrition is combustion, limbs are levers, joints are ball-in-socket. The exercise world does not make any notable conceptual declaration that we are mechanical men and women. We already were that, at least as far as our science is concerned. Rather it expresses a will, on the part of each and every individual, to discover and regulate the machinelike processes in his own body.

And we go to this hard labor with no immediate reward but our freedom to do it. Precisely this kind of freedom may be enough. Exercise machines offer you the superior mastery of subjecting your body to experimentation. We hide our reasons for undertaking this labor, and thoughtlessly substitute a new necessity. No one asks whether we want to drag our lives across a threshold into the kingdom of exercise.

Exercise is no choice. It comes to us as an emissary from the realm of biological processes. It falls under the jurisdiction of the obligations of life itself, which only the self-destructive neglect. Our controversial future is supposed to depend on engineered genes, brain scans, neuroscience, laser beams. About those things we have loud, public, sterile debates, while the real historic changes are accomplished on a gym's vinyl mats, to the sound of a flywheel and a ratcheted inclined plane.

In the gym you witness people engaging in a basic biological process of self-regulation. All of its related activities reside in the private realm. A question, then, is why exercise doesn't stay private. It could have belonged at home with other processes it resembles: eating, sleeping, defecating, cleaning, grooming, and masturbating.

Exerciser, what do you see in the mirrored gym wall? You make the faces associated with pain, with tears, with orgasm, with the sort of exertion that would call others to your immediate aid. But you do not hide your face. You groan as if pressing on your bowels. You repeat grim labors as if mopping the floor. You huff and you shout and strain. You appear in tight yet shapeless Lycra costumes. These garments reveal the shape of the genitals and the mashed and bandaged breasts to others' eyes, without acknowledging the lure of sex.

Though we get our word "gymnasium" from the Greeks, our modern gym is not in their spirit. Athletics in the ancient institution were public and agonistic. They consisted of the training of boys for public contests. The gymnasium was closest to what we know as a boxing gym, with the difference that it was also the place adult men gathered to admire the most beautiful boys and, in the Greek fashion, sexually mentor them. It was the preeminent place to promote the systematic education of the young, and for adults to carry on casual debates among themselves, modeling the intellectual sociability, separated from overt politics, that is the origin of Western philosophy. Socrates spent most of his time in gymnasia. Aristotle began his philosophical school in the covered walkway of a gymnasium.

The Socratic and Peripatetic methods could find little support in a modern gym. What we moderns do there belongs to mute privacy. The Greeks put their genuinely private acts into a location, an *oikos,* the household. To the household belonged all the acts that sustained bare biological life. That included the labor of keeping up a habitation and a body, growing food and eating it, bearing children and feeding them. Hannah Arendt interpreted this strong Greek distinction of the household from the public sphere as a symbol of a general truth, that it is necessary to keep the acts that sustain naked life away from others' observation. A hidden sphere, free from scrutiny, provides the foundation for a public person — someone sure enough in his privacy to take the drastic risks of public life, to think, to speak against others' wills, to choose, with utter independence. In privacy, alone with one's family, the dominating necessity and speechless appetites could be gratified in the nonthought and ache of staying alive.

Our gym is better named a "health club," except that it is no club for equal meetings of members. It is the atomized space in which one does formerly private things, before others' eyes, with the lonely solitude of a body acting as if it were still in private. One tries out these contortions to undo and remake a private self; and if the watching others aren't entitled to approve, some imagined aggregate "other" does. Modern gym exercise moves biology into the nonsocial company of strangers. You are supposed to coexist but not look closely, wipe down the metal of handlebars and rubber of mats as if you had not left a trace. As in the elevator, you are expected to face forward.

It is like a punishment for our liberation. The most onerous forms of necessity, the struggle for food, against disease, always by means of hard labor, have been overcome. It might have been naive to think the new human freedom would push us toward a society of public pursuits, like Periclean Athens, or of simple delight in what exists, as in Eden. But the true payoff of a society that chooses to make private freedoms and private leisures its main substance has been much more unexpected. This payoff is a set of forms of bodily self-regulation that drag the last vestiges of biological life into the light as a social attraction.

The only truly essential pieces of equipment in modern exercise are numbers. Whether at the gym or on the running path, rudimentary calculation is the fundamental technology. As the weights that one lifts are counted, so are distances run, time exercised, heart rates elevated.

A simple negative test of whether an activity is modern exercise is to ask whether it could be done meaningfully without counting or measuring it. (In sports, numbers are used differently; there, scores are a way of recording competition in a social encounter.) Forms of exercise that do away with mechanical equipment, as running does, cannot do away with this.

In exercise one gets a sense of one's body as a collection of numbers representing capabilities. The other location where an individual's numbers attain such talismanic status is the doctor's office. There is a certain seamlessness between all the places where exercise is done and the sites where people are tested for illnesses, undergo repairs, and die. In the doctor's office, the blood lab, and the hospital, you are at the mercy of counting experts. A lab technician in a white coat takes a sample of blood. A nurse tightens a cuff on your arm, links you to an EKG, takes the basic measurements of your height and weight — never to your satisfaction. She rewards you with the obvious numbers for blood pressure, body fat ratio, height, and weight. The clipboard with your numbers is passed. At last the doctor takes his seat, a mechanic who wears the white robe of an angel and is as arrogant as a boss. In specialist language, exacerbating your dread and expectation, you may learn your numbers for cholesterol (two types), your white cells, your iron, immunities, urinalysis, and so forth. He hardly needs to remind you that these numbers correlate with your chances of survival.

How do we acquire the courage to exist as a set of numbers? Turning to the gym or the track, you gain the anxious freedom to count yourself. What a relief it can be. Here are numbers you can change. You make the exercises into trials you perform upon matter within reach, the exterior armor of your fat and muscle. You are assured these numbers, too, and not only the black marks in the doctor's files, will correspond to how long you have to live. With willpower and sufficient discipline, that is, the straitening of yourself to a rule, you will be changed.

The gym resembles a voluntary hospital. Its staff members are also its patients. Some machines put you in a traction you can escape, while others undo the imprisonment of a respirator, cueing you to pump your lungs yourself and tracking your heart rate on a display. Aided even by a love that can develop for your pains, this self-testing becomes second nature.

The curious compilation of numbers that you are becomes an aspect of your freedom, sometimes the most important, even more preoccupying than your thoughts or dreams. You discover what high numbers you can become, and how immortal. For you, high roller, will live forever. You are eternally maintained.

The justification for the total scope of the responsibility to exercise is health. A further extension of the counting faculty of exercise gives a precise economic character to health. It determines the anticipated numbers for the days and hours of one's life.

Today we really can preserve ourselves for a much longer time. The means of preservation are reliable and cheap. The haste to live one's mortal life diminishes. The temptation toward perpetual preservation grows. We preserve the living corpse in an optimal state, not that we may do something with it, but for its own good feelings of eternal fitness, confidence, and safety. We hoard our capital to earn interest, and subsist each day on crusts of bread. But no one will inherit our good health after we've gone. The hours of life-maintenance vanish with the person.

The person who does not exercise, in our current conception, is a slow suicide. He fails to take responsibility for his life. He doesn't labor strenuously to forestall his death. Therefore we begin to think he causes it.

It may be a comfort to remember when one of your parents' acquaintances dies that he did not eat well or failed to take up running. The nonexerciser is lumped with other unfortunates whom we socially discount. Their lives are worth a percentage of our own, through their own neglect. Their value is compromised by the failure to assure the fullest term of possible physical existence. The nonexerciser joins all the unfit: the slow, the elderly, the poor, and the hopeless. "Don't you want to *live?*" we say. No answer of theirs could satisfy us.

Conceive of a society in which it was believed that the senses could be used up. Eyesight worsened the more vivid sights you saw. Hearing worsened the more intense sounds you heard. It would be inevitable that such a conception would bleed into people's whole pattern of life, changing the way they spent their days. Would they use up their powers on the most saturated colors, listening to the most intoxicating sounds? Or might its members refuse to move, eyes shut, ears covered, nursing the remaining reserves of sensation? We, too, believe our daily lives are not being lived but eaten up by age. And we spend our time desperately. From the desperate materialist gratifications of a hedonistic society, commanding immediate comfort and happiness, we recoil to the desperate economics of health, and chase a longer span of happinesses deferred, and comforts delayed, by disposing of the better portion of our lives in life preservation.

Exercise does make you, as a statistical person, part of different aggregate categories that die with less frequency at successive ages. It furnishes a gain in odds. This is the main public rationale for those billions of man- and woman-hours in the gym. The truth, however, is also that being healthy makes you feel radically different. For a segment of its most ardent practitioners, exercise in its contemporary form is largely a quest for certain states of feeling. A more familiar phenomenon than the young person who is unhappy physically from never exercising is the young exerciser who suffers from missing one or two days of exercise. The most common phenomenon may be the individual who judges, in his own mind if not out loud, the total healthiness of his state at each moment based on what he ate, what he drank, how much he exercised, when, with what feelings as he was doing it, and with what relation to the new recommendation or warning he just heard on the news hour's health report. One feels healthier even when the body doesn't feel discernably different. Or the body does begin to feel different — lighter, stronger, more efficient, less toxic — in ways that exceed the possible consequences of the exercises performed. This may be a more important psychic "medicalization of human life" than anything a doctor can do with his tests.

The less respectable but even more powerful justification for day-to-day exercise is thinness. It involves the disciplining of a depraved will rather than the righteous responsibility to maintain the health of the body-machine and its fund of capital.

Women strip their bodies of layers of fat to reveal a shape without its normal excess of flesh. Despite the new emphasis on female athleticism, the task of the woman exerciser remains one of emaciation. Men thin themselves too, but more importantly bloat particular muscles, swelling the major clusters in the biceps, chest, and thighs. They awaken an incipient musculature that no work or normal activity could bring out in toto. Theirs is a task of expansion and discovery. Women's emacation is a source for feminine eye-rolling and rueful nicknames: the "social x-ray," the actress as skin and bones. Men's proud expansion and discovery of six muscles of the lower abdomen, reminiscent of an insect's segmented exoskeleton, likewise become a byword and a joke: the "six-pack," bringing exercise together with the masculinity of drinking.

Unlike the health model, which seems to make a continuous gain on mortality, thinness and muscle expansion operate in a cruel economy of accelerated loss. Mortality began when the first man and woman left the Garden. Everyone has to die, but no one has to shape a physique, and once body altering begins, it is more implacable than death. Every exerciser knows that the body's propensity to put on weight is the physical expression of a moral fall. Every exerciser knows that the tendency of the body to become soft when it is comfortable or at rest, instead of staying perpetually hard, is a failure of discipline. This is the taste of our new Tree of Knowledge. In our era of abundance, we find that nutrition makes one fat rather than well fed, pleasures make one flabby rather than content, and only anorexics have the willpower to stop eating and die.

Exercise means something other than health to a young person who conceives sexual desirability as the truth about herself most worth defending. And youth is becoming permanent in the demand that adults keep up an outward show of juvenile sexuality. The body becomes the location of sexiness, rather than clothes or

wit or charisma. This is less true for society — which values personality still — than for the exerciser herself, who imagines an audience that doesn't exist. Saddest of all is the belief that an improved
body will bestow bliss on the unloved.

The shock troops of modern exercise are women just past the
college years. Only recently the beneficiary of a sexually mature
body, and among our culture's few possessors by native right of the
reduced body type we prefer — which we daily prefer more openly,
more vehemently — the girl of twenty-two is a paradoxical figure
as an exemplar of exercise. She is not yet among the discounted.
But she knows her destiny. She starts immediately to get ahead in
the race to preserve a form that must never exceed the barest minimum of flesh. A refreshing honesty can exist among exercisers
who are not yet caught up in the doctrine of health. The rising incidence of smoking among young women, which worries public-
health advocates, is coincident with the rising incidence of gym
exercise, which doesn't. While the cigarette suppresses appetite
(rebelliously), the StairMaster attacks calories (obediently). Each
can become intensely, erotically pleasurable, and neither is really
meant for health or longevity.

The doctrine of thinness introduces a radical fantasy of exercise
down to the bone. It admits the dream of a body unencumbered by
any excess of corporeality. Thanatos enters through the door
opened by Eros, and exercise flirts with a will to annihilate the un-
attractive body rather than to preserve its longevity. Without an accompanying ideology of health, thinness would in fact liquidate all
restraints, generating a death's-head vision of exercise. Health curiously returns as the only brake on a practice that otherwise would
become a kind of naked aggression against the body.

With health in place, the aggression is more likely to be carried
on psychically. It pools, then starts an undercurrent of hatred for
this corrupt human form that continually undoes the labor you invest in it. One hundred twenty pounds of one's own flesh starts to
seem like the Sisyphean boulder. Yet the bitterness of watching
your body undo your work is restrained by a curious compensation
that Sisyphus did not know. If the hated body is the scene of a battle, a certain pleasure still emerges from the unending struggle,
and in a hedonistic order divided against its own soft luxuries, at
least *this* pleasure, if no other, can be made to go on forever.

*

An enigma of exercise is the proselytizing urge that comes with it. Exercisers are always eager for everyone else to share their experience. Why must others exercise if one person does?

No one who plays baseball or hockey demands that everyone else play the sport. Sports are social. Their victories become visible in the temporary public arrangements of a game. Perhaps accomplishments recognized by others in the act of their occurrence can be left alone. The gym-goer, on the other hand, is a solitary evangelist. He is continually knocking on your door to get you to recognize the power that will not give him peace. You, too, must exercise. Even as he worries for your salvation, nevertheless he has the gleam of someone who is ahead of you already, one chosen by God.

Running is most insidious because of its way of taking proselytizing out of the gym. It is a direct invasion of public space. It lays the counting, the pacing, the controlled frenzy, the familiar undergarment-outergarments and skeletal look, on top of the ordinary practice of an outdoor walk. One thing that can be said for a gym is that an implied contract links everyone who works out in its mirrored and pungent hangar. All consent to undertake separate exertions and hide any mutual regard, as in a well-ordered masturbatorium. The gym is in this sense more polite than the narrow riverside, street, or nature path, wherever runners take over shared places for themselves. With his speed and narcissistic intensity the runner corrupts the space of walking, thinking, talking, and everyday contact. He jostles the idler out of his reverie. He races between pedestrians in conversation. The runner can oppose sociability and solitude by publicly sweating on them.

No doubt the unsharability of exercise stimulates an unusual kind of loneliness.

When exercise does become truly shared and mutually visible, as in the aerobics that come close to dance, or the hardcore bodybuilding that is always erotic and fraternal, it nears sport or art and starts to reverse itself. When exercise is done in a private home, or in untenanted landscapes, or without formal method, apparatus, or counting, it recovers certain eccentric freedoms of private techniques of the self.

However, the pure category of modern exercise is concerned with neither the creative process of reproduction (as in activities-in-common) nor the pure discoveries of solitude (as in private eccentricity). It pursues an idea of replication. Replication in exercise recreates the shape and capabilities of others in the material of your own body, without new invention and without exchange with others or crossing over of material between selves.

It is a puzzling question, in fact, whether "you" and "your body" are the same in exercise. If on the one hand exercise seems strongly to identify exercisers with their bodies, by putting them to shared labor, on the other hand it seems to estrange them from the bodies they must care for and manage. Where does "fitness" actually reside? It seems to be deep inside you; yet that inside has risen to a changeable surface. And this surface is no longer one you can take off, as you did a costume in earlier methods of improving your allure. Fashion historians point out that women freed themselves from corsets worn externally, only to make an internal corset, as they toned the muscles of the abdomen and chest, and dieted and exercised to burn away permanently the well-fed body that whalebone stays temporarily restrained. Though the exerciser acts on his *self,* this self becomes ever more identified with the visible surface. Though he works on *his* body, replication makes it ever more, so to speak, *anybody.*

Does this critique imply a hatred of the body? On the contrary. The ethos of gym exercise annihilates the margin of safety that humans have when they relate to their own bodies. Men and women seem more ashamed of their own actual bodies in the present environment of biological exposure than in a pre-gym past. An era of exercise has brought more obsession and self-hatred rather than less.

A feminist worry becomes important. It is certainly possible to make people used to displaying to others' eyes the biological processes of transformation. And this has been, at times, the aim of feminists, who intended to attack a patriarchy that vilified the natural body or that made biological processes a source of shame and inferiority. But the forms of exposure that have recently arisen are not in line with feminist liberation of the unconditioned body.

Patriarchy made biology a negative spectacle, a filth that had to be hidden. The ethos of exercise makes it a positive spectacle, a competitive fascination that must be revealed. The rhetoric of "loving the body" can thus be misused. With the extension of the cliché that one should "not be ashamed" of the body, people are less able to defend themselves against the prospect that their actual bodies, and biological processes, may be manifest at every moment, in new states of disciplining neither public nor private. It becomes a retrogression, a moral failing, in these people to wish to defend against exposure, or to withdraw their health, bodies, arousal, and self-regulation from the social scene, as if privacy of this kind were mere prudery or repression.

Once subjected to this socialization of biological processes, the body suffers a new humiliation no longer rooted in the distinctions between the revealed and the hidden, the natural and the shameful, the sexual ideal and the physical actuality, but in the deeper crime of merely *existing* as the unregulated, the unshaped, the unsexy, the "unfit."

Our practices are turning us inside out. Our hidden flesh becomes our public front. The private medical truth of bodily health becomes our psychic self-regard. Action in public before strangers and acquaintances has disappeared from the lived experience of the citizen and been replaced by *exercise* in public, as speech gives way to biological spectacle.

Your exercise confers superiority in two contests, one of longevity and the other of sex. Facing mortality, the gym-goer believes himself an agent of health — whereas he makes himself a more perfect patient. Facing the sexual struggle, the gym-goer labors to attain a positive advantage, which spurs an ever-receding horizon of further competition.

The technical capabilities of gym exercise in fact drive social ideals and demands. The exerciser conforms, in our era's most virulent practice of conformism. But exercise itself pushes medicine and sexual allure toward further extremes. The feedback does not stabilize the system but radicalizes it, year by year. Only in a gym culture does overweight become the "second leading cause of death" (as the news recently reported) rather than a correlation, a relative measure, which positively covaries with the heart attacks, the cancers, the organ failures and final illnesses that were formerly our killers. Only in a gym culture do physical traits that were formerly considered repellent become marks of sexual superiority.

(We are hot now for the annihilation by exercise and dieting of once voluptuous feminine flesh, watching it be starved away in natural form and selectively replaced with breast implants, collagen injections, buttock lifts. We've learned to be aroused by the ripped, vein-popping muscles that make Incredible Hulks of men who actually push papers.) Because health and sex are the places we demand our truth today, newly minted ideals must be promulgated as discoveries of medical science or revelations of permanent, "evolutionary" human desires.

The consequences are not only the flooding of consciousness with a numbered and regulated body or the distraction from living that comes with endless life-maintenance, but the liquidation of the last untouched spheres of privacy, such that biological life itself becomes a spectacle.

"You are condemned. You are condemned. You are condemned." This is the chant the machines make with their grinding rhythm inside the roar of the gym floor. Once upon a time, the authority of health, and the display of our bodies and biological processes, seemed benign, even liberating. We were going to overcome illness, we were going to exorcise the prudish Victorians. But our arrows were turned from their targets, and some of them punctured our privacy.

The thinness we strive for becomes spiritual. This is not the future we wanted. That prickling beneath the exerciser's skin as he steps off the treadmill is only his new self, his reduced existence, scratching the truth of who he is now, from the inside out.

EDWARD HOAGLAND

Small Silences

FROM HARPER'S MAGAZINE

WANDERING TO THE EDGE of Dr. Green's woods, next door to our new house, at the age of eight, I found a little brook running — my first, because we had just moved from the city to the country. The floating twigs and leaves, the ripples, and yet the water's mirroring qualities, and the tug on my fingers or feet when I dipped them in, plus the temperature, so remarkably different from the air's, fascinated me. We, like the other neighbors, had some brush and untrimmed trees in back of our lawn, so the brook picked up interesting flotsam before entering Dr. Green's pines, where except for scattered boulders or stones the ground was less varied, all needly. The sounds the stream made, thocking and ticking, bubbling and trickling, were equally beguiling, however, and like the wind-nudged boughs twisting overhead, never precisely the same.

This was in Connecticut during World War II, so we kept a dozen brown hens for their eggs, and I watched their pecking order develop, and other habits, endlessly. But the brook was a near second for curiosity, and because it was undomesticated I recognized in it a wilder power. I felt like part of the flock — feared for them at nightfall, when they would duck inside the coop through an entrance I never forgot to close, and rejoiced with them when a New Hampshire Red rooster was acquired to trumpet their accomplishments. But the woods were an adventure, more mysteriously reverberant. By nine I was probably daring enough to follow the stream (knee-high, so nobody was afraid I might drown in it) through the forest far enough to catch sight of Dr. Green's pond and approach its spongy inlet. I must have heard about its existence, but no one had taken me there — my father golfed, my mother gardened. The distance is now elastic in my mind's eye, but no roads or houses intervened and my discovery caused no alarm. My parents, retracing the path, notified Dr. Green, a retired and retiring widower whose given name I never learned. They owned two acres; he, I would guess in retrospect, at least fifteen. Then there was Miss Walker's estate, in back of both properties, and lending them a bit more wildlife, such as the foxes that threatened my chickens. She was a fiftyish spinster, with servants, who may have had about three times as much land. My parents had never met her, but she caught me trespassing as a "nature boy" once or twice — climbing the spruces in her overgrown fields — and summoned me inside her manorial stone house (ours and Dr. Green's were white clapboard) and gave me and the friend who was with me a proper glass of apple juice with chocolate chip cookies. A real estate agent who wanted to subdivide the place surprised me too and was less friendly, afraid that I might start a wildfire, but I would sooner have harmed myself, and I think Miss Walker surmised as much and knew you couldn't stop a boy from crossing stone walls and wire fences.

The pond was the great revelation, after, first, the stream and before I could climb a sixty-foot Norway spruce and swing with the wind. Amber, black, and silver, with moss on one bank and cattails on another, it had frogs plopping — leopard and green frogs and bullfrogs with large eardrums who said *jugarum*. I saw crayfish and a ribbon snake, yellow-striped, and a muskrat swimming in a moving V. Greenish pollywogs and salamanders. The pines, in retrospect, were red pines, and red squirrels of course were chattering in them from all angles, much more vociferous than the gray squirrels that nested in the maple shade trees in front of our house. Also my dog, Flash, an English setter and constant companion, who barked at them, sniffed out an opossum, long-haired, long-nosed, pouched like a miniature kangaroo, who promptly swooned and played dead when I picked it up by the tail, just as it was supposed to do. The pines, with their thousand jewely shards of light as you looked up on a sunny day, didn't like wetting their feet and gave way to white birches whose curling strips of bark you could write on not just with a pencil but with your fingernail if you had to, and dark hemlocks, droopy-branched and unbelievably tall and somber, in the soggy ground, while the pond itself might be as bright as a lens of glass, with tree crowns, mackerel clouds, and blue sky reflected on its surface.

I was a good student and not as friendless or solitary as this may sound. My trouble was a bad stutter that made Flash's companionship and the flock of chickens and communing out-of-doors important to me. But I generally had an intimate friend of my own age whom I could lead to these precious places — Miss Walker's lordly spruces, like the beanstalk that Jack climbed, or Dr. Green's miraculous, jam-packed pond — discovering, however, to my astonishment that they didn't matter as much to him. He would prefer listening to Mel Allen broadcast the Yankee games with me, gossiping about our class, inventing piratical schemes. Ice-skating, yes, we shared, or throwing rocks into the water to watch the thumping splash, but when we were past the volcanic stage, why go? Dr. Green was a cranky, softhearted soul almost too old to walk to his pond by the time I discovered it, but he made the effort to inspect both me and it when he heard from his gardener that I was there, telling me not to treat the frogs inhumanely or to fall through the ice. Brooks, the silent Irishman whom he had long employed, had no interest in woods or ponds, so I seldom encountered him, and he was easy to avoid, sitting smoking in his chilly greenhouse — just nodded at me as an authorized visitor if we did chance to meet.

I saw a mink trap an eel, and a musk turtle diving out of reach on the bottom, and tree frogs in the bushes, and "pumpkinseeds," or sunfish; learned how to fish with a worm and a pole. A blue heron bigger than me would sometimes flap over from the larger ponds (Dr. Green's, though huge to a ten-year-old, may have been scarcely an acre in size) after amphibians. Or on my repeated expeditions I might see a kingfisher diving for shiners. Nobody could spot me from the road as I circled the water, looking at the strange jointed plants called horsetails, or ferns at the margins. The ordeal of stuttering at school seemed distant indeed, and I was learning how to swim well enough at my parents' country club not to be a danger to myself if I fell in. I was cautious anyway, as stutterers must be if they are to survive — bicycled home after swimming lessons before I'd have to try to talk to people on the patio. I could talk to Flash with absolute abandon, and loved Mel Allen and Tommy

Henrich, "Old Reliable," the Yankees' right fielder, and watched the New Hampshire Reds' social goings-on like a budding ethnologist, though I tended to downplay my various excitements in the house lest they be restricted or used against me. It was not a silly instinct, because my parents did soon tell me I was reading too much, and by prep school were telling my favorite teachers that I was too intrigued by nature and writing; that these were dodges due to my handicap and might derail a more respectable career in law or medicine — angering the teachers who nurtured me.

I was an only child until, at ten, we adopted a three-month-old baby girl named Mary Elizabeth, from Chicago. So this event may have been another force pushing me into the woods. Within a few years she and I became close, though in the beginning I used to proclaim that she wasn't my "real sister" in order to watch my mother's distress. And from the pond, after school, I would often go uphill, not back along the stream, to Dr. Green's house, skirting both Brooks and, in particular, the doctor himself. That is, he was always indoors, but I would take care not to be heard in his bedroom or sitting room upstairs, and knock softly instead at the kitchen door so that Hope alone heard me. She, as cook, like Brooks, had worked for Dr. Green for many years but had not established the same fellow feeling. She was brown-skinned and tacitly more intelligent and ironic than Brooks was, and took good care of her employer without receiving the hearty although formal daily greetings Brooks did. He was white and had a family in town to repair to, which also made him more of an equal, perhaps, than a large-waisted, large-breasted, light-colored Negress in a pink uniform, far from wherever her grown-up children were located, or other friends. Being small and mute, I never inquired of Hope where she had originated. I was grateful for her kindness in inviting me in, to sit on a white chair, with the kitchen clock ticking and the scents of baking. Like the pond, it soon became a dependable sanctuary where nobody asked me to speak. We simply sat quietly, she with her hands in her ample lap, while Flash and the doctor's cocker spaniel lay down together on the back porch. Sometimes I forgot my handicap, but if we talked for a minute it was in low tones so that the lonely doctor wouldn't tromp downstairs and interrupt us, asking angrily why I hadn't come to see him. To a little boy he appeared formidably crabby and diagnostic — naturally wanting to hear, analyze, and cure my stutter.

Jimmy Dunn, in the house on the other side of ours, was a good playmate for cards and chess and imaginary games; and Tommy Hunt, at whose house the school bus stopped, was a likable guy — he eventually became a minister — more mature than us, who worked on a jalopy about as much as I went to the pond and had a crush on the girlfriend of our football quarterback, who became an airline pilot after high school and college, when she married him. By eighth grade I had a silent crush on her too; she was our most down-to-earth, approachable blonde. Though nobody picked on me, some of the other boys collected at Tommy's after the bus dropped us off for BB-gun fights or to drive that hoodless jalopy around and around Tommy's parents' vacant field or to squeeze each other's balls in the bedroom in a manhood test or to tie each other up or masturbate their dogs, including mine if they could catch him (to my cowardly shame). I sometimes hunted rats with Flash in our relic barn with my own BB gun, after I had ceased to need to seek out Hope so much. But the wonder isn't why these kids didn't beat me up — even the Kane boys, sons of a drunken "black Irish" gardener, gap-toothed, tricky and sly, who threw stones at cars and went to the public school, not ours, did not, though I was certainly warier when crossing their employer's meadow — as much as why nobody ever has. Not when I honeycombed Boston on foot for years and New York for decades in late-night walks, or in five trips to Africa and nine to Alaska, and so on. I don't need to belabor the point, but neither cowardice nor caution alone explains it. A naturalist's and a stutterer's intuition maybe more so — I've swung around and looked into an approaching mugger's eyes occasionally, which caused him to sheer off — and a berserk streak that I have when sufficiently angered that perhaps sets other people back on their heels long enough for a bad situation to defuse. Stutterers learn to distinguish genuine danger from the ersatz, and also to manipulate their anger for the fluency that a shot of adrenaline will momentarily bestow. And they may develop a well of empathy that, again, deflects the rage of sufferers looking for someone to attack, and learn to distinguish the fulcrum of power in any group. While bullies, for example, will persecute the closest target, real predators look into the middle distance — as I learned in my late teens when taking care of lions and tigers in the Ringling Bros. and Barnum & Bailey Circus. So you avoid a bully, but stand in closer proximity to a predator and join him in gazing out.

Girls were another puzzle. One of my sister's babysitters would coax me to lie on the sofa with my head in her lap, before I was ready to, so that she could practice what she wanted to do when she was with her boyfriend. Or she would ask me to reach for something on a high shelf, then press her breasts against my back, as if to help. At a dancing class another girl taught me to cut in on her when she was burdened with a partner she didn't like, but after I took this to mean she was partial to me, she got mad because I cut in on her when she was fox-trotting with a boy whom she *did* like. Dr. Green died while I was away at boarding school, so I can't recall whether Hope retired somewhere down south, being of an age to, or sought other employment. But she was authentically welcoming to me, and suitably erotic to a prepubescent too, sitting catty-corner to me across from the big old-fashioned stove and oven — with invariably a roast in it for the solitary old man upstairs — and her hands loosely clasped, a gentle expression, big hips, lax bosom, and her uniform collar unbuttoned. I was never interrupting anything; she'd have the clock to listen to, the radio on low, a newspaper the doctor had finished with folded on the counter. Live-in maids in our neighborhood, black or not, had no cars to visit one another and would not have been permitted by the police to walk the roads. I took care not to trigger my stammer by telling her I had just seen watercress, water striders, eelgrass, mudpuppies, duckweed, pickerelweed, horned pout, and water with trembling algae, wavy larvae, and waterlogged trees like slumbering alligators three feet down. The clouds had piled up like smoke signals over the pond and the pines, and I had nibbled rock tripe and touch-me-nots. One winter I'd accidentally angered a friend by grabbing at him as I fell through the ice, pulling him into an icy bath. Our families thought, oh, dirty water, but I knew that, no, it was where life lived, and part of my heart. By twenty I would be climbing unobserved into a mountain lion's cage, but already I trusted my faith in nature and was biking to larger ponds, then every week or two basking in my secret refuge at Hope's kitchen. I didn't eat there or stay as long as an hour, just dropped in to decompress, resting.

*

Hope was not the first colored person I'd known. (The term "black" then was an epithet of insult, equivalent to "nigra.") When my mother brought my baby sister home on the train from the Chicago adoption agency, she had hired a woman from the South named Arizona, much younger than Hope, vigorous, boisterous, taller, darker, and less acclimated to the behavior expected of servants in an upscale WASP suburb up north. She was a blithe spirit, as I remember her, assertive, gleeful, expansive, loud, and goofy with me when, to tease her, I'd pull on the bow of her apron strings — which, though I was about ten or eleven, quickly alarmed my Missouri-born father as, I suppose, proto-miscegenation. In a few years he would begin boycotting the Metropolitan Opera for permitting the great black contralto Marian Anderson to sing on its stage. Arizona had big buttocks under the thin fabric of her uniform that made the butterfly of the bow doubly tempting, and he perceived a sexual element in our giggles. My mother, not being from a former slave state, was more startled by Arizona's guileless tales of growing up barefoot in a hovel, and chewing her own babies' meals for them when she couldn't afford to buy prepared food. It sounded unsanitary, barbarian, "African," like her strangely untrammeled name (evocative to me now of wanting to "light out for the Territories") and her maid's-day-off visits every Thursday to Harlem by taxi and train. Goodness knows what diseases she might bring back to her attic room and our dishes and pantry. My mother rang a tinkly bell at the dining room table, rather than possibly interrupt a polite conversation with guests, to call Arizona to clear each course off the table, but Arizona didn't seem to fathom the gentility of the ritual; was likely to holler out helpfully to ask what was wanted. So they got rid of her, my father believing afterward that it reduced a property's value, at least in Connecticut, if a colored person had ever lived in it, even in a servant's capacity.

I learned from the episode not to betray to a third party affection for anybody who might get fired because of it, or to divulge any passion that might thereafter be denied me. "I'm going to the pond," I'd say casually to my mother; then dodge carefully past the stolid, deracinated Brooks (like a tug-on-the-forelock-when-the-gentry-go-past footman), toward the trillium and columbine, the toadstools and fairy-ring mushrooms, the nematodes and myriapods, the blueberries or blackberries, near the opaque yet shiny stretch of hidden water, deep here, shallow there, with the wind ruffling the surface to conceal such factual matters, and cold at its inlet but warm where it fed into a creek that ran to the Silvermine River and finally the ocean. Getting hold of a live-trap, I caught a couple of weasels that screamed at me through the mesh until I released them, and a burglar-masked coon, and the inevitable beautifully white-caped skunk, who didn't let me have it when I let him go.

The plopping raindrops, wobbly riffles, crosscurrent zephyrs, the penny-sized and penny-colored springs that replenished the margins of the pond from underground, pluming hazel-colored, endlessly rising-and-falling individual grains of sand, irislike around the black pupil of the actual hole, lent variance to the velvet water, near dusk, or bright mornings, when it shone in the mini-forest like a circlet of steel. During a thunderstorm it seethed, fingered madly. Then when the clouds cleared off, in the batty moonlight, the shadows seemed crafted differently than might be cast by any sun. I was delighted watching bats flutter after hatching mosquitoes in the wetland that bulwarked the pond, and thrilled when the pair of barn owls that nested in an abandoned water tower on the hill would shriek as they skimmed across Miss Walker's second growth. It was more frightening to be alone upstairs in my own house at night than to tiptoe about the woods. Nor was it as scary peering at a copperhead on a ledge one noontime that a schoolmate whose mother was a birdwatcher took me to see. And I loved the whirligig beetles and water boatmen, the damselflies and fireflies, the sticklebacks and freshwater snails. My favorite turtles were the wood turtles, *Clemmys insculpta*, seven or eight inches long, that have almost disappeared from New England now, with their sculptured carapaces, like Cellini's metalwork, and salmon-red legs, which I would watch breed in the stream in the spring, but that roamed the fields until hibernation time, when they'd return again to the streambed's leaves and mud.

Snappers lurked in the muck of the pond year-round, platter-sized, but didn't bite if you left them there, even if you happened to step quite close or purposely touched their serrated tails: only if you picked up a female on her big day in June when she left the water to lay her eggs. The bottom, when you waded, was painted with fallen leaves and so varied you'd stand with one foot sucked ankle-deep and the other supported on hard feldspar sand — little fish angrily nipping at you because you had begun to infringe on their nesting terrain — and one warm but one chilled, and a branch knifing out of the water alongside you much like a fin. Wood frogs and peepers were to be found in the bushes, and a water snake tasseled in lovely russets and tans somewhere down the bank. A green frog or bullfrog couldn't survive the snake's visits simply by holding its breath underwater; it had to swim in zigzags or leap fast. But speed was not a defense when the great blue heron, gangly-legged, slow-flapping, maneuvered down from the sky. It had a spear beak and watched as sternly as a sentinel, once it had landed, for the first frog buried in mud that needed some air. Similarly, a mama duck might be clever at concealing her ducklings in the reeds from me — but not from the mama snapping turtle, who grabbed them one by one through the late spring before laying her own eggs. Even a seagull dropped by from Long Island Sound to forage on crappies or whatnot, and Mrs. Morris, my sixth-grade biology teacher, told me that my eels, too, had migrated in from the sea. The Canada geese barked like beagles, going north or south.

On sunny days a certain woodchuck liked to clamber up onto the leaning bough of an apple tree next to the stream and straddle it as comfortably as if she thought she were not just a matriarch but an arboreal creature. I'd face the ethical dilemma of whether to notify Flash and provide him some fun at the expense of panicking her miserably. An old apple tree's outreach, like that one's, carries an idiosyncratic eloquence because season by season the weight of its fruit has twisted each individual limb. This generosity speaks, whereas a white spruce's symmetry is more visually generous, and climbing high to rock with the wind was to plumb a power no truck tire roped like a pendulum to a maple or an oak tree could approach. I'd lie on my back on a patch of moss watching a swaying poplar's branches interlace with another's, and the tremulous leaves vibrate, and the clouds forgather to parade zoologically overhead, and felt linked to the whole matrix, as you either do or don't through the rest of your life. And childhood — nine or ten, I think — is when this best happens. It's when you develop a capacity for quiet, a confidence in your solitude, your rapport with a Nature both animate and not so much so: what winged things possibly feel, the blessing of water, the rhythm of weather, and what might bite you and what will not. In the circus a tapir, a tiger, a mandrill, a rhino, but building really upon the calm that Dr. Green's modest woods and pond, forty-five miles out of New York City, had bestowed on me.

Nature indoors — that plump bobbysoxer stroking my hair while holding my head in her lap to practice up for her boyfriend — made me more jittery, but I was not really somebody who "liked animals more than people," as the cliché goes. Animals didn't sometimes smile sardonically or in wonderment when I stuttered and avert their eyes, turn their backs, but I had close friends and was enjoying my sister's presence now too. I loved her, and even found she was deflecting about the right amount of attention away from me in family politics (but not too much). I didn't go swimming in crashing surf or lightning flashes or climb cliffs with ropes and pitons or kayak in white-water rapids or spelunk claustrophobically. I wasn't trying to conquer nature or prove my testosterone. But nature as simply night or a height or a lonely menagerie animal or a small limestone cave to crawl down in or the lip of the crest of an unpretentious mountain to hunker on for an hour felt just right, and often as if my throttled mouth and bottled-up emotions had engendered a sort of telepathy in me. Not of course to warn of inanimate events, like a flash flood or a rock slide, but the bear around the bend or the desired milk snake in the woodshed. My sixth sense was unstoppered.

I never totaled a car (machines may not have interested me enough) or broke my bones, and had an upbeat view of life, experiencing the kindness of many strangers when I hitchhiked, for instance. I speculated as to what the anthropological purpose could be of the brimming, broad-gauge affection people like me felt when watching a wriggling tadpole or clouds wreathing a massif — sights that have no reproductive or nutritional aspect. Call it "biophilia" or *agape;* it wasn't in response to a hunter's blunt hunger, or kinship-protective, or sexual in some way. Was it a religious wellspring, then? Silence and solitude are fertile if the aptitude is there, and love in its wider applications is also, I think, an aptitude, like the capacity for romantic love, indeed — stilling for a few minutes the chatterbox in us. That massif wreathed in clouds, or the modest pond that has been left in peace to breed its toads, is not a godhead. Like sparks flung out, each perhaps is evidence instead (as are our empathy and exuberance), but not a locus. And yet a link seems to need to take hold somewhere around nine, ten, or eleven — about Mowgli's age, in Kipling — between the onset of one's ability to marinate in the spices of solitude, in other words, and puberty, when the emphasis will shift to contact sports, or dress and other sexual ploys and fantasies, or calculations.

But nine was fine; and when you came to feel at home in Connecticut's woods, New Hampshire's were not a large step up the ladder, or Wyoming's expansive mountains after that, then California's by twenty, building toward British Columbia's and Alaska's, Africa's and India's, in the course of the future. The sea was different, however. I admired it from the beach or a steamship but never acquired the nonchalance required for solo sailing; was afraid of drowning. On the other hand, having been born in New York City and then returned to live there as an adult, I loved metropolises and saw no conflict between exulting in their magnetism and in wild places. Human nature is interstitial with nature and not to be shunned by a naturalist. This accidental ambidexterity enriched my traveling because I enjoyed landing and staying awhile in London on the way to Africa, or exploring Bombay and Calcutta en route to Coimbatore or Dibrugarh. Didn't just want to hurry on to a tribal or wildlife wilderness area without first poking around in these great cities, which I rejoiced in as much. Although there are now far too many people for nature to digest, we are all going to go down together, I believe. We are part and parcel of it, and as it sickens, so will we.

In the meantime, joy is joy: the blue and yellow stripes of a perfect day, with green effusive trees and the dramatic shapes of the streaming clouds. Our moods can be altered simply by sunlight, and I found that having cared for primates, giraffes, and big cats in the circus made it easier to meander almost anywhere. Few people were scarier than a tiger, or lovelier than a striding giraffe, or more poignant than our brethren the chimps and orangutans, and you can often disarm an adversary if you recognize the poignancy in him. Nevertheless, I preferred to step off the road when I was walking in the woods at night and saw headlights approaching. Better to take one's chances with any creature that might conceivably be lurking there than with the potential aberrations of the drive-by human being behind the wheel. It may seem contradictory that for reverence and revelation one needs a balance. You can be staggered by the feast of sensations out-of-doors, but not staggering. Your pins ought to be under you and your eyes focused. As in music, where beauty lodges not in one note but in combining many, your pleasure surges from the counterpoint of saplings and windthrow, or the moon and snow. Both are pale and cold, yet mysteriously scrimshawed — the moon by craters, mountains, and lava flows, the snow by swaying withes or maybe a buck's feet and antler tines. Although like snow the moon will disappear predictably and reappear when it's supposed to, moonlight is an elixir with mystical reverberations that we can pine and yet grin over, even when "empty-armed." It's off-the-loop, a private swatch of time, unaccountable to anybody else if we have paused to gaze upward, and not burdened with the responsibility of naming birdcalls, identifying flowers, or the other complications of the hobby of nature study. One just admires a sickle moon, half-moon, full moon that, weightless and yet punctual, rises, hovering. Sometimes it may seem almost as if underwater, the way its dimensions and yellow-ruddy coloring appear to change — butter, or russet, or polar. The Hungry Moon, Harvest Moon, Hunter Moon, are each emotional, and expertise about their candlepower or mileage from the earth a bit extraneous. Although our own cycles are no longer tied to whether they are waning or gibbous, we feel a vestigial tropism. This is our moon. *It's full*, we'll murmur; or *It's a crescent*, or like a cradle lying partly tipped. And a new moon is no moon.

Twilight, the stalking hour, itself can energize us to go out and employ that natural itch to put our best foot forward and "socialize." The collared neck, the twitching calf, and tumid penis will respond to daylight's variations or the moonrise, as we gulp raw oysters and crunch soft-shelled crabs that still possess that *caught* quality, not like precooked pig or processed cow. If we've lost the sense of astrological spell and navigational exigency that the stars' constellations used to hold, we at least present fragrant bouquets and suck the legs of briny lobsters like savages on important occasions. The stunning galaxies have been diminished to blackboard equations that physicists compute, and our dulled eyes, when we glance up, instead of seeing cryptic patterns and metaphors, settle rather cursorily for the moon.

Water does retain a good deal more of its ancient power to

please or panic us. Bouncing downhill in a rocky bed, shouldering into any indentation, and then nurturing fish, mirroring a spectrum of colors, or bulking into waves that hit the spindrift beach at the inducement of the wind, it's the most protean of life's building blocks, the womb of the world. "My god, there's the river!" we will say, in pure delight at the big waterway willows, the glistering currents bounding along like a dozen otters seizing ownership of the place, as we walk within sight. Our bodies, seventy percent water (and our brains more), only mimic the earth's surface in this respect. And we want a mixed and muscular sky, bulging yet depthless, and full of totems, talismans, in the clouds: not every day, but when we have the energy for it, just to know that we're alive. Rising land of course will lift our spirits too. Hills, a ridgeline, not to begin toiling right up today but the possibility of doing so, perhaps discovering unmapped crannies up there and trees as tiny as bonsai on the crest, yet dips for the eyes to rest in as we look.

We already think we know too much about too much, so mountains are for the mystery of ungeometric convolutions, a boost without knowing what's on top. Awe is not a word much used lately, sounding primitive, like kerosene lamps. What's to be awed about — is this the Three Wise Men following the Star? — what hasn't been explained? Actually, I don't know what *has* been explained. If we are told, for example, that ninety-nine percent of our genes are similar to those of a mouse, does that explain anything? Apprehension, disillusion, disorientation, selfishness, lust, irony, envy, greed, and even self-sacrifice are commonplace: but awe? Society is not annealed enough. Trust and continuity and leadership are deteriorating, and the problem when you are alone is the clutter. Finding even a sightline outdoors without buildings, pavement, people, is a task, and we're not awed by other people anymore: too much of a good thing. We need to glimpse a portion of the axle, the undercarriage, of what it's all about. And mountains (an axis, if not an axle) are harder to be glib about than technological news reports. But if you wait until your mature years to get to know a patch of countryside intimately, thoroughly, your responses may be generic, not specific — just curiosity and good intentions — and you will wind up going in for golf and tennis and power mowers, bypassing nature, instead.

*

No man was complete without a parrot on his shoulder, I used to think. Pirates had them — or perhaps a monkey with a string knotted around its waist — and far-flung sailors, and naturalists searching the tropics for undiscovered plant and animal species. An Orinoco toucan or an orange-epauletted Amazon or hyacinth macaw nibbled at an earlobe or chatted in their ear. At the mouth of the Congo River or the Amazon, hotels had to post a sign saying no parrots were allowed here, and the birds lived so long that in tamer harbors like the USA you might never know who had taught yours to cry, *What's that down between your legs, big boy?* In the port area of lower Manhattan, which later became the World Trade Center, I used to see foulmouthed merchant seamen's big-billed birds for sale in a cigar store that also proffered shrunken human heads with pained and puckered faces and sewn-up lips, which sailors on the coffee or United Fruit banana boats had purchased from tribes such as the famous head-hunting Jivaros of Ecuador. Both the brilliant-colored parrots and the Indians' heads, suspended behind the counter by their greasy black braids of hair, had been jungle-born, except of course for the especially valuable blond-tressed heads of white women and their missionary husbands: although, buyer beware, you were supposed to be careful about fakes — maybe monkeys that had been treated and bleached.

And there was a kind of "leopard store," as I thought of it, named Trefflich's, in a brownstone at 215 Fulton Street, close to where a lot of other ships came in to dock from Joseph Conrad countries. It sold jaguar cubs, anacondas, margay cats and ocelots, aoudads and addaxes, baboons, pangolins, gibbons, adolescent elephants — importing wholesale stuff for zoos to a warehouse in New Jersey. But you could walk around the several floors, if you were with your father, and look at giant Seychelles tortoises, reticulated or Burmese pythons, black panthers peering between the slats of cargo crates, and wheedling monkeys whose organ grinder might have died. Carnival owners stopped by in the spring in painted trucks to purchase an iron cage with a sun bear already in it or rent a half-trained lion or a bunch of monkeys. "When it comes to monkeys," a placard boasted, "we pledge ourselves to give full cooperation to all operators interested in giving the public their monkey's worth!" Beasts in makeshift confinement — an arctic wolf, a rainbow boa, a baby camel — crammed every corner, and then in season might be touring the nation's midways, living on roadkills or sick chickens the drivers stopped to pick up, the panther on foundered horses or dead dogs from a pound, the monks on fruit the public bought.

Parrots did not remain a priority for me because I sensed that they were delicate and in considerable peril, though squawking harshly and nipping fingers. Even when a fancier hamstrung them by scissoring their flight feathers, as if to bauble-ize them, they continued to emit untamable screams and like a peg-leg pirate moved about laboriously by grabbing footholds with their beaks and chimneying up or belaying down in mountaineer fashion. Their shrieks might bring the neighborhood's blue jays to the owner's window, as if to try to help a friend in need, and double the noise. Then you'd see the guy abandon a thousand-dollar pet to his local flower shop, where at least it had the ferns and ficus trees for company. Or I've known a parrot or two that escaped from captivity and shimmied high into a fir tree next to the house, and even in the wintertime simply refused to come down. Up, up, the pinioned bird hitched with claws and beak, watching the hollering jays and crows circling around and screaming gleefully with them. Although of course it couldn't fly, it ate a few tart bits of bark or cone in freedom at their level. The drama continued for hours — pleas and commands from the ground, and hullabaloo from the whirling wild birds. Then a soft snow started falling as night settled down. The native flocks — warmly plumaged and observing the newcomer's crippled condition — flew away to their sheltered roosts while the parrot, in its bright jungle colors, climbed poignantly, stoically higher, to wait in silence to nibble needles and freeze.

I went to summer camp in the Adirondacks, helped out at an animal hospital near my home, and, with a friend's family, visited a little dude ranch in the Wind River range at Dubois, Wyoming, going out by train when I was fourteen. This showed me that whole tiers of land exist that most of us never reach; just look at, perhaps. My horse could scramble by switchbacks for a short way, like a badger galumphing. Horses were more independent-minded than a dog, preferring the open range as a grubstake to any barn and wintering there for six months as uncosseted as the elk or mule deer. The ranch hands wintered pretty tough, too — not just drank a lot but practically hibernated in snowed-over cabins, living on a wad of cash secreted in a coffee can, not a bank account, and snaring jackrabbits, eating root-cellar turnips and steaks axed off a frozen side of beef, by a hissing Coleman lantern. They lost their teeth sooner than easterners, and the men got gimpy at an early age from being thrown or kicked. Not only the rodeo types: many ordinary wranglers were fallen on, stepped on, in breaking horses, roping calves, rassling a steer, or had slid off an icy road in a Chevy and limped for miles with a broken bone. Help was so damned far off.

The bristling, pelagic scale of the landscapes, skyscapes, exhilarated me, plus the chance to catch sight of a cougar by peering up a box canyon, or the coyotes that howled after dark from the same creekbed where I had walked an hour before. In these late 1940s the Good War was barely over, evil had been defeated, but a tremor of risk and early death still prickled the mood of many people of middle age: veterans who wouldn't speak of what they'd done, and for whom foreign travel had involved stifling weeks on a troop ship to places they never wanted to lay eyes on again. They squinted and bit their lips, thinking back. Fred, the one cowhand I got to know somewhat — who taught me to ride in a roundup and shoot ground squirrels, and talked confidingly toward the end — was both mild in manner and steadfast, yet lamed internally, with a cowboy's kidney disabilities and a flat-wallet winter to look ahead to. As with Hope, I can't reconstruct our conversations from sixty years ago, except that there were many factualities for me to learn, glued to yearnings Fred might even help me fulfill. Our talk was less inchoate. Childless from knocking around the West all his life, he was sympathetic to my wish to hear stories of megawildlife, trapper-hermits, gold prospecting, Bigfoot myths, and not just rehearse my saddle skills like the other dudes. That West was already threadbare but not skeletal, and I learned that when somebody in the know recognizes what you care about, he may earnestly try to help. Antelope, moose, and marmots — "whistlers" — we looked for, and falling-down cabins in draws that had yarns attached to them. Fred was slightly built, like a person who dealt with creatures so large that heft itself hardly mattered, compared with logic and telepathy. He sized up people quietly too, and minimized his reactions if he could, the way you would with a haywire heifer or bull.

Act purposefully but minimally and keep your reasons under wraps, was a lesson he taught me. Not the whole formula for life, but quite a beginning, because love and openness to what you love are fragile and yet will flower if cupped and sunlit: as will a free-lance toughness and survivability, when you need that. Like a certain helicopter pilot in the Brooks range in Alaska who flew me around decades later, Fred grounded my enthusiasms at the same time that perhaps mine reinforced his. I couldn't help him face an old age of penury, but we were wistful when this summer interlude wound up. Teasing so many memories out of his mind had cheered him up, made him feel that they were worth it, and as in a relay race, he was passing along nuggets to me, not necessarily from his own life but that turn-of-the-century horse wranglers had conveyed to him. Just so, we elasticize our lives — as you'll see a tiny school of fish do in an aquarium. As quick as mercury and multidirectional, they impart a darkly silver, wriggly sorcery to the cubic inches of the tank. Instead of gallons, it becomes like having a mini-planetarium in the house, because the stars also sometimes seem to swim in the sky, not just hang in suspension there.

Pets in containers, or loose as catty companions or doggy slaves, can hardly fill in for the immensity of wind, stars, and trees, the infinity of unlobotomized animal species, the intricacy of landscapes, the galaxy of scents and shapes in natural creation, that we are losing or just no longer sense or see. A planetarium is not the heavens, or an aquarium the southern oceans, and our own intricacy — our bristly whiskers, flaring nostrils, our fingerpads flicking in and out as ceaselessly as gills, our curling pinnae and peripheral vision and intuitive antennae, all seeking connections — perhaps demands them. Only two percent of Americans are farmers now, and yet the rest of us are still avid for spring's green-up and weather forecasts. Without the primeval dangers that formed us, we tune in bruising professional football or pore through the tabloids for raunchy murders, sexual triangles and kidnappings, news of disease, greedy scandals. We actually learn skills of the chase and the feint from these, learn about insanity and bad judgment and to control our spates of rage, to cushion our marriages, downsize our fantasies, put the brakes on our Neanderthal instincts. The tabloids are appetite-rich and Darwinian. We read them for meat and war games, or watch the tube for boobs that we can't ogle in real life, and truth or consequences — robbers punished — while rejiggering our minds' chemistry with pills, replacing an aging hip with titanium, and exercising on a gym machine, or face-lifting our long-suffering skin.

But I seem to have gained, around eight, nine, or ten, the rather precious sense of continuity that knows that when you come out of the woods into a house it's only temporary; you will be going back out again. People are less amphibious or ambidextrous in this regard than they used to be. A thousand or so may have topped Mount Everest ("Well, we knocked the bastard off," Sir Edmund Hillary famously said after conquering it in 1953), and plenty run marathons or balance on surfboards. Yet a more authentic affinity with what we call nature is being lost even faster than nature itself. Into the void slips obsessional pornography, fundamentalist religion, strobe-light showbiz (no Bing Crosby or Frank Sinatra, who blazed on forever), and squirmy corporate flacks such as the old power brokers seldom employed. If gyms don't substitute for walking, it's hard to find a place to walk, as houses line every beachfront and scissor every patch of woods with culs-de-sac for real estate. You may prefer the ubiquity of electricity to seeing fields of stars after dark, but losing constellation after constellation in the night, and countless water meadows along uncontoured rivers, and bushy-tailed horizons, may be a titanic change. Our motors similarly wipe out the buzz and songs of insects, birds, the sibilation of the breezes that hunters used to front, always stalking into the wind and studying the folds of the terrain for how it flowed, because meals were won by knowing the intimacies of the wind. To lose moonlight, and compass placement, and grasshoppers telling us the temperature by the intensity of their sound, poses the question of whether we *can* safely do away with everything else. The ecology of solitary confinement on this planet may be calamitous, not to mention the sadness. To assuage the emotional effects, already one notices an explosion of plant nurseries, pet stores, computer-simulated androids, and television animations. We've boarded up our windows so as to live interiorly with just our own inventions — though sensing too that we are in the grip of a slow, systemic illness, somehow pervasive — as meanwhile chimpanzees are being eaten up wholesale in Africa as "bushmeat," the elephants butchered, the lions poisoned.

I knew these signature animals by the age of eighteen because I worked for two summers in a circus where we had in our charge some of the most glorious and legendary wilderness creatures. Asian elephants, Sumatran and Siberian and Bengal tigers, a cheetah, a hippo, a jaguar, pythons and boas, three lowland gorillas, a rhino, and an orangutan. My mentor then was a Mohawk Indian, from a culture that was comparably endangered. Indeed, he finished out the remainder of his years as a groom at the riding stable that services New York's yuppie equestrians who ride in Central Park, before having his ashes scattered off of the George Washington Bridge into the Hudson River, which are immemorial waters for the Mohawks. But the survival of wild places and wild things, like the permanence of noteworthy architecture, or the opera, a multiplicity of languages, or old shade trees in old neighborhoods, is not a priority for most people. They are on their way out, and you simply love and love them as you, too, shuffle along.

But the elephants, wrinkled in their sagging hides, appeared to recognize the tenor of events. They were not optimistic — at least I thought not — and forty years later, seeing shattered herds in India and Africa, I was surer still that they realized that the road for them shambled off downhill. Their anxiety was more than jumpy; it seemed demoralized. Their bizarre hugeness only doomed them further. We generally discover important things late: like how very closely the great apes' genome resembles ours. This was obvious to the naked eye and won't prevent wild ones from being eaten in Africa, but makes their treatment here in captivity more appalling. And thus it was with elephants' infrasonic communications, which supplement the squeals and trumpeting we hear. It took a former whale biologist, Katie Payne, who had helped record the high frequencies humpbacks sometimes use, beyond the capacity of a human ear, to figure out that elephants also talk at acoustic (though subsonic) levels we can't detect, and that these deep sound waves travel as messages for surprising distances, from herd to herd (yet nothing like what the ocean's physics can accomplish for certain whales' low-voiced emotings).

The more complexities we come to know about a fellow being, the less cavalier we're going to feel when its kin are wiped out. Most species that disappear, of course, have never been examined or "discovered" at all. But with the jumbo kind — formerly demonized as rogues, or boat swampers and living oil wells — we have a good deal less excuse. Indeed, in the circus, decades before Katie Payne's breakthrough, I had experienced intimations that within our single herd, animals a hundred yards apart could convey their politics or frustrations by sounds below the lowest range that people heard. They would be clearly communing across the field, looking at each other, swinging their trunks convivially and swaying with eloquent body language, until after a minute or so the session ended with a strain of sound finally edging up into a low-pitched groan. I was eighteen, nineteen, not a scientist, and these insights were accompanied by a swarm of others about our giant, protean, poignant beasts — Ruth and Modoc and twenty others — whose feet I liked to lie close to, testing my trust in the rapport I thought I had with their rhythms and whims. Acoustics were not the reason I was touched or central to what I was trying to comprehend, even when they stood there forthrightly and frontally, broadcasting sounds I sometimes intuited but couldn't hear.

In East Africa on two trips during the 1970s, I saw pristine herds on the vastness of the veldt, browsing slowly among the thorn trees as creatures do when engaged in being themselves. Although they were being poached, the horizons were huge, and the scale of ivory-hunting an attrition they could bear. Their humor, gait, and dignity were intact, the tutoring of the calves, the playfulness of bathing, the virtuoso trunks spraying dust when insects annoyed them, or plucking an epicurean shoot, or squealing at a stork. By the 1990s, however, when I returned twice again, the splintered groups, targeted by Somalis with Kalashnikovs, had witnessed so much butchery and anguish — their numbers more than halved — that they acted as if danger were everywhere. They drank at the water holes twitchily, hastily, and migrated between their feeding groves without the ambling ambience of old. Like the chimps I saw, they didn't just react to immediacies, as, for instance, the big cats did, but appeared to worry in advance. They weren't freewheeling personalities anymore, and it was a relief to meet a noncommittal aardvark or a snoopy jackal on the track.

Nature throbs in us through our digestive gases, sweaty odors, wrist pulse, unruly penis or bloody vulva, and nervy tics. We flinch, gasp, fuck, cluck, grin, blink, panic, run, fight, sleep, wake, and wolf a meal like animals. Our official seven deadly sins are rather animal, too, and so is bliss, I think: not only lust but that out-of-body happiness you may feel when being quite still, yet aware and self-contained. Nature is continuity with a matrix and not about causing a stir in the world, and as we destroy our links to other forms of life, it's like whittling at our heels and shins and toes. You can do it for a while until you cut a tendon, nick a bone, and find you limp. And we've now done that. Life turns into more of a riddle when not braided together with other manifestations of energy, grace, scale, and harmonics or tempo and all the rest. Humanity all alone can be constricting, and I've met more blithe spirits in frontier situations than anywhere else. They weren't the quickest conversationalists or the most educated, and inevitably there were also augured souls who had fled to the mountains to get as far away from other people as they could. But as George Orwell remarked at the end of his diaries, "At fifty, everyone has the face he deserves" (alas, he didn't live that long); and these guys from the era of the First World War or the Depression, living on the Skeena River or the Stikine, in British Columbia and Alaska — the Spatsizi or the Omineca, the Klappan or the Kuskokwim, the Tanana or the Porcupine — when you hollered to them from the footpath and they came out of their cabins, looked blithe. They were likely to wear long johns all year round, and light the woodstove every morning regardless of how warmly the sun might be going to shine, because you never know. Anyway, smoke and long johns discourage mosquitoes, and if you've ever been profoundly cold, you won't mind being overwarm.

They were on the lookout for gold colorations in the creekbeds as we walked about, and before fall got well started they would be laying in a mammoth woodpile, and extra rations under the floorboards, and boiling and re-scenting their fur traps, then, after a hard frost, throwing caribou carcasses up on the pitched roof, where they'd keep. I made sure not to take them unawares — because was this an individual who lived out here with the elements because he had abandoned everybody who had ever trusted him, or because of what he'd *sought?* With men thirty years older than me and at home with the tessitura of the wilderness in the 1960s, you didn't need to be a psychologist to arrive at some swift conclusions, mostly cheerful ones. A general competence, plus maybe the yearly salmon runs, had enabled them to ride out the six months of winter, as well as the specters that can afflict a solitary mind. If a man's smile looked to be guyed out as securely as a well-staked tent, it meant he probably grinned a lot, if only to himself, and wasn't about to blow away.

My hunches in the main worked out, and more importantly I escaped the confines of my stutter and gradually became able to talk to people as easily as to animals. Being a humanist, I was not as interested in animals but, in the Whitman mode, aspired to contain multitudes, which included being a mutt and hybrid oneself, snaky, fishy, foxy, and as Afro-Indo-European as our far-trekking forefathers. Although I was living in New York City by this time and married, and therefore swinging as if in a bathysphere into some of these roadless valleys in the far Northwest with my pack and sleeping bag, I felt at home on a moose path too. My spirit keyed into the tuning fork of old melodies — not simply the sense of trust I had acquired in Dr. Green's woods, but the narratives, I think, behind us all. In back of Gilgamesh and Beowulf, Homer, Hardy, and Melville, lie impulses of animism that personified the sweet wellsprings and ominous cliffs, the mountaintops and antique trees as godlings for our ancestors, and the fact that primates are talking to lions even today. Baboons are arguing with them on a Tanzanian plain and fathoming their reactions much as I was often doing half a century ago in the Ringling Bros. Circus. We sleep in edgy surges of a few hours that we manage to combine into a night's civilized schedule, yet would have more logic for a chimp in the forest or a baboon on the veldt, rousing from each nap to glance around for a leopard's dappled coat creeping through the gloaming.

Life is so elastic that people whose circumstances appear to be about the same may measure themselves as almost anywhere on a continuum from misery to elation, and nature herself is invoked to justify fidelity or infidelity, tolerance or violence. I've never thought of nature as a guardian angel, but rather as a polychromatic thrum you sway and hum along with and therefore are not caught by surprise by a sudden juddering in the weather, a hyena on a kill, or a soggy bowl of landscape when you're hiking. Although never a daredevil, I didn't believe that we can live quite wholeheartedly if we are overly afraid of dying, but on the other hand didn't think if life gets boring you have to climb a hairy mountain. Just pick your calluses off and refresh your sensibilities. The airiest scenery I've been privileged to see was in the Himalayan foothills of Arunachal Pradesh, between Assam and Tibet in northeast India. Yet I didn't stand there yearning to scale and "top" the greenly rising and then vertiginous ridges that towered toward snow peaks like laddered but amorphous ghosts, muscular and portentous beyond the mists. I wanted to let them be. And similarly I plan not to be cremated, so that the proverbial worms can do a recycling job on me after I die, rather than be rendered into tidy, sterile minerals in an undertaker's furnace: a less juicy fate.

Now, animals live even more in the present than we do. They are geographic or hierarchical in organization, operating by rote or scented memories of previous hazards and good fortune, seeking food with smaller brains but not wistful about it, as you'll notice watching a fox glance up at suet in a birdfeeder without wasting energy in pining after a bite of it. Short and brutish has been a description of their lives ("brutish" being somewhat tautological), but certainly the lives of what are called the megafauna are getting shorter while ours grow longer. Some people scarcely know what to do with their bonus time — doubled life spans, plus the round-the-clock availability of artificial light — because nature doesn't deal in bonuses. The sun rises and sets when it did a million years ago, with daylight altering by immemorial increments as the planet rolls. It doesn't award you an extra hour if you have a deadline. *Can you make it?* nature asks instead, if it says anything at all. But secondly, and curiously, I think, it speaks in terms of glee. Glee is like the froth on beer or cocoa. Not especially necessary or Darwinian, it's not the carrot that balances the stick, because quieter forms of contentment exist to reward efficiency. Glee is effervescence. It's bubbles in the water — beyond efficiency — which your thirst doesn't actually need.

Bubbles are physics, not biology, and glee, if the analogy is to carry far, may be an artesian force more primordial than evolutionary. To me, it's not a marker for genetic advantages such as earning more, but an indicator that life — the thread of Creation, the relic current that has lasted all this way — is ebullient. Still, you might argue that the choosiest females select not just for strength and money or its zoological equivalents but for the superfluous energy

that humor and panache imply. The woodpecker drumming an ir-
regular tattoo on my tin roof in the spring is not mechanistic in his
ritual, as if merely to prove that he could dig big bugs out of a tree
and bring them to his mate. His zest and syncopation is like when
you watch two fawns gamboling with a doe, or a swaggering vixen
mouth three meadowmice that she has killed to fit them all between her teeth for the trip to her den. Such surplus moments
relax us and serve a tonic function — triumphal for the vixen, ton-
ing the fawns' reflexes, letting the woodpecker pause unexpect-
edly to listen for an answer.

The gamboling, like a kitten's stalk, prepares an animal for the
hunt or being hunted, and the youngster that enjoys it most may
wind up savviest. But the glee I mean is less utilitarian, more spontaneous, and a kind of elixir that needs a bit of peace to germinate.
How does one account for the passive, concentrated happiness of
listening by a lake to the lap and hiss of rustling water, watching
the leaves jiggle, the poplars seethe and simmer? The lake is
ribbed with ropes of wind and strands of sun between cloud shadows. The contours of three hills delineate the comely way that
brooks feed into its blue bulk, and otters, loons, mergansers, animate it (the far mile curving out of sight), so that you'd hardly
need to invent a loch "monster" for drama. And yet you can wake
up nearly anywhere and experience a comparably high-pitched se-
renity. Glee is not complacency — in the middle of a roaring city it
may seize you — and I think of it as possibly generated at life's origins, like a filament from, or footprint of, that original *kick*. Nature
seems more than evolution, punctuated or otherwise, and the
creationists may be on to something when they insist that it is an effusion of God's glory. Their god isn't mine, but glee may be a
shard of divinity.

Nature, although more inclusive than fundamentalism allows
for, seems to me infused with joy. Even the glistering snow is evidence, though burdensome by March, and October's dying leaves,
parched by an internal trigger before the first frosts, turn gratu-
itously orange, red, and yellow, as beautiful as any plumage — yet
what mating purpose does that serve? When outdoors with a dog,
anybody can observe the gulping relish with which it quaffs evocative smells, then punctiliously may leave its own before hounding
on. I have been watching colonies of animals, from chickens, mice,

and garter snakes to some of the megafauna, for sixty years, and when they are not under stress you see plenty of delight and exuberance, particularly when young ones are splitting off and diligently getting a new group started. Biochemistry drives hunger and explains why animals consume one another. But what explains the elation, exuberance — this surplus snap of well-being that animals as well as naturalists feel, and people in Calcutta as much as in New York, or Arunachal Pradesh, for that matter?

Joy sprouts from squalor as well as in the middling classes, a perennial as well as a primitive emotion, as if propelled by a spin originating from the ur- or ultra-density of the Big Bang. Or should we claim that amphibians acquired a capacity for glee only after they became lizards? Or lizards only after they evolved into birds? Where and when did the perception of beauty begin? Most of us nowadays agree that the birds that sing at dawn in the spring are expressing some degree of gladness in their surging notes, not merely a mechanical territoriality. But for a person like me, who considers the toads' sparkling, twinned-note, extended song on warm days in May and June to be actually the loveliest of all, the answer is not that easy. I can't swallow the notion that I — but not the toads — find it so lovely. (I also think I've seen and heard alligators and seen turtles enjoy themselves.) However, then the question shifts to whether amphibians that sing, such as frogs and toads, began to respond to warmth and what we call beauty only after they left the constancy of the water and ceased being fish. Not a sureshot answer there either, unless you discount the evidence of your eyes when you're closely watching fish. And water is an unboxed, undulant medium. What does it mimic when it sloshes?

That crucial age when I opened up and trusted myself to nature, back in Connecticut in 1942, is about when most children start perceiving the world beyond themselves in nuanced, revelatory ways. I later tried sport hunting and gave it up, sport climbing and gave it up, preferring not to lord my ego over what I saw, as in those chill, steep rain forests of Arunachal Pradesh — like Alaska's, multiplied several times over — with footbridges woven of vines stretching across the cataracts and thatched houses perched on stilts and white peaks suspended above it all. To be immersed was sufficient, without attempting to "knock the bastard off."

If we're not immersed, we're likely to try to simulate the hubbub of a tribal encampment by collecting cats or dogs (butchering countless horses in order to feed them), or barbecue sets and fishing tackle, off-road vehicles or quirky Web site monikers. We'll fly in bales of greenhouse flowers from low-wage tropical countries, which are being denuded of their natural flora, to present as symbols of we hardly know what. That is, yes, for anniversaries, marriages, courtship, holidays, graduations: but why *flowers?* Are we bees or bears, or are they somehow akin to the mysteries of glee and orgasm and why small boys stand by the conundrums embedded in the mud of a pond, then reach from the bank or roll their pant legs up and wade after salamanders, water snakes, pollywogs, and perhaps a reflection of what have you?

We reach for where we came from, our older folk a bit homesick: the nights not being starry anymore and distances not quite real. Is there anything untoward that we don't take a pill or press a button for? Nature envelops us, nonetheless, in the piquancy of cottage cheese, the giggle of thunder in the next county. Our lewdness and acquisitiveness bray to prove how recidivist we are, still with our feet in the primal muck. I live alone at the moment, and would smell piquant after a stroke if I weren't discovered immediately. Nor, when I laugh, do I feel in the twenty-first century — I could be Babylonian. And my rapport with friends is more a refinement of ancient habituations than contemporary. Nature, when abused, may react eventually like a tiger whose tail has been pulled. We shall see, indeed, if that is the case. We will definitely find out. But in the meantime we live like those amphibians: sometimes on the dry beach of modernity and sometimes swimming in the oceans that were here eternally before.

TED KOOSER

Small Rooms in Time

FROM RIVER TEETH

SEVERAL YEARS AGO, a fifteen-year-old boy answered the side door of a house where I once lived, and was murdered, shot twice by one of five people — two women and three men — who had gone there to steal a pound of cocaine. The boy died just inside the door, at the top of a staircase that led to the cellar where I once had set up my easel and painted. The robbers — all but one still in their teens — stepped over the body, rushed down the steps, and shot three people there, a woman and two men.

Somebody called the police, perhaps the people who rented the apartment on the second floor. The next day's front-page story reported that the three in the basement were expected to survive. The boy's father, who was somewhere on the first floor and out of the line of fire, had not been injured.

It's taken me a long time to try to set down my feelings about this incident. At the time, it felt as if somebody had punched me in the stomach, and in ways it has taken me until now to get my breath back. I'm ashamed to say that it wasn't the boy's death that so disturbed me, but the fact that it happened in a place where my family and I had once been safe.

I recently spent most of a month building a Christmas surprise for my wife, a one-inch-to-one-foot scale replica of her ancestral home in the Nebraska sandhills. The original, no longer owned by her family, was a sprawling fourteen-room, two-story frame house built in 1884. Her great-grandparents and grandparents lived there. Her great-aunt, still living and 108 years old at the time I am writing this, was born there. Her father and his brothers and sister chased through those rooms as small children, and as a girl my wife and her younger sister spent summers there, taking care of their invalid grandmother.

Day after day as I worked on this dollhouse, pasting up wallpaper, gluing in baseboards and flooring, I would feel my imagination fitting itself into the little rooms. At times I lost all sense of scale and began to feel grit from the sandhills under my feet on the kitchen linoleum, to smell the summer sun on the porch roof shingles. I had never lived in that house, but I lived there during those moments, and as I worked, the shadows of wind-tossed trees played over the dusty glass of the windows. Now and then I would hear footsteps on the porch, approaching the door.

Immediately upon seeing the dollhouse on Christmas Eve, my wife began to recall the way it had been furnished when she was a girl, to talk about this piece of furniture being here and that one there. I watched her feed the goldfish in the dirty aquarium and sit down on the stiff, cold leather of the Mission sofa. I saw her stroke-damaged grandmother propped in her painted iron bed under the eaves. Listening to my wife, watching her open the tiny doors and peer into the tiny closets, I began to think about the way in which the rooms we inhabit, if only for a time, become unchanging places within us, complete in detail.

I clipped the article about the shooting and must have read it a hundred times those first few days. In a front-on photograph, like a mug shot, there stood the house, sealed off by yellow police tape, looking baffled, cold, and vacant. Next to the picture was a row of slack-faced mug shots of the five arrested. They looked as empty as the house.

I mailed a copy of the article to my first wife. I wanted her to share the shock that I was suffering, like a distant explosion whose concussion had taken years to reach across a galaxy of intervening happenstance. At the site where only the most common, most ordinary unhappiness had come to us — misunderstandings, miscommunications, a broken marriage like thousands and thousands of others — there had been a murder, three people had been wounded, and five were on their way through the courts and into prison, all for the want of a pound of cocaine that the article reported had never been there.

For several years in the early 1960s we'd rented the first floor, which included the use of the cellar that I used as a study. We'd been married for three years and were then in our early twenties. Diana was a schoolteacher in a nearby town, and I worked as a clerk at an insurance company. While we lived there, Diana became pregnant, our son was born, and when we brought him home from the hospital we carried him in through that same side door where the murder took place.

I remember matted orange shag carpet inside the door and continuing down the steps to the cellar, and more of the same carpet on the damp concrete floor and glued to the walls. (I can't think of it now without seeing bloodstains.) At the foot of the stairs, in a mildewed, overstuffed chair I'd bought at a thrift shop, I studied for night classes at the university. In that room I painted a few amateur pictures by bad basement light, one of a towering grain elevator that I thought was pretty good but which I mislaid long ago. A life-sized nude of Diana disappeared while we were packing to leave that house for another across town. I wonder if someone doesn't have it nailed up over their basement bar. Perhaps over cocktails on football Saturdays their guests try to guess who that pretty young woman might have been.

Two quiet Latvian women rented the upstairs apartment. They had emigrated from Europe during the Second World War and spent spring, summer, and autumn on their knees beside beds of annual flowers they'd put in along the driveway. Olga was the older, then I suppose in her sixties. She had a badly curved spine, a shy smile, and from a forest near Dresden had seen wave after wave of Allied bombers. She told me that a thousand feet over the city the atmosphere stood in red columns of flame. Alida was handsome, dark-eyed, dark-haired, younger than Olga. Of the two, she was the less approving of the young couple who lived downstairs, who drank too much, who had a very barky dog.

When I think of the exterior of that house, their flowers are always in bloom — petunias, asters, pansies, bachelor's buttons, phlox — but when I remember Diana and me living there, it is always winter and we are closed in by heavy snow. The side door where the boy was killed opened onto the driveway, and the first thing I did on those blizzardy winter mornings was to open it to let out our black Schipperke, Hagen, and watch him wade through the snow to pee and then turn back, a miserable look on his sharp little face. It was a cheap aluminum storm door with loose glass panes, icy to the touch. As I waited there I could hear the kitchen radio behind me, turned up loud so that Diana, who dreaded the twenty-mile drive when the roads were bad, could catch the list of schools that were to be closed for the day.

In a few weeks' time I could build a miniature version of that house, using the approximate measurements of memory, and as I worked with plywood and paper and glue I would be able to gradually remember almost everything about it. But I won't need to do that; since the murder I have often peered into those little rooms where things went good for us at times and bad at times. I have looked into the miniature house and seen us there as a young couple, coming and going, carrying groceries in and out, hats on, hats off, happy and sad.

As I stared at the article, every piece of our furniture took its place in the rooms. I could have reached in through the door of that photograph and with the tip of a finger rolled our antique dental chair over the floor. A friend's big painting of the Rolling Stones hung on the opposite wall. On the living room floor was the plush white carpet I'd bought with money from a literary prize. It was always dirty. Down the hall and through a door to the left, our bed, rumpled and unmade, stood right where it stood when we were young parents, with Jeffrey's crib nearby, and by leaning a little forward I could hear the soft, reassuring sound of his breath.

It has been more than thirty years since we lived at 2820 R Street, Lincoln, Nebraska. I write out the full address as if to fasten it down with stakes and ropes against the violence of time. I hadn't thought about it often, maybe a few times a year. But it was our house again the minute I opened the paper that morning and saw its picture and the faces of the people who had struck it with terrible violence. They didn't look sorry; they looked like they'd do it again if they could.

Now and then since the murder, I find myself turning into that decaying neighborhood and down that street, slowing to look at our house. The window shades are drawn on what were once such bright, welcoming rooms. Nobody lives there now, as far as I can tell. On snowy days there are no tracks up the drive to that flimsy side door.

*

I lean down, I try to fit myself inside. Even after thirty years there still might be the smell of Olga and Alida's salt herring being cooked upstairs, and on the first floor the fragrance of phlox, a few stalks in a water glass. For thirty years I had put it all firmly behind me, but like a perfect miniature it had waited in a corner of my heart, its rooms packed with memories. The murder brought it forward and made me hold it under the light again. Of course I hadn't really forgotten, nor could I ever forget how it feels to be a young father, frightened by an enormous and threatening world, wondering what might become of him, what might become of his wife and son.

Only a year after Diana, Jeff, and I moved away and into another house across town, our marriage came apart, and I began to learn to be a single father. From time to time Jeff came to visit me at the home of friends who had taken me in. The dead boy, too, had gone to visit his father.

If my luck in this life had been worse, I might have been that other father, occupied by some mundane task, perhaps fixing a leaky faucet, when my son went to answer the door. But I was lucky, and my son was lucky, and today, long after the murder, finding myself imagining that damp cellar room, peering down into it as if looking into a miniature cellar, I don't hear shots or see blood on the steps. I hear only soft sounds: my breath as I sit with my book, Diana's stocking feet as she pads along the hall above me, and water running into the bathtub as she gets ready to give our baby a bath.

The landlord, who owned a little doughnut shop, died many years ago. He had once lived in that house. His wife had Alzheimer's disease and sometimes arrived bewildered at our door, wanting us to let her in. She too is gone. If I were building a miniature of that house, I would stand her at the door, clenching her purse in both hands, her hat on crooked.

The flowers that grew along the driveway are thirty years past their season and their beds are only dust today. My friend who painted the Rolling Stones has died. Olga and Alida, having survived the horrors of war to come to the New World and take a little pleasure in simple flowers, they too are gone. I've noticed lately when I've driven past that the porch has begun to slope toward the street, as if to pour our ghosts out the front door and onto the buckled sidewalk. And I am not that young father anymore, but a man in his sixties who is slowly becoming a baffled old woman who hammers and hammers at a door, wanting to be let in again, knowing by instinct that something good must still be waiting just inside.

JONATHAN LETHEM

Speak, Hoyt-Schermerhorn

FROM HARPER'S MAGAZINE

WHEN YOU'RE A CHILD, everything local is famous. On that
principle, Hoyt-Schermerhorn was the most famous subway station
in the world. It was the first subway station I knew, and it took years
for me to disentangle my primal fascination with its status as a
functional ruin, an indifferent home to clockwork chaos, from the
fact that it was, in objective measure, an anomalous place. Personal
impressions and neighborhood lore swirled in my exaggerated regard. In fact the place was cool and weird beyond my obsession's
parameters, cooler and weirder than most subway stations anyway.

My Brooklyn neighborhood, as I knew it in the 1970s, was an
awkwardly gentrifying residential zone. The Hoyt-Schermerhorn
station stood at the border of the vibrant mercantile disarray of
Fulton Street — once the borough's poshest shopping and theater
boulevard. Fulton had suffered a steep decline, from Manhattan-
esque grandeur to ghetto pedestrian mall, through the fifties and
sixties. Now, no less vital in its way, the place was full of chain outlets and sidewalk vendors, many selling African licorice-root chews
and "Muslim" incense alongside discount socks and hats and mittens. The station itself gave testimony to the lost commercial greatness of the area. Like some Manhattan subway stops, though fewer
and fewer every year, it licensed businesses on its mezzanine level:
a magazine shop, a shoeshine stand, a bakery. Most telling and
shrouded at once were the ruined shop-display windows that lined
the long corridor from the Bond Street entrance. Elegant blue-
and-yellow tilework labeled them with an enormous L — standing
for what, exactly? The ruined dressmakers' dummies and empty
display stands behind the cracked glass weren't saying.

The station was synonymous with crime. A neighborhood legend held that Hoyt-Schermerhorn consistently ranked highest in arrests in the whole transit system. Its two border streets, Hoyt and Bond, were vents from the Fulton mall area, where purse snatchers and street dealers were likely to flee and be cornered. The station also housed one of the borough's four Transit Police substations, a headquarters for subway cops that legislated over a quarter of Brooklyn's subway system, so perhaps it was merely that suspects nabbed elsewhere in the system were brought there to register their actual arrest? I've never been able to corroborate the legend. The presence of cops and robbers in the same place has a kind of chicken-and-egg quality. Or should it be considered as a Heisenbergian "observer" problem — do we arrest you because we see you? Would we arrest you as much elsewhere if we were there?

However ridiculous it may seem, it is true that within sight of that police substation my father, his arms laden with luggage for a flight out of JFK, had his pocket picked while waiting on line for a token. And the pay phone in the station was widely understood to have drug-dealers-only status. Maybe it does still. I myself was detained, not arrested, trying to breeze the wrong way through an exit gate, flashing an imaginary bus pass at the token agent, on my way to high school. A cop gave me a ticket and turned me around to go home and get money for a token. I tried to engage my cop in sophistry — how could I be ticketed for a crime that had been prevented? Shouldn't he let me through to ride the train if I were paying the price for my misdeed? No cigar.

Undercover transit policemen are trained to watch for "loopers" — that is, riders who switch from one train car to the next at each stop. Loopers are understood to be likely pickpockets, worthy of suspicion. Even before that, though, loopers are guilty of using the subway *wrong*. In truth, every subway rider is an undercover officer in a precinct house of the mind, noticing and cataloguing outré and dissident behavior in his fellow passengers even while cultivating the apparent indifference for which New Yorkers are famous, above and below ground. It may only be safe to play at not noticing others, because our noticing senses are sharpened to trigger-readiness. Jittery subway shooter Bernhard Goetz once ran for mayor. He may not have been electable, but he had a constituency.

As it happens, I'm also an inveterate looper, though I do it less these days. I'll still sometimes loop to place myself at the right exit stairwell, to save steps if I'm running late. I've looped on the 7 out to Shea Stadium, searching for a friend headed for the same ball game. More than anything, though, I looped as a teenager, on night trains, looping as prey would, to skirt trouble. I relate this form of looping to other subterranean habits I learned as a terrified child. For instance, a tic of boarding: I'll stand at one spot until a train stops, then abruptly veer left- or rightward, to enter a car other than the one for which I might have appeared to be waiting. This to shake pursuers, of course. Similarly, a nighttime trick of exiting at lonely subway stations: at arrival I'll stay in my seat until the doors have lain open for a few seconds, then dash from the train. In these tricks my teenager self learned to cash in a small portion of the invisibility that is not only each subway rider's presumed right but his duty to other passengers, whose irritation and panic rises at each sign of oddness, in exchange for tiny likelihoods of increased safety.

Other peculiarities helped Hoyt-Schermerhorn colonize my dreams. The station featured not only the lively express A train, and its poky but serviceable local equivalent, the CC, but also the erratic and desultory GG, a train running a lonely trail through Bedford-Stuyvesant and into Queens. The GG — shortened today to the G — had the sorry distinction of being the only subway line in the entire system never to penetrate Manhattan. All roads lead to Rome, but not the GG. Hoyt-Schermerhorn also hosted a quickly abandoned eighties transit experiment, the Train to the Plane — basically an A train that, for an additional fare, made a quick express run to the airport. For my friends and me, the Train to the Plane was richly comical on several grounds — first of all, because it didn't actually go to the airport: you had to take a bus from the end of the line. Second, for its twee and hectoring local-television ad — *"Take the train to the plane, take the train to the plane,"* etc. And last because the sight of it, rumbling nearly empty into Hoyt-Schermerhorn with the emblem of an airplane in place of its identifying number or letter, suggested an inglorious subway train that was fantasizing itself some other, less earthbound conveyance.

The Train to the Plane was actually the younger cousin to a more successful freak train, also run out of Hoyt-Schermerhorn:

the Aqueduct Racetrack special, which ran horseracing bettors out to the track on gambling afternoons. Begun in 1959, it flourished, as wagering's infrastructure tends to, until in 1981 it became a casualty of the even more efficient Off-Track Betting, known as OTB, the walk-in storefront gambling establishments that soon dotted the city. Both the Train to the Plane and the Aqueduct Racetrack special made use of Hoyt-Schermerhorn's most fundamentally strange feature: its two quiescent tracks and dark spare platform, that parallel ghost haunting the live platforms. As a kid, I took that dark platform for granted. Later, I'd learn how rare it was — though there are whole ghost stations, dead to trains, and famously host to homeless populations and vast graffiti masterpieces, only a handful of active stations in the entire system have a ghost platform.

Even if I'd known it, I wasn't then curious enough to consider how those two unused tracks and that whole spare platform spoke, as did the ruined display windows, of the zone's dwindled splendor, its former place as a hub, a center. Where I lived was self-evidently marginal to Manhattan — who cared that it was once something grander? What got me excited about Hoyt-Schermerhorn's eerie fourth platform was this: one summer day in 1979, I found a film crew working there, swirling in and out of the station from rows of trucks parked along vacant Schermerhorn Street. Actors costumed as both gang members and high school students dressed for prom night worked in a stilled train. The movie, I learned from an assistant director standing bored with a walkie-talkie at one of the subway entrances, was called *The Warriors*. My invisible, squalid home turf had been redeemed as picturesque. New Yorkers mostly take film crews for granted as an irritant part of the self-congratulatory burden of living in the World Capital. But I was more like a small-town hick in my delight at Hoyt-Schermerhorn's being deemed lensworthy. I was only afraid that, like a vampire or a ghost, the station wouldn't actually be able to be captured in depiction: What were the odds this crappy-looking movie with no stars would ever be released? By picking my turf, the crew had likely sealed their doom.

The origins of the New York underground rapid transit, like those of the city itself, reflect a bastard convergence of utopian longing and squalid practicality — land grabs, sweetheart deals, lined pockets. The city's first, thwarted subway was no different: a Jules Verne dream, one instantly snuffed by Tammany Hall, that paradigmatic political machine. The story has the beauty of a Greek myth: a short length of pneumatic subway built in 1870 *in secret* beneath Broadway by a gentleman engineer determined to alleviate the choking daylight nightmare of New York's foot, pig, horse, stagecoach, and surface railway traffic, against the status quo wishes of Tammany's Boss Tweed, who as commissioner of public works rolled in troughs of money extorted from trolley and omnibus companies. The tube's builder, Alfred Ely Beach, ought to be the hero of one of those elegiac novels of Time Travelers in Olde New York — one of the first editors of *Scientific American,* architect of American patent law, he was also a health nut and an opera buff, and the man in whose office Edison first demonstrated the phonograph ("Good morning . . . How do you like the talking box?"). In fifty-eight nights of covert digging, Beach's crew created a 312-foot tunnel, then assembled an elegant wooden, horseshoe-shaped subway car, pushed by an enormous electric fan. When he unveiled his miracle to the press — in an underground waiting room fitted with curtains, frescoed walls, stuffed chairs, a grandfather clock, a fountain, and bright zircon lamps — his demonstration subway made a sensation, drawing four hundred thousand visitors in 1870. Boss Tweed, aghast at what had been hatched beneath his feet, roused a legal and entrepreneurial assault against Beach's tunnel, investing his influence — and New York City's immediate future — in elevated lines rather than subways. The life was gradually squeezed out of Beach's dream. His tunnel was rented for wine storage, then sealed, then forgotten. When in 1912 diggers excavating for what would become the BMT line stumbled unwittingly into Beach's intact waiting room, his drained fountain and extinguished lamps, his stilled wooden car, they must have felt like intruders on Tut's tomb.

I became a regular customer in 1978. That year I began commuting from Brooklyn to Harlem, an hour away in the upper reaches of Manhattan, to attend Music and Art, a venerated public high school created by Fiorello La Guardia. (Music and Art, with its sister campus, Performing Arts, was immortalized in the movie *Fame* during my years there, but since I was studying painting and no painters were portrayed in the film, I didn't take it personally.) The A train out of Hoyt-Schermerhorn was now my twice-daily passage, to and from. My companion was Lynn Nottage, a kid from the block I grew up on, a street friend. Lynn was from a black middle-class family; I was from a white bohemian one. We had never gone to school together in Brooklyn — Lynn had been at private school — but now were high school freshmen together, in distant Harlem. Lynn had the challenge of getting to school on time with me as her albatross. Some mornings the sound of her ringing the doorbell was my alarm clock.

Lynn and I had habits. We stood in a certain spot on the platform, boarding the same train every morning (despite an appearance of chaos, the system is regular). Most mornings we rode the same subway car, the conductor's car. Had we been advised to do this by protective parents? I don't know. Anyhow, we became spies, on the adults, the office workers, tourists, beggars, and policemen who'd share segments of our endless trip. We took a special delight in watching the bewilderment of riders trapped after Fifty-ninth Street, thinking they'd boarded a local, faces sagging in defeat as the train skipped every station up to 125th, the longest express hop in the system. Also, we spied on our own conductor. The conductor's wife rode in with him to work — she'd been aboard since somewhere before Hoyt-Schermerhorn — then kissed him goodbye at a stop in the financial district. Two stops later, his girlfriend boarded the train. They'd kiss and moon between stops until she reached her destination. Lynn and I took special pleasure in witnessing this openly, staring like evil Walter Keane kids so the conductor felt the knife edge of our complicity.

This was the year another student, a talented violinist, had been pushed from a train platform, her arm severed and reattached. The incident unnerved us to the extent that we were able to afford to maintain it as conscious knowledge: we couldn't, and so didn't. There were paltry but somehow effective brackets of irony around our sense of the city's dangers. Lynn and I were soon joined by Jeremy and Adam, other kids from my street, and we all four persistently found crime and chaos amusing. The same incidents that drew hand-wringing from our parents and righteous indignation from the tabloids struck us as merry evidence of the fatuousness of grownups. Naturally the world sucked, naturally the authorities blinked. Anything was possible. Graffiti was maybe an art form, certainly a definitive statement as to who had actually grasped the nature of reality as well as the workings of the reeling system around you: not adults but the kids just a year or three older than you, who were scary but legendary. The entire city was like the school in the Ramones' movie *Rock 'n' Roll High School,* or the college in *Animal House* — the dean corrupt and blind, the campus an unpatrolled playground. Our own fear, paradoxically, was more evidence, like the graffiti and the conductor's affair, of the reckless, wide-open nature of this world. It may have appeared from the outside that Lynn and Jeremy and Adam and I were cowering in this lawless place, but in our minds we romped.

The names of the three limbs of the subway — the IRT (Interborough Rapid Transit), the BMT (Brooklyn Manhattan Transit, changed from the original BRT, for Brooklyn Rapid Transit), and the IND (Independent) — are slowly falling from New Yorkers' common tongue, and the last enamel signs citing the old names will soon be pried off. Slipping into shadow with the disuse of those names is the tripartite origin of the subways, the fact that each of the three sets of trains was once a completely separate and rival corporation. The lines tried to squeeze one another out of business, even as they vied with now extinct rival forms: streetcars and elevated trains. On this subject, the language of the now unified citywide system, the official maps and names, has grown mute. But the grammar of the train lines and stations themselves, with their overlaps and redundancies, their strange omissions and improvised passageways, still pronounces this history everywhere.

The early subways pioneered in crafty partnership with realtors and developers. Groping for new ridership, the early owners threw track deep into farmland, anticipating (and creating) neighborhoods like Bensonhurst and Jackson Heights. The latecomer, the IND(ependent), contrary to its name, was a political instrument, conceived from within a mayor's feud with transit's maverick owners. James Hylan, elected mayor in 1917, was widely understood to be a puppet of the Hearst newspapers — a man who, according to Robert Moses, "swelled instead of growing" in office. His credo — "the preservation of democracy and the retention of the 5-cent fare" — is only a glimpse into the scope of his obsession with transit interests, whom he accused of wishing to rape New York "like the conquered cities of old."

The legacy of Hylan's bullying was the eventual merging of this chaotic system into a confederated public trust. When subway unification came, in 1940 under Fiorello La Guardia, it was the largest railway merger in the history of the country — of, I suppose, the world. Under Hylan's own watch, though, the IND was a city-sponsored rival to the private interests, one nonetheless forced to run in the black and therefore to cling to established population centers, unlike its more adventurous precursors. The IND's circumscription within the city's previously established transit routes alienated the realtor lobby, previously the subway's great secret weapon. The city's destiny was no longer horizontal but vertical, perhaps fractal, a break with the American frontier motif in favor of something more dense and strange.

Construction of new subway stations and tunnels in a city already webbed with infrastructure was a routine marvel. According to Stan Fischler's *Uptown, Downtown,* tunneling for the IND required, among other astonishing statistics (22 million cubic yards of rock and earth displaced, 7 million man-days of labor), the *relocation* of 26 miles of water and gas pipes, 350 miles of electrical wire, and 18 miles of sewage pipes. What's striking, though, in photographs documenting that work, is the blithe indifference in the faces of passersby, even at such preposterous scenes as workers tunneling beneath a street where both a surface trolley and an elevated train are being kept in continuous operation above. Construction of the Sixth Avenue tunnel at Thirty-fourth Street was an engineering marvel of its day, the tunnel having to be threaded under the Broadway BMT subway and over the Pennsylvania Railroad (now Amtrak) tubes, as well as an even more deeply buried water main. This, according to Groff Conklin, author of *All About Subways,* "the most difficult piece of subway construction which has ever been attempted," is almost impossible to keep in mind on an F train as it slides blandly through Herald Square today.

A scattering of photos of the Hoyt-Schermerhorn dig are available in the archives in the basement of the MTA's building on Livingston Street, just a couple of blocks from the station. The excavation method was typical: it was a "cut-and-cover" job, where an elaborate temporary roadway is constructed of wood and girders. The majority of the pictures document a not-quite-catastrophe: the collapse after a rainstorm of a portion of the wooden roadway into the tunnel, swallowing several cars and streetlamps but no lives. In several photos the landmark Quaker Meetinghouse is seen hovering on the crumbled brink of the hole. Another few feet and it would be undermined. The only newspaper account I could locate treated the collapse so glancingly it was occasion only for an admiring photograph of a crane picking a car from the pit, labeled with a brief caption.

Alfred Kazin, in *A Walker in the City*, wrote: "All those first stations in Brooklyn — Clark, Borough Hall, Hoyt, Nevins, the junction of the East and West side express lines — told me only that I was on the last leg home, though there was always a stirring of my heart at Hoyt, where the grimy subway platform was suddenly enlivened by Abraham and Straus's windows of ladies' wear." When a friend directed me to this passage, thinking he'd solved the mystery of those deserted shop windows in the Hoyt-Schermerhorn station, I at least had a clue. I searched the corporate history of Abraham & Straus — Brooklyn's dominant department store and a polestar in my childhood constellation of the borough's tarnished majesty, with its brass fixtures and uniformed elevator operators and the eighth floor's mysterious stamp- and coin-collectors' counters. In the A&S annals I found the name of a Fulton Street rival: Frederick Loeser's, one of the nation's largest department stores for almost a century, eventually gobbled by A&S in a merger. The 1950s were to such stores as the Mesozoic was to the dinosaurs — between '52 and '57 New York lost Loeser's, Namm's, Wanamaker's, McCreery's, and Hearn's; the names alone are concrete poetry.

I'd nailed my tilework L: Loeser's created display windows in the new Hoyt-Schermerhorn station to vie with A&S's famous (at least to Alfred Kazin) windows at Hoyt. Kazin's windows are visible as bricked-in tile window frames today, but like the smashed and dusty Loeser's windows of my childhood, they go ignored. Meanwhile, aboveground on Fulton Street, the name Loeser's has recently reemerged like an Etch A Sketch filigree on some second-story brickwork, as lost urban names sometimes do.

*

The abandoned platform was a mystery shallower to penetrate than Loeser's L — in fact, it is the station's bragging point. The extra track connects the abandoned platform to an abandoned station, three blocks away on Court Street. This spur of misguided development was put out of its misery in 1946 and sat unused until sometime in the early sixties, when the MTA realized it at last had an ideal facility for renting to film and television crews. The empty Court Street station and the curve of track between it and the ghost platform at Hoyt-Schermerhorn allowed filmmakers to run trains in and out of two picturesque stations along a nice curved wall without disturbing regular operations. For this distinction Hoyt-Schermerhorn sporadically stars in human-interest stories in the *New York Times* Metro section: Who doesn't enjoy reading about film stars slumming in urban locations? The nonpareil among thirty-six movies made utilizing subway property just between 1970 and 1975 is the subway-hijacking-hostage thriller *The Taking of Pelham One Two Three*. It was in Hoyt-Schermerhorn's approach tunnels that Robert Shaw and his cohort stripped off fake mustaches and trench coats and, clutching bags of ransom money, made their hopeless dash for daylight, and it was in Hoyt-Schermerhorn's approach tunnels that Shaw, cornered by crusading MTA inspector Walter Matthau, stepped on the third rail and met his doom.

And then there is *The Warriors*. The film is based on a novel by Sol Yurick, itself in turn based on Xenophon's *Anabasis,* an account of a band of Greek mercenaries fighting their way home, against impossible odds, through enemy turf. Yurick translated Xenophon into New York street gangs. His book is a late and lofty entry, steeped in the tone of Camus's *The Stranger,* in the "teen panic" novels of the fifties and sixties. Walter Hill, a director whose paradigm is the Western, turned Yurick's crisp, relentless book into the definitive image of a New York ruled by territorial gangs, each decorated absurdly and ruling their outposts absolutely.

The movie inspired reports of theater-lobby riots during its theatrical run. It's a cult object now, fetishized on Web sites, celebrated in hip-hop by Puff Daddy and the Wu-Tang Clan, and cherished by New Yorkers my age — we who preen in our old fears — for mythologizing the crime-ruled New York of the seventies more sweetly and absurdly than *Kojak* or *The French Connection.* For, in the film, it is the gang members themselves who become the ultimate victims of the city's chaos. Even the Warriors wish they'd stayed home.

For me, a fifteen-year-old dogging the steps of the crew as they filmed, it was only perfect that a fake gang had occupied Hoyt-Schermerhorn's fake platform. The film was etching my own image of the city into legend, and for me it had begun its work even before its public life. (In fact, I couldn't imagine that anyone would want to see it.) Yurick's book has just been reissued again, with a movie still on the jacket and a long new introduction, detailing the classical and existentialist roots of the project, and fascinating for its rueful and erudite perplexity that this least ambitious of his books should be the one to survive: "There hasn't been one film made in the United States that I would consider seeing five times, as many who loved the film version of *The Warriors* did." Years later, by chance, I met the wizened Yurick on a train platform, though not the subway. We disembarked together in Providence, Rhode Island, each a guest at the same literary conference, and, unknowingly, companion riders on an Amtrak from New York. Our hosts had failed to meet our train, and as the locals all scattered to their cars, the family members or lovers to their reunions, we were left to discover each other and our dilemma. Yurick shrugged fatalistically — should we have expected better? He summed up his perspective in a sole world-weary suggestion: "Wanna nosh?"

Michael Lesy's 1973 book *Wisconsin Death Trip* is a mosaic of vintage photographs and newspaper accounts of eccentric behavior and spastic violence in turn-of-the-century rural Wisconsin. It makes a case, not polemically but by a flood of miniature evidence, that stirring just under the skin of this historical site is mayhem, sexuality, the possibility of despair. The book is a corrective to homilies of a pastoral American countryside, a catalogue of unaccountable indigenous lust, grief, revenge, and sudden joy.

As my newspaper clippings accumulated, I began to imagine my equivalent: *Hoyt-Schermerhorn Death Trip*. "TWO ARE KILLED BY POLICE IN GUN BATTLE, 1/23/73: Neither of the slain men was immediately identified. But the police said that one of them had been wanted for several bank robberies and for allegedly shooting at policemen last Wednesday night in the Hoyt-Schermerhorn Street subway station . . ." "WOMAN HURT IN SUBWAY

FALL, 6/19/58: A 55-year-old woman was critically injured yesterday when she fell or jumped in front of a southbound IND express train at the Hoyt-Schermerhorn Street station in Brooklyn . . . Service on the southbound tracks of the A line was interrupted for fifty-three minutes." "37 HURT IN CRASH OF TWO IND TRAINS, One Rams Rear of Another in Downtown Brooklyn During Evening Rush, 7/18/70: . . . there was a rending of metal at the crash, she said, and then the car tilted. All the lights went out. She said there were sparks and the car filled with smoke. The girl said she was thrown to the floor and, terrified, began screaming . . ." "YOUTH ARRESTED WITH GUN, 5/26/89: A 13-year-old Brooklyn youth was arrested yesterday morning with a fully loaded 9-millimeter handgun, and he showed up later in the day to ask the New York City Transit Police when he would get his gun back." "STRANGER PUSHES WOMAN TO DEATH UNDER A TRAIN, 2/2/75: A 25-year-old woman was thrown to her death in front of an onrushing subway train in Brooklyn yesterday evening by a man who apparently was a total stranger to her, the police said . . . The incident took place at about 6:15 P.M. in the Hoyt-Schermerhorn Street IND station, which was crowded with shoppers at the time. According to witnesses, including the train motorman . . . [the] man suddenly stepped up to the victim, who had her back to him, and pushed her forward in front of the train without saying a word . . ." "400 BOYCOTTING STUDENTS RIOT, HURL BRICKS, BEAT OTHER YOUTHS, 2/18/65: Four hundred boycotting Negro students broke through police barricades outside Board of Education headquarters in Brooklyn yesterday in a brick-throwing, window-breaking riot . . . The disturbances spread over a two-mile area and onto subway trains and stations . . . A group of 60 youths attacked a group of six white high school students on the Clinton-IND's GG line . . . They were apprehended at the Hoyt-Schermerhorn station by 15 transit policemen . . ." "300 IN SUBWAY HELP TILT CAR AND RELEASE BOY'S WEDGED FOOT, 9/2/70: A rescue team of subway passengers, hastily organized by three transit patrolmen, tipped back a 54-ton subway car last night to free an 11-year-old boy whose foot was wedged between the car and the platform at a downtown Brooklyn station. The boy . . . was running for an IND A train when his leg was caught between the platform and train at the Hoyt-Schermerhorn station."

Contemplation of the density of meanings at a given site becomes, in the end, like Lesy's scrapbook, a tidal experience. The lapping of successive human moments forms a pulse or current, like the lapping of trains through the underground tunnels, or like the Doppler-effect fading of certain memories from the planet as they're recalled for the penultimate time, and then the last: When will the last person to have purchased pantyhose or a razor at Loeser's pass from the earth? When will the last of those three hundred who rocked the train car off the boy's pinned leg, or the last of those four hundred Negro boycotters, be gone?

A kid raised inside the liberal sentiments of a middle-class family yet living in an area fringed with crime and poverty met a choice. It was possible to identify with and assimilate to the harsher truths of the street, and so toughen, somewhat, to fear. Alternately, a kid could carry his parents' sensitivities and standards with him, out-of-doors. The price was obvious. Most of us, whether we ended in one camp or another, wavered. I was a "good" kid, and a bullied one, yet I recall dozens of moments when I slid briefly across the separation line. It was on a basketball court directly across from Hoyt-Schermerhorn's entrance where I allowed myself to meld complicitly into a crowd of Puerto Rican kids, with whom I'd been playing, as they briefly halted our game to harass and threaten a single Asian man, a gay man, off a neighboring court. I wasn't violent; the incident hardly was. But the man was the boyfriend of a pal of my mother's, and I'd been a guest in their elegant townhouse. When my mom's friend, a gay man considerably huskier than his young lover, returned to the court with a baseball bat and, bellowing at us, broke up the game, sent us scurrying, his eyes met mine and I was disgraced, wrenched between concurrent selves.

  The moment was precursor to a worse one. This was the summer between high school and college, which is to say the verge of my escape from Brooklyn for most of fifteen years. I've come to understand how fraught that moment was for me, as I considered or refused to consider what I was involuntarily carrying with me out of the particulars of my childhood environment. My girlfriend was from upstate New York but living in my city, my neighborhood, for that summer before we both embarked to college. She worked nights as a waitress in Manhattan and rode, yes, the A train, into Hoyt-Schermerhorn. She was frightened, as she perhaps should have been, to walk the several blocks home from that station after eleven, and so I'd promised always to meet her. I often lightly mocked her fear — but that bit of overcompensation, lousy as it sounds, wasn't my crime.

My crime was that one night, going to the station to pick her up, I impulsively waited in shadow by the entrance instead of making myself visible. I had no plan. I was fooling around. She looked for me, evidently afraid to stand there waiting alone, as she absolutely should have been: it was a different thing to walk swiftly home than it was to linger. I could have stepped forward easily, but instead my stupid jape distended, and I just watched her. And then, as she began walking home without me, I followed her.

I think I was certain she'd turn and see me, and that it would be oddly funny, but she never did. She was afraid to turn to see whose footsteps followed her, of course. I trailed her home, compounding my mistake with each accelerating footstep until I at last overtook her just outside the door. While I tried to explain, she trembled, in fear that had converted immediately, and rightly, to rage. Denial has covered any recollection of my words by now, but I know they were hopelessly inadequate to repair what I'd told myself was a harmless joke — though I was walking behind her, I'd still been protecting her, hadn't I? — and was actually such a cruel joke it wasn't a joke at all. Although I'd hardly claim to be Patty Hearst, there was a touch of the Stockholm syndrome in my behavior. I was bestowing on another a trace, or more than a trace, of fears I'd absorbed for years.

Here's where I am: in the subway, but not on a train. I'm standing on one platform, gazing at another. Moaning trains roll in, obscuring my view; I wait for them to pass. The far platform, the one I'm inspecting, isn't lit. The tiles along the abandoned platform's wall are stained — I mean, more than in some ordinary way — and the stairwells are caged and locked, top and bottom. Nothing's happening there, and it's happening round the clock.

I've been haunting this place lately, though the more time I spend, the further it reels from my grasp. And, increasingly, I'm drawing looks from other passengers on the platforms, and upstairs, at the station's mezzanine level. Subway stations — the platforms and stairwells and tunnels, the passages themselves — are

sites of deep and willed invisibility. Even the geekiest transit buffs
adore the trains, not the stations. By lingering here, I've set off
miniature alarms in nearby minds, including my own. I've allied
myself with the malingerers not on their way to somewhere else.
My investigation of this place reeks of a futility so deep it shades toward horror.

By the same law of meticulously observed abnormalities that
causes loopers to stand out, my spying at Hoyt-Schermerhorn trig-
gers a rustle of disquiet. I'm not here for a train. What I'm trying
to do maybe can't be done: inhabit and understand the Hoyt-
Schermerhorn station as a place. Worse, I'm trying to remember it,
to restore it to its home in *time*. There's no greater perversity, since
a subway station is a sinkhole of destroyed and thwarted time. By
standing here trying to remember Hoyt-Schermerhorn I've only
triggered its profoundest resistance: I'm using it wrong.

Yet I'm stubborn. This was my first subway memory, the tunnel,
those ruined Loeser's windows. I've returned to reclaim the seed
of a lifelong romance, a New Yorker's typical romance with our
limitless secret neighborhood, the one running beneath all the
others. Nothing subsequent, not hundreds of high school days, not
The Warriors, not my own feeble crimes, can displace this memory's
primacy or fade its color. I held my mother's hand. I was being
taken to her office in Manhattan. Perhaps it was a day off from
school, I don't know. I rode the subway for the first time I can recall, but I don't remember the train. I remember the station.

E. J. LEVY

Mastering the Art of French Cooking

FROM SALMAGUNDI

I HAVE NO PHOTOGRAPH of my mother cooking, but when I recall my childhood this is how I picture her: standing in the kitchen of our suburban ranch house, a blue-and-white-checked terry cloth apron tied at her waist, her lovely head bent over a recipe, a hiss of frying butter, a smell of onions and broth, and open like a hymnal on the counter beside her, a copy of Julia Child's *Mastering the Art of French Cooking.*

The book's cover is delicately patterned like wallpaper — white with miniature red fleurs-de-lis and tiny teal stars — the title and authors' names modestly scripted in a rectangular frame no larger than a recipe card: a model of feminine self-effacement.

This unassuming book was my mother's most reliable companion throughout my childhood, and from the table laid with a blue cotton cloth, not yet set with flatware and plates and glasses of ice water, not yet laid with bowls of broccoli spears, *boeuf bourguignon,* potatoes sautéed in butter, I observed her as she sought in its pages an elusive balance between the bitter and sweet.

It is a scene less remembered than invoked, an amalgam of the many evenings when I sat and watched my mother cook at the copper gas stove whose handles glowed a soft, burnished, too human pink. Tall and remote as statuary, dressed stylishly in cashmere and pumps, a chestnut bouffant framing her face and its high cheekbones, her pale blue eyes cast down, my mother consulted her recipes night after night. It is a scene suffused in memory with a diffuse golden light and a sense of enormous safety and an awareness that beyond that radiant kitchen lay the shadow-draped lawn, the cold, starry night of another midwestern autumn.

My mother had few pleasures when I was growing up. She liked to read. She liked to play the piano. She liked to cook. Of these, she did a good deal of the first, very little of the second, and a great deal of the third. She was of that generation of women caught in the sexual crossfire of women's liberation, who knew enough to probe for their desires, but not enough to practice them.

Born into the permissive sixties, raised in the disillusioned seventies, the third of three children, I came of age in a world where few rules were trusted, few applied. Of those that did, the rules contained in my mother's cookbooks were paramount.

The foods of my childhood were romantic. *Boeuf bourguignon. Vichyssoise. Salade niçoise. Bouillabaisse. Béarnaise. Mousseline au chocolat.* Years before I could spell these foods, I learned their names from my mother's lips, their smells by heart.

At the time I took no notice of the gustatory schizophrenia that governed our meals. The extravagant French cuisine prepared on the nights my father dined with us; the Swanson TV dinners on the nights we ate alone, we three kids and my mother, nights that came more frequently as the sixties ebbed into the seventies. On those nights we ate our dinners in silence and watched the Vietnam War on television, and I took a childish proprietary delight in having a dinner of my own, served in its aluminum tray, with each portion precisely fitted to its geometrical place. These dinners were heated under thin tinfoil and served on plates, and we ate directly from the metal trays our meals of soft whipped potatoes, brown gravy, sliced turkey, cubed carrots and military-green peas.

Had I noticed these culinary cycles, I doubt that I would have recognized them for the strategic maneuvers they seem to me in retrospect. Precisely what my parents were warring over I'm not sure, but it seems clear to me now that in the intricate territorial maneuvers that for years defined their marriage, cooking was my mother's principal weapon. Proof of her superiority. My father might not feel tenderness, but he would have to admire her. My mother cooked with a vengeance in those years, or perhaps I should say she cooked for revenge. In her hands, cuisine became a martial art.

*

My mother spent herself in cooking. Whipping egg whites by hand with her muscular forearm, rubbing down a turkey with garlic and butter and rosemary and thyme, she sublimated her enormous unfeminine ambition in extravagant hubristic cuisine. Disdainful of the Sisyphean chores of housecleaning, she threw herself into the task of feeding us in style. If we were what we ate, she was hell-bent on making her brood singular, Continental, and I knew throughout my childhood that I would disappoint her.

In the kitchen, my mother could invent for herself a coterie of scent and flavor, a retinue of exquisite associates, even though she would later have to eat them. What she craved in those years was a companion, not children; but my father was often gone, and I was ill suited to the role.

I lacked utterly the romance my mother craved. Indifferent to books, unsociable, I could not master French. Though I would study the language for five years in high school, I would never get beyond the rudiments of ordering in restaurants and asking directions to the municipal pool (*Je voudrais un bifteck, s'il vous plaît. Où est la piscine?*). In the face of my mother's yearning, I became a spectator of desire, passive, watchful, wary. Well into my twenties I remained innocent of my tastes, caught up in observing my mother's passions and fearful too that I might betray her, call into question her unswerving desires with desires of my own.

Julia Child was the only reliable companion my mother had in those years, other than the woman who came once a week to clean the house. Across the street the Segals had a "live-in girl," a local college student who came in to watch the children in the afternoons while Mrs. Segal nursed a nervous breakdown. Each year these live-in girls changed: now blond, now brunette, with names like Stacy and Joanne. They taught us how to shoot hoops, how to ride bikes, how to appreciate soap operas. In our house there was no "live-in girl," there was only Mrs. Williams, the "cleaning lady."

I was quiet on the days when Mrs. Williams came to clean, embarrassed that we needed someone to help us keep our lives in order, embarrassed too by the fact that she was black and we were white. On the afternoons she came to clean I could not help but see my family as White People, part of a pattern of white folks who hired black folks to pick up after them. I felt ashamed when I saw my mother and Mrs. Williams chatting over coffee at our kitchen table. I saw their silhouettes against history, and they made an ugly broken line. I read in it patronage, condescension, exploitation, thwarted rage.

I thought at the time that it was misapplied gentility that prompted my mother to sit with Mrs. Williams while she ate lunch. Their conversations seemed to me a matter of polite routine. They spoke generally. Of the latest space launch, Watergate, the price of oil. The conversation was not intimate. But they shared it. Later, when Mrs. Williams was dying of breast cancer, she told my mother that my mother had been her best friend. Her *best* friend. My mother told me this with wonder, as if she were amazed that anyone had ever considered her a friend. Now I wonder if the declaration moved her too because she understood its corollary, that Mrs. Williams had been her best, perhaps her only, friend.

Cooking was not the only medium in which my mother excelled. She organized birthday parties on an epic scale — fashioning piñatas out of crepe paper and papier-mâché, organizing haunted houses and games of smell and memory — and she made us prize-winning costumes well beyond the point at which we should rightly have given up masquerading.

I was fifteen when I won the final prize in a series of prizes won for her costumes, for a banana suit she'd made me, a full-length, four-paneled yellow cotton shift, worn over a conical cardboard cap to shape the crown, and yellow tights. My mother had ingeniously designed the suit with a triangular front panel that could be secured with Velcro to the crown or "peeled" down to reveal — through a round hole in the cloth — my face.

The prize for this costume, my father reminds me, was a radio designed to look like a box of frozen niblet corn — a square, yellow plastic radio with an authentic Green Giant label. This was the late seventies, and in America you could buy a lot of things that looked like food but weren't. You could buy a scented candle in the shape of a chocolate sundae, sculpted in a tulip glass with piles of frothy false whipped cream and a perfect wax cherry. You could buy a soda glass tipped on its side, out of which a carbonated cola-colored liquid spilled into a puddle of clear plastic. There was shampoo that smelled of herbs or lemons; tiny soaps in the shape of peaches and green apples; paperweights shaped like giant aspirin, four inches in diameter, cast in plaster; the plastic simulacrum of a slice of pineapple or a fried egg dangling at the end of a key chain.

It was an era of food impersonation. A cultural critic might dismiss this as conspicuous consumption: possessed of abundance, we could mock necessity. Food, for us, could be a plaything — revenge for all those childhood admonitions not to play with your food. But I think that there was in this as well a sign of political disaffection — an ironic commentary on the unreliability of appearances in the wake of Watergate and Vietnam (in South Africa such objects were also popular at the time, a Fulbright scholar from Zimbabwe would tell me years later) — and a measure of spiritual dislocation. As if, glutted with comfort and suspicious of appearances, we had lost touch with what sustains us and had relinquished faith in even the most elementary source of life. Food.

Mixed marriage. The phrase itself recalls cuisine: mixed greens, mixed vegetables, "mix carefully two cups sifted flour with . . ." As if marriage were a form of sentimental cookery, a blending of disparate ingredients — man and woman — to produce a new and delectable whole. "She's my honey bun, my sweet pea, my cookie, sugar"; "You can't make an omelet without breaking a few eggs."

English is spiced with phrases that attest to our enduring attachment to food as metaphor, and point to our abiding faith in affection's ability to sustain us as vitally as food does. But the phrase "mixed marriage" also suggests the limits of love, its inability to transform difference, and is a warning. In the mythic goulash of American culture, the melting pot is supposed to inspire amity, not love. One should melt, it seems, not mix. Marriage of the kind my parents ventured to embrace — between gentile and Jew — went, according to the conventions of the time, too far.

It was in part because of their differences that my mother married my father. He must have seemed to her exotic, with his dark skin, jet eyes, his full sensuous mouth. At seventy he will look like Rossano Brazzi, but at age thirty-one, when my parents meet at the University of Minnesota, on the stairs of Eddy Hall, as my beautiful mother descends from a library in the tower where she has finished her day's research and my father ascends to his office where he is a young professor of psychology, he is more handsome even than a movie star — I can see this in photos from the time — because his face is radiant with expectation for his future.

For my father, the son of Russian and Latvian immigrants, marrying my mother must have seemed like marrying America itself. Her ancestors had come over in 1620 on that first and famous ship, and though my mother's family was of modest means, her speech and gestures bespeak gentility. Her English is precise, peppered with Latinate words and French phrases; her pronunciations are distinctive and slightly Anglicized (not *cer-EE-bral,* she corrects me, *CER-eh-bral*). She possesses all the Victorian virtues: widely read, she is an accomplished pianist and a gifted painter; she speaks French and Czech, is knowledgeable in art and history, physics, physiology, and philosophy. Although she is a passionate conversationalist, she has a habit of concluding her sentences on a slight descending note, as if she has discovered partway through speech that it is too wearying to converse after all, and so gives up. My mother's verbal inflections are the telltale signs of class in classless America, and marrying her, my father crossed the tracks. He could not know how he would resent the crossing; she could not know how she would resent the role of wife.

My mother's enormous ambitions were channeled by her marriage into a narrow course — like a great roaring river forced against its nature to straighten and be dammed, resulting in floods, lost canyons — and her desires became more powerful for having been restrained. It seemed to me only a matter of time before she'd reassert her claim to wilder, broader terrain. Throughout my childhood, I waited for my mother to leave.

Given the centrality of culinary concerns in my childhood, it is unsurprising perhaps that my first act on leaving home was to codify my eating. My first term at college, I eschewed the freshman ritual of room decoration — the requisite Manet prints, the tacky O'Keeffes — in favor of regulations: I tacked a single notice to the bulletin board beside my desk, specifying what I could and could not eat. My schema was simple: one thousand calories each day, plus, if absolutely necessary, a pack of sugarless gum and as much as a pound of carrots (my skin, in certain photos from the period, is tinted orange from excess carotene). I swam my meals off each morning with a two-mile swim at dawn, followed by a cold shower.

My saporous palette was unimaginative and highly unaesthetic and varied little from an essentially white and brown motif: poached white fish, bran cereal, skim milk, egg whites, with the occasional splash out into carrots. I practiced a sort of secular asceticism, in which repression of desire was for its own sake deemed a virtue.

In time I grew thin, then I grew fat. My senior year, by an inverse of my earlier illogic, I ate almost without cessation: lacking authentic desire to guide me, I consumed indiscriminately. Unpracticed in the exercise of tastes, I lumbered insensibly from one meal to the next. I often ate dinner twice, followed up by a pound bag of M&M's or a slice of pizza. The pop psychology of the day informed me that my eating habits were an effort to "stuff rage," but it seemed to me that I was after ballast. Something to weight me to the world, as love was said to do. Despite my heft, I felt insubstantial as steam, airy and faint as an echo.

Therapy was merely insulting. One waiflike counselor, who had herself been anorexic and spoke in a breathy, childlike voice, insisted earnestly and frequently, whenever I confessed to a thought, "That is your bulimia speaking." She said this irrespective of my statements, like a spiritualist warning of demons in the ether. I raged, I wept, I reasoned. But it was not me, she averred, but my bulimia — *speaking*. She made it sound as if I had a troll living inside me. And I knew it was a lie. I told her I thought this whole thing, my eating and all, was about desire, about being attracted to women. But she set me straight.

In the space of two years I would pass through half a dozen women's hands (none of them a lover's) — therapists, social workers, Ph.D. candidates, even a stern Irish psychiatrist, who looked unnervingly like the actress Colleen Dewhurst — and all of them in short order would assure me that I was not desirous of women. As if it were unthinkable, a thing scripted on the body at birth, a thing you could read in the face, the hands; as if sexual desire were not after all an acquired taste.

I was twenty-five before I went to bed with a woman, and when I did, I found that all along I had been right. Though it strains credulity, the following morning I woke and found that I had lost ten pounds in the night and had recovered my sense of taste. I never again had trouble with food, though my tastes surprised me. Things I never knew I liked suddenly glowed on the gustatory horizon like beacons. Plump oily avocados. The dainty lavender-sheathed teeth of garlic. Ginger. Tonic and Tanqueray gin. Green olives. Blood oranges. Pungent Italian cheese.

If education is ultimately the fashioning of a self through the cultivation of discernment and taste, this was my education, and with it came an acute craving for books and music and film. I discovered in that summer the writings of Virginia Woolf and the films of Ingmar Bergman, the paintings of Jasper Johns and Gertrude Stein's prose and John Cage's symphonies, Italian wines and sex. And I began, tentatively, fearfully, to write (though even the effort to keep a journal was an ordeal; I was tortured by doubt: How could I know what was worthy of recording, what I liked enough, what mattered enough to note and keep?).

"Do you love him?" I once asked my mother, when I was thirteen and still young enough to think that was a simple question, a thing one had or didn't have, the thing that mattered; when I did not yet understand all the other painful, difficult things that bind people more surely than love ever will.

"I like your father," she said. "That is more important."

I do not misremember this. It remains with me like a recipe I follow scrupulously, an old family recipe. And when in my first year of graduate school my lover asks me if I love her, I try to form an answer as precise as my mother's before me; I say, "I am very fond of you, I like and respect you," and watch as pain rises in her face like a leavening loaf. I have learned from my mother and Julia Child how to master French cooking, but I have no mastery when it comes to love. It will take me a long time to get the hang of this; it will take practice.

In my second year of graduate school, I enroll in an introductory French class. The instructor is a handsome man from Haiti, and the whole class is a little in love with him. In Minneapolis, the home of the sartorially challenged, where a prominent uptown billboard exhorts passersby to "dress like you're not from around here," he is a fashion oasis. An anomaly in these rooms of unmodulated beige, he is dressed this drear January morning in a black turtleneck, chinos, belt, heavy gold chain, ring, watch. He looks like he might go straight from this 11:15 A.M. class to a nightclub — or as if he has just come from one.

Born thirty miles east of Cap Haitien, the second-largest city in Haiti, he is an unlikely figure in these rooms filled with privileged white kids from the suburbs. His own education, he recalls, was "sketchy," snatched from stints in a *lycée* (the equivalent of an American secondary school) in Cap Haitien. His parents did not live together, and life under Duvalier was difficult; he did, he says, what was necessary to survive.

All my adult life I have sought out people like this, people who I sense can instruct me in how to live in the world. Who know how to survive, to hustle. How to make it from one day to the next. The things my mother and father couldn't teach me or never knew. I will spend my twenties and early thirties seeking out people like this, like a junkie; I can't get enough of certitude or attitude.

The questions you ask in an introductory language class are always the important ones, the original ones that the raw fact of language inspires, the ones we ask as children, then forget when we grow up. On the first day of class I dutifully copy into my notebook the questions the instructor has written on the board: *Qui suis-je? Qui êtes-vous?* It is only later, while scanning the pages of this notebook, that I am startled to see the questions I have scribbled there, demanding an answer: Who am I? Who are you?

I had been in junior high or high school when I first began to imagine that my parents would separate as soon as their children left home. I had come to expect this, so when my siblings and I did leave I was genuinely shocked, even disappointed, that my parents stayed together. I didn't understand that they were, after all those years, if not fond of each other, at least established; that they were afraid of loneliness; that, approaching sixty, approaching seventy, they were too tired to fight and so perhaps could make room, as they hadn't previously, for tenderness. I didn't understand that it is not that time heals all, but that in time the simple fact of having survived together can come to outweigh other concerns, that if you're not careful, you can forget that you ever hoped for something more than sustenance.

"Your parents seem so comfortable," a friend of mine commented after we had dined with my parents in New York City a few years back, when my folks were visiting me. "Yes," I said, with something like regret, recognizing in that moment for the first time their surrender in a long-waged battle. "I think they are." These days my mother orders in Thanksgiving dinner from a restaurant in St. Paul. She orders unlikely foods: in place of the traditional turkey with trimmings, there is a large, squat, hatbox-shaped vegetable torte with marinara sauce, green salad, cranberries from the can. At dinner, she presides from the head of the table, opposite my father, smiling. Sedate as a pudding.

In college, I met a young woman who had corresponded throughout her childhood with Julia Child. It was from her that I first heard that Child had been an alcoholic and often was drunk on the set. My mother, if she recognized drunkenness for what it was, nevertheless cast the story differently: she laughed about how Child, having dropped a chicken on the floor during a taping, had had the aplomb to pick it up and cook it anyhow. This delighted my mother, this imperturbability, the ability in the face of disappointment to carry on.

I have asked my mother if she regrets her marriage, her choices, and she has told me it is pointless to regret. That she did what she could do. What more can we ask of ourselves? I want to tell her, but do not, that we must ask for so much more, for everything, for love and tenderness and decency and courage. That we must be much more than comfortable, that we must be better than we think we can be, so if in some foreign tongue we are confronted with those childhood questions — *"Qui êtes-vous?" "Qui suis-je?"* — we will not be afraid to answer.

A few weeks ago, I came across a copy of *Mastering the Art of French Cooking* in a secondhand shop, unused, for $7.49. I bought it and took it home. Fingering its rough pulpy pages, consulting its index for names that conjured my long-ago abandoned childhood, I scanned the book as if it could provide an explanation, as if it were a secret record of my mother's thwarted passion. I held it in my lap, hesitant to read it, as if it were after all a private matter, a diary of those bygone days when it still seemed possible in this country, in our lives, to bring together disparate elements and mix them — artfully, beautifully — and make of them some new and marvelous whole.

MICHAEL MARTONE

Contributor's Note

FROM FLYWAY

MICHAEL MARTONE was born in Fort Wayne, Indiana. He is the author of several books of fiction and nonfiction, and in the course of publishing and promoting those books, Martone has, upon occasion, given readings of his work at various venues, including colleges and universities, bookstores, churches, and YMCAs. Martone's worst experience as a public reader of his own work happened at a YMCA in Cambridge, Massachusetts. Having given several readings by this point, Martone made sure, in a pre-reading ritual, that the pages of his manuscript were in order. It always irritated Martone (when he was in the audience for a reading given by other writers) to have to witness the seemingly nervous habits of readers, shuffling through the pages, searching for the right piece to begin. Admittedly this happened more often with poets, but the practice spurred Martone to always have his pages in order. So that night, right before he began his reading at the Y in Cambridge, as he forced himself to yawn (an ancient platform speaker's trick to relax the voice), Martone carefully noted the order of his pages by flipping through his manuscript, recounting the numbers in the top right-hand corner. What made the evening such a disaster was that after reading, in order, the first eighteen pages of his story, Martone discovered, as he turned to the final page, that the final page was not there. Looking at the artificial wood grain of the podium before him, Martone, chagrined, announced that he seemed to be missing the final page and then summarized haltingly the missing information to a bemused and embarrassed audience. Since then, Martone always checks to make sure that his pages are not only in order but all there. Over the years, Martone has also had occasion to organize and host reading series as well. He has found that the conversation he has before the reading with his visiting readers inevitably turns to stories of other reading disasters and mishaps. Martone (while collecting these anecdotes in the hope of one day publishing an anthology of readers' worst readings) noticed that one particular set of circumstances seemed to befall several poets. It concerned, with slight variations, the visiting poet showing up to read at a college or university only to discover that his or her host is ill or is taking care of someone who is ill, and so excuses him- or herself before the poet's introduction. The poet is then left in a room alone to discover only a few distracted people in the audience, and often one of them is described as a homeless man and the remaining two or three as undergraduate students. The sparsity of the turnout, added to the host's departure, ratchets up the bleakness of the event. But of course, it then gets even worse. The poet introduces him- or herself to the scant audience and reads his or her first poem, and then, in the patter that follows, suggests, as the crowd is so small, that it would be better if they just had an intimate conversation about poetry. The climax is always that one member of the audience asks how long this is going to take, since they, the students, are only here to study. The homeless man (if he is in the story) then eats the stale snack crackers and chunks of dried-out cheese from the pitiful reception table. Martone has heard this story delivered by several poets as their worst reading experience. He realizes it is either an extraordinary coincidence or a widely shared urban tale or an anxious Jungian dream. Everyone agrees, however, that this is indeed the best of the worst reading stories, that it contains all the excruciating elements of fear and embarrassment inherent in this public occasion for participants who are, by nature, shy of public occasions. When it comes to readings, Martone thinks often of water. Water in a cup or bottle the only prop available to the platform reader beyond the pages of the manuscript and the occasion to futz with the microphone. Bottled water seems to be replacing the paper cup or glass tumbler. Bottles have eliminated the need for a pitcher, too, which only revealed the degree of nervousness in the tremor of pouring. A glass of water seems more refined than the now more prevalent plastic bottle. The construction of that vessel creates a dramatic gesture. The reader must tip the bottle up completely, one's lips affixed to the narrow opening, manipulating the glugging management of air and liquid, a pantomime of fellation. Martone, unscrewing the cap of the proffered bottle of water at his own readings, can't help but think of that as he tips his head back, the image feeding back to amplify his already active self-consciousness and embarrassment. Water, Martone thinks. As an organizer or host of various series of readings throughout his career, Martone has worried about water — the providing of it and its delivery devices. The task is made most difficult when there is more than one reader. Will the first reader drink out of both glasses, thereby "contaminating" the other reader's prepared and waiting glass? Martone has watched (admittedly with some horror) a reader hesitate when deciding which glass to take up, having forgotten where that reader had set down the drink after first imbibing. Martone has watched the looks of consternation cross the faces of readers in that position, gamely attempting to maintain the informative patter between swallows. This confusion does not depend on an evening with two or more readers. Proprietary glasses can be confused simply between the reader and the person introducing the reader, who might have his or her own supply of water that is or isn't touched (introductions being relatively short in comparison to the readings themselves). Martone, when it is his role to introduce, usually remembers to take back to his seat his glass or bottle of water after the introduction, thereby leaving a clear, unambiguous field of play water-wise, as it were, for the introduced reader. Though this practice — the retrieval of the introducer's water by the introducer once the introduction has been made — creates an additional moment of awkwardness when the introducer and the introducee pass on the stage (one heading back to the seats and the other going to the podium) during the obligatory polite, applause-covered exchange between the introducer and the reader. The moment is already fraught. A handshake? A hug? A hug and kiss on the cheek? A high-five? It is the dramatized moment of appreciation for the introduction, a physical launch after the verbal one that has just ended. Martone, in the introductory role, complicates matters when his hands are full at that moment of contact, with the notes of his introduction and now the water and its apparatus retrieved to avoid the future confusion of the speaker. Few readers ever finish all of their water during their reading. They are good at rationing it out over the course of the evening's performance, not wanting to be caught short during the crucial crescendo moments of the delivery. There is nothing worse than the dry mouth (both the syndrome and the symptom), Martone knows. Martone, in his role as host of a reading, is often faced with what to do with the leftover water of his guests who, after greeting the enthusiastic listeners before the stage, signing some books, and shaking hands, are taking off for the evening's reception. Martone is left behind to secure the room, coil the microphone cables, clean up, kill the lights. Part of the cleaning-up part has always included the disposing of the evening's water. Often the lecture halls and auditoriums are not outfitted with a sink. Indeed, the whole point of the headache of providing water in the first place has been the fact that the hall is not in close proximity to a source of water. So Martone has found that he has fallen into the habit of finishing the water himself, drinking the dregs from the glasses or bottles left by the readers, like a priest ingesting the leftover Eucharist at the end of Mass. Martone does this more out of a sense of neatness and order, but, he supposes, there is some of the spirit involved as well. He has witnessed some really amazing performances, listened to the work of famous and remarkably gifted writers. And he has drunk their leftover water. Perhaps a part of him believes some of that talent and skill will find their way into his own metabolism through this communion with greatness. It is a kind of inoculation, by means of this tainted fluid, with the cooties of the greatest. Martone hopes, as he drinks, that its inspirational properties, if not the medicinal ones, have "taken."

DAVID MASELLO

My Friend Lodovico

FROM THE NEW YORK TIMES

TEN YEARS AGO, upon breaking up with someone after an embarrassing public argument in Central Park, I went to see Lodovico Capponi. I needed his approval and reassurance. He was also one of the first people I visited a few days after September 11. Whenever friends are in from out of town, I often take them to meet him, and if I find myself in his Upper East Side neighborhood, I can rarely resist dropping by.

Lodovico lives in the Frick Collection, the mansion-museum on Fifth Avenue. He is a portrait, painted in the 1550s by Agnolo Bronzino, the celebrated Florentine artist employed as a court painter to the Medicis; the 500th anniversary of Bronzino's birth is being celebrated this year. In this four-foot-high oil, Lodovico is shown with wavy, red-brown hair, a flawless complexion, and a wandering left eye.

I have known Lodovico for twenty-three years, as long as I have lived in New York. And after all these years, I keep asking myself the same question: Why do I continue to visit this mute, overdressed, imperious young man? Many people to whom I introduce him find him austere, even humorless. Others consider another Bronzino young man, who hangs on a wall at the Metropolitan Museum of Art, handsomer and more engaging.

When I was close to Lodovico's age, about twenty-two, some people said I resembled him; my right eye wanders lazily in the way his left does; his nose appears to be equally ample and Italian. I suppose it's natural that we are attracted to those who remind us of ourselves. Years ago, after I sent a postcard of the portrait to my father in Florida, he called to mention that he had taped Lodovico to his refrigerator as a reminder of me. "He looks like you, only without your eyeglasses," my father said. "And get a haircut — you could be as clean-cut as this kid."

Lodovico was a constant in my early years in New York. I knew always where to find him, in the West Gallery of the Frick. Being a painting, he would never change or age. At a time when I still had few friends and a fragile self-confidence as a young man in a new city working in an office job for a book publisher, I admired Lodovico's regal bearing, his unblinking confidence, and his solid ownership of a defined station in life.

Much has changed since we met. I am now twice as old as he is in the painting; I've had careers and I've been happily involved with a partner for years. Yet I need the unspoken advice that Lodovico still supplies. When I visit the Frick, his portrait is what I go to first, striding purposefully to the work, and leaving the museum after only several minutes, sometimes even before the coat checker has hung up my garment. I have never visited the Frick without spending some time with Lodovico.

He wears a high-collared, velvet-striped taffeta jacket over a white satin shirt, sleeves embellished with fisheye cutouts. A long swag of luxurious black velvet swoops from his right shoulder down to his billowing breeches, which seem fashioned from shimmering ribbons. In his right hand he pinches a cameo with the mysterious inscription "*Sorte*" (fate, or fortune, in Italian), and in his left he clasps neatly folded brown gloves, which I had long mistaken for a wallet until the audio-guide narrator enlightened me one day.

The space where he dwells is a retreat not only from Manhattan streets but from all concerns in life, although every passion, from lust and jealousy to murder and love, is on display. Even before reaching the galleries, some visitors are seduced by the trickling fountain in the interior courtyard, where they wind up spending contemplative hours listening to the water instead of looking at the art works. This is where I sat those many years ago after my romantic breakup; rather than confront Lodovico in tears, I collected myself beside the waters before presenting myself to him for consolation.

Despite his calm demeanor, Lodovico was living through trying times when his portrait was being painted. While on the job as a court page, he fell in love with a young girl, Maddalena Vettori, whom his employer, Duke Cosimo I de' Medici, had chosen as a bride for one of his cousins. Upon learning of their courtship, the duke forbade the couple to meet. The duke's wife, Eleonara of Toledo, empathized with the young couple and lobbied on their behalf. After three years the duke acquiesced, but stipulated that unless the couple married within twenty-four hours, they would be forever separated. They wed immediately and produced eight children.

One reason I go to see Lodovico is because he is an expert creation. I marvel at the folds in the fabric and the resulting shadows, the shimmer of material, the smoothness of skin, and the absence of brush strokes, an almost photographically flawless application of color. I love the literal cloak of mystery created by the green material. I can imagine a marble palazzo just behind the folds, corridors bustling with court pages, ladies-in-waiting lifting skirts as they walk, busybody Eleonara passing messages between Lodovico and Maddalena.

Lodovico and I have maintained an odd relationship. We don't speak, and when together, we stare each other down. Yet I can look at him indefinitely. And I miss him quickly if too many weeks go by without a visit. I break my gaze only when another visitor approaches.

He neither smiles nor frowns, seems judging or indifferent, appears happy or sad. Lodovico is just as he is. There is nothing else in the painting but him; no alluring snippets of late Renaissance cityscapes, beloved pets, fanciful furniture. He is simply a young, well-dressed, attractive man who has taken the time to stand for us over what must have been many weeks.

Lodovico is my Dorian Gray. Because he will never age or fade, neither will my memories of life in New York in my early twenties, when Lodovico was one of the first figures I met and came to know.

If he could see me, he would have discerned over the years a portrait of me standing before him, alone, with various mates, as they entered and left my life, with friends (some of whom died in the eighties during our version of the black plague), and with strangers who share their thoughts about the painting. He would have seen me wearing ties as wide as napkins, later ones ruler-narrow, glasses in every style from granny to aviator.

I can't claim that an image in a painting became one of my first real friends in New York, but I can say that I visited the painting so often when I was new to the city that, as an object, it became friendly and familiar. The painting and the room where it hangs became, and remain, constants in my life.

Lodovico and I are equally removed from each other's time, and I worry increasingly about the growing gulf in our ages. Will his youth eventually intimidate me? Yet I know that if he came to life somehow, we would eagerly teach each other the ways of our time. I wouldn't know how to negotiate the intrigues of Renaissance Florentine court life, and he wouldn't understand whole-wheat pasta. But I'm sure our friendship would be an easy one. We would be, as they say in Italian, simpatico.

DANIELLE OFRI

Living Will

FROM THE MISSOURI REVIEW

WILBUR RESTON WAS already in the intensive care unit of the tiny Florida hospital when I arrived at two-thirty A.M. I had been doing a series of temp jobs after having completed my medical residency at New York City's Bellevue Hospital and now found myself in a small town on the Gulf Coast. The breathing tube in Mr. Reston's throat and his heavy sedation precluded formal introductions. But there was a typewritten summary of his medical history that his wife had left with the nurses: a two-page, single-spaced account that chronicled the rebellion and demise of each organ in this sixty-one-year-old white man. He had survived three heart attacks and seven strokes. One kidney had been removed. He suffered from diabetes, high blood pressure, and congestive heart failure. He had emphysema, glaucoma, severe migraines, and arthritis. His medical history included pancreatitis, diverticulitis, pyelonephritis, sinusitis, cholelithiasis, tinnitus, and ankylosing spondylitis. The typed paper also mentioned gastroesophageal reflux, vertigo, and depression. I quickly glanced over to the man hooked up to the ventilator to verify that he was indeed alive.

His wife had told the ER physicians that he'd stopped taking his water pills several days ago. Eventually he could no longer breathe. He possessed a living will stating that he did not want any life-sustaining procedures. In the ER, however, he had apparently agreed to be intubated. It had taken an enormous amount of sedation to get the breathing tube in, and then his blood pressure bottomed out. He was now unconscious in the ICU, on multiple pressor medications to support his blood pressure and augment his weak heart. In Bellevue terminology, he was a "train wreck."

Mr. Reston had been admitted to East General Hospital at two A.M. My colleagues in the small private practice where I was working had instructed me *never* to go to the hospital in the middle of the night. "Give your orders over the phone and see the patient in the morning," they advised. But I was still too new at this kind of medicine to be that confident; I had to at least lay eyes on the patient before I could decide on any medical orders.

I couldn't take a history from Mr. Reston, since he was at present unarousable because of all the sedation. My physical exam was brief. Mainly I plowed through the typed medical summary, converting it into a concise admission note. I handed my admitting orders to the nurse, and then there was nothing for me to do. In this small community hospital, the nurses were used to, and entirely comfortable with, working without any doctors around. How unlike Bellevue, where interns and residents roamed the halls twenty-four hours a day, deeply and intricately involved in the minutiae of medical care. Here the nurses took most of the doctors' orders over the phone and did everything themselves: drew blood, inserted IVs, did EKGs, obtained blood and urine cultures, sent patients for x-rays, followed up on test results, and so on. The doctors, with their busy private practices, usually visited once a day, either very early in the morning or late, after their office hours. The emphasis was on remembering to sign verbal orders within twenty-four hours. Not surprisingly, the head nurse was taken aback and almost alarmed when I showed up in the middle of the night for Mr. Reston's admission.

It was now nearly four A.M. as I drove back to the hotel in my rental car. The main roads of the town were deserted. I rolled down the windows and was quickly enveloped in humid, orange-scented fog. Stretches of flat, boring landscape were broken up periodically by strip malls. Neighborhoods of low-slung, white stucco houses were dotted with pickup trucks and palm trees. The smell of blossoms had not been fully eradicated by the burgeoning construction industry.

Southwest Florida was nothing like West Palm Beach, which I had assumed represented all of Florida. This area was rural, with acres of fields farmed by itinerant workers, mostly from Central America. I had just returned from Guatemala, so I was eager to practice my Spanish, but in the private practice where I worked, I rarely had the opportunity, except for the time when I was called upon to explain to a Honduran fruit picker that we couldn't treat his high blood pressure because he didn't have medical insurance. The hospital emergency room had called me when he'd shown up there needing prescriptions, and I'd said sure, send him over right now. When he arrived at the office, however, the practice manager informed me that we could not treat patients without insurance except for medical emergencies. Since I was the only one in the office who spoke passable Spanish, the duty of telling him fell to me. My verb-conjugating ability floundered, and my pronouns disagreed with their antecedents. My vocabulary in Spanish — and in English for that matter — had never included such phrases as "We cannot take care of you. You must go to a different doctor." I suddenly longed for Bellevue, for the chaos of the emergency room there, with its bubbling tumult of languages, ethnicities, colors, and socioeconomic classes, and its assumption that everybody received medical care regardless of ability to pay.

But aside from that one incident, the office was a pleasant place to work. Three doctors had started this practice several years ago, and they were now extremely successful. They had built an impressive clientele of devoted patients, mainly older but many middle-aged. They had equipped their office with a tiny pharmacy and a stress-test machine, and had arranged for weekly visits from an ultrasound technician, who performed all their sonograms. They'd even opened a small gym next door, in which they sponsored exercise classes for the elderly and rehab classes for their patients with emphysema. The doctors were in their forties, looking for ways to cut down on hours and enter semi-retirement. They were more than happy to hand over a third of the office patients and one hundred percent of the inpatient hospital duties. They gladly acceded to my request for paid prep time so that I could read patients' charts in advance of their appointments, all in a comfortable office with an experienced, full-time nurse to assist me. It was the lap of luxury. Within a week they offered me a permanent, full-time position with a salary that was four times what I'd earned as a resident for half the working hours, plus a share in the practice.

The patients were pleasant and apparently particularly happy to have a woman doctor, something new to that practice. And for the first time in *my* life, medicine was not a struggle: I could practice the best medicine I wanted without having to fight for anything. Coming from the trenches of Bellevue, where medicine felt almost like warfare, I found the ease of practicing good medicine almost disconcerting. I couldn't deny that the job offer was tempting.

But I could never leave Manhattan — certainly not to live in such a tiny town.

The town was a speck on the map in southwest Florida that no one I knew had ever heard of. The pace was unhurried, and the locals were unceasingly friendly and helpful, traits that were sometimes unsettling to a native New Yorker. Overly polite strangers made me suspicious, though everyone assured me that this was the normal style in the South. There was no place to get sushi, but the two-room library across the street from my office did stock Spanish-lesson tapes, and I was able to study a semester's worth of grammar on my way to work each day. Much to my dismay and disbelief, the library did not subscribe to the *New York Times*. A very weak consolation was the *Wall Street Journal* — only available, however, the following day.

The private practice was affiliated with East General, an eighty-eight-bed community hospital. I'd never seen a hospital that small. Eighty-eight beds was one floor at Bellevue, and Bellevue sported twenty-one floors. East General Hospital reminded me of my elementary school — spread out over two wings, each only two stories high. The elevator seemed redundant. Some of the services that I was used to from Bellevue, like twenty-four-hour-a-day access to cardiac catheterization and hemodialysis, were not available, but there were other advantages. With a maximum census of eighty-eight patients, there was never any waiting time for anything I ordered. Stress tests, sonograms, CT scans, pulmonary consults, social-work requests — I had only to jot a request in the chart and it would be completed by the end of the day. The staff was small, but everyone seemed competent and extremely friendly. Within a week even the housekeepers were greeting me by name, and the phone operators recognized my voice when I called.

The following morning Mr. Reston was awake but extremely uncomfortable. He had tried to pull out his breathing tube several times, so the nurses had tied his arms down. I apologized to him for the wrist restraints and explained that I would try to get the tube out as soon as possible. I was self-conscious about my words because Wilbur Reston's body was sentient. He heard and understood everything I said, but the tube and the restraints prevented him from speaking or even gesturing; my awkward reassurances met with no response. I spent the morning in the ICU weaning Mr. Reston off the ventilator and draining fluid from his lungs. When the nurses were rolling him over to change the sheets, he managed to dislodge his own breathing tube and set himself free.

There is an entire scientific literature on the most appropriate time to extubate a patient, based on pulmonary function tests, blood gas values, and chest x-ray findings. But the Bellevue ICU's wisdom was that a patient was ready to be extubated when he or she reached over and yanked the damn tube out. Mr. Reston proved this to be true, since enough fluid had been removed from his lungs that he was able to breathe, if a bit huskily, without the tube. His condition was still tenuous, though, and he was too exhausted from his ordeal to talk much. I waited a while for his wife to arrive, but she never showed up.

Thirty-six hours after his admission I was finally able to actually "meet" Mr. Reston. He was a burly fellow who looked surprisingly robust for a patient with such a thick medical record. I would have expected a shriveled old man, but he had beefy arms and a hefty belly. There was a tattoo of an alligator on his left biceps. The ICU bed sagged slightly under his weight whenever he shifted or turned.

Mr. Reston's face was pulled low on his neck by meaty jowls, and dark bags weighed his eyes down. He had lived his entire life in this small town on the west coast of Florida. He was a veteran of the Korean War, with a specialty in artillery. After the war he'd worked as a police officer and spent some time training guard dogs.

His voice was surprisingly soft and somewhat morose. In slow, deliberate phrases he described a lifetime of progressively declining health. His arthritic pains and severe headaches seemed to have taken a greater toll on him than his many strokes and heart attacks. He was confined to his house, unable even to walk down the driveway to retrieve his mail.

Did he have any hobbies? He heaved a melancholic sigh. "I fancied myself a carpenter. I built miniature furniture for dollhouses. Always used the best wood."

I imagined this bearlike man hunched over delicate divans and bedroom sets.

"Can't do it anymore. My hands." He threw up his gnarled, arthritic paws for inspection.

"I also collect Civil War memorabilia. Once found a belt buckle from the second battle of Bull Run," he said with a puff of pride. "They had it in the museum for a while." But his recollection of his former glory was brief. "My wife thinks it's a stupid hobby," he said.

What about depression? "I've never *not* been depressed," he sighed ruefully. "Ever since college, I suppose." His records showed that he'd been treated at the VA psychiatric clinic with both psychotherapy and antidepressant medications for more than twenty years. His only daughter had died of a brain tumor the year before. His mother and sister had both died in the past five years. So had his dog.

Had he ever attempted suicide? "I'm handy with guns, you know. I have at least five in the house," he said dryly. "Different models. Always keep a loaded one at my bedside."

Did he ever use it? "Well, I stuck the barrel in my mouth. Didn't pull the trigger, though. Too messy. Just stopped taking my pills."

I had an image of Mr. Reston sitting on the side of his bed, shoulders sagging, cradling the gun in his hand. Perhaps he'd raised the gun to his head several times, each time not able to bring it close enough. But then he'd take a quick, dry swallow and, squinting, slide the gun into his mouth. I imagined that he might be startled at how comforting the gun felt in his mouth. But then that very comfort would make him shudder, and he'd rip the gun out, stuff it back into the nightstand drawer, and slam the drawer shut.

Then he'd be left staring at the pill bottles lined up on that nightstand, loaded with promises of good health. He'd finger them, recalling what ill each was meant to cure. And cure they did. And then what?

I envisioned him opening that drawer again and, with the crook of his clublike arm, sweeping the bottles in, their hard plastic clattering against the gun as they came to rest at the bottom. He'd sink his head into his hands, forgetting to shut the nightstand drawer.

What about his wife, I asked. "She's busy with that volunteer work. She don't have time for me and all my pills," he said sadly. An uneasy silence settled in. I could see moisture accumulating at the edges of his soulful eyes. "We haven't shared a bed in fifteen years," he whispered.

His voice was plaintive but resigned. "Why should I live this life? I can't walk, my wife don't speak to me, I can't do nothing. What's the point?" He fixed his mournful gaze upon me. "*You* tell *me.*"

It was both a plea and a demand. His simple statement had caused the space between us to evaporate, and I suddenly felt naked. Without my clinical armor to shield me, I was just one human facing another, squinting before the raw question. What *was* the point? What were the reasons for him to go on living?

I struggled to come up with one. Mr. Reston's body had withered sufficiently to keep him in perpetual pain but not enough to let him die. He had no friends; his wife was estranged. His daughter, mother, and sister had died and abandoned him. He was too weak to walk out of his house. He could no longer do any of the things that brought him pleasure. Why should he want to live? I could see why he had stopped taking his pills.

I didn't have an answer for him, but the law dictated what I had to do: actively suicidal patients must be prevented from harming themselves.

Like all good emergencies, this one occurred late on a Friday afternoon. Unlike Bellevue, there was no residency program in psychiatry to supply immediate consultations. There were several psychiatrists in the community, but they were busy with their private practices during the day and rarely made after-hours calls. But the staff of this tiny hospital was resourceful and helpful. They got me in touch with the local mental health agency, which was able to dispatch a psychiatric nurse practitioner. She agreed with my concerns and helped the nursing staff arrange a round-the-clock "suicide watch" over Mr. Reston. I could have Mr. Reston transferred to a psychiatric hospital once his medical condition stabilized if I felt he was still in danger of hurting himself. The nurse practitioner explained the procedures to invoke the Baker Act, the state legislation that allowed involuntary psychiatric commitment in such circumstances.

Over that weekend Mr. Reston's medical condition slowly improved, but his mood did not. Why should it? I thought. What did he have to look forward to? As much as I tried, I could not bring myself to utter flimsy platitudes about the value of life and how

things would be better tomorrow. They weren't going to get better
— he knew it and I knew it. Although he was clearly depressed, Mr.
Reston was perfectly lucid. Despite his many strokes, his mind
seemed to be working just fine. He could do all the tasks in the
mental status exam: spell "world" backward, count down from one
hundred by sevens, name the president, interpret the proverb "A
rolling stone gathers no moss."

Although Mr. Reston seemed to have a reasonably realistic grasp
on his situation, I wasn't so sure I had a grasp on mine. Doctors
aren't supposed to agree with their patients who say they want to
kill themselves, but I found myself overwhelmed by the utterly dis-
mal facts of Mr. Reston's situation. Whom did Mr. Reston have left
to live for? Even his dog had died.

I tried to imagine pacing the blank landscape of an empty life.
How could I survive if every source of pleasure was denied? How
could I live if the flavors, colors, and textures that made life palat-
able were flattened into a monochrome gray? If I were Mr. Reston,
I might have pulled that trigger.

To complicate matters, he was in a rather unique medical situation. Although he had multitudes of medical problems, he was not
yet terminally ill. He had a long list of diseases, but none was close
to killing him. He was sick enough to be miserable but not sick
enough to die. He was still able to eat, care for himself, and communicate with others. There were plenty of services and options
for people on the verge of death, but Mr. Reston was not sick
enough to qualify. His body, honed from years in the military and
police force, was holding on too tenaciously. It left him stranded,
strung too far from the shores of either health or death. Mr.
Reston had severe physical pain, apparently unresponsive to various treatments, but more important, he was being eaten away by
psychic pain.

The medico-legal issues were clear: a suicidal patient is prevented from committing suicide, even against his will, period. But
the shades of gray needled me. My patient didn't want his life, and
I wasn't sure it was ethical to force him to continue living it.

These issues plagued me for the remainder of the week.
Ashamed to reveal my heresies to anyone, I secretly toyed with my
doubts, picking at them as one does a loose tooth, perversely finding pleasure in its pain. What if I let him go home to his household

of loaded guns? What if I discharged him, knowing full well that he'd stop taking his life-saving medicines? What if I turned my head and let him kill himself, as he so desperately wanted to do? There are those who say that all suicidal thoughts are products of depression, but Mr. Reston had been assiduously treated with medications and psychotherapy for decades. Perhaps he was being entirely rational. Who was I to stand in his way?

Then the toothache would burrow down to the raw nerve: What kind of evil doctor was I to even *consider* not protecting my patient from his violent tendencies? How could I be so negligent?

As I drove back and forth to work each day, this dilemma nagged at me. Lulled by the bland landscape, my mind would wander from the Spanish vocabulary coming from the car's tape deck to Mr. Reston languishing in his bare hospital room. Could there ever be any happiness for him? What if I found him a new hobby, one that he could manage with his disabilities? Stamp collecting — that wouldn't require much mobility. But probably his fingers couldn't manipulate the fragile paper stamps. Maybe he could take up painting. Large, easy brushes with hefty tubs of paint — he could manage that. Perhaps there was an artist waiting inside his weary body.

Traffic was stopped as a cumbersome tractor-trailer backed out of a construction site, attempting to turn around. A grove of orange trees had just been plowed, probably for a new strip mall. The trailer was open on top, and I could see the stacks of shimmering steel girders. The driver backed up a few feet, and then the trailer swung in the opposite direction, blocking his turn. The workers on the road waved their hands, shouting contradictory instructions: "Pull back a bit." "Swing to the right." "Turn your wheels on a sharp left." The driver edged forward and back, craning his neck out the window, then up toward his rearview mirror, as he tried to extricate himself from the tight spot. The steel girders flashed in the sunlight each time he changed angles. The smell of fresh, damp earth blended with the intoxicating sweetness of the orange blossoms, something I'd never smelled in New York City.

The metallic clanking and the competing shouts, along with the glare of the sunlight and the overpowering fragrance, made me feel heady and somewhat faint. I leaned my head into the steering wheel, and suddenly I saw the hole in Mr. Reston's armor: he had let himself be intubated. This man, who possessed a living will explicitly refusing all life-sustaining procedures, had *voluntarily* allowed a breathing tube to thrust air into his drowning lungs. He had reached for a life preserver.

I picked my head back up, feeling the murkiness begin to clear. Despite all of Wilbur Reston's misgivings and doubts, a desire to live had somehow percolated through.

As I leaned back in my seat, I wondered how that had come to pass. Was it simply the life-grabbing instinct that springs forward in such moments of near doom? Or was it truly evidence of Mr. Reston's ambivalence, of a desire to be saved and cared for?

Clearly, I had no way to know — I doubted if he himself would even know — but it seemed to me that Mr. Reston had given himself permission for a second chance. Now that he had done so, I had the opportunity, perhaps even the obligation, to allow that chance to flourish. If this second chance wasn't nourished, there probably wouldn't be a third. As if to confirm my realization, the tractor-trailer veered to the left and finally pulled itself out of its trap. The traffic snarl cleared, and I jammed on the accelerator, flying down the road with the breath of orange blossoms sweeping against my face.

When his medical condition stabilized, Mr. Reston was involuntarily committed to a VA psychiatric facility. He didn't protest when I informed him. He just nodded his head, his baggy jowls bobbing. During his entire stay, I'd never once met his wife; her occasional visits never seemed to coincide with mine.

The VA doctors assumed care of Mr. Reston, and I had no more contact. The private practice was busy, and I saw many patients every day. My mind was filled with Shana Elron's brittle diabetes and Henry Shaw's uncontrolled hypertension. There was the couple who lived in Pennsylvania during the summer but spent winters down south, and I was helping them coordinate his prostate cancer treatment between the two locations. I had recommitted myself to Spanish and spent my evenings conjugating verbs. I planned to leave for Mexico as soon as this stint in Florida was over, and I wanted to have the conditional tense under my belt. I had to decide if I wanted to start my trip in Guadalajara and end it in

Chiapas, or vice versa. Or maybe just fly straight to Oaxaca and enroll in the Spanish school there. And then there was that shell-
beach peninsula set against a tangle of mangroves twenty minutes
from my hotel which beckoned me every night after work. I soon
forgot about Mr. Reston.

Several weeks later, as my assignment in Florida was drawing to a
close, some paperwork concerning Mr. Reston's original hospital
admission turned up in my office needing a signature. Wilbur
Reston's morose face flickered in my mind, and I thought about
his miniature doll furniture. I wished I were still his doctor.

    Besides giving himself a second chance, Mr. Reston had granted
me the opportunity to tease out some of the more subtle aspects of
medicine. He forced me to see beyond his imposing résumé of disease to his simple, hurting human self. The patient is not simply
the sum of his illnesses, Wilbur Reston taught me. It is far more —
blessedly far more — intricate than that.

    After a labyrinth of phone calls through the VA bureaucracy, I
finally tracked down his psychiatrist. Mr. Reston had just been discharged a few days ago. The psychiatrist described the long weeks
and the laborious effort it had required to get Mr. Reston to take
responsibility for simple things like brushing his teeth. By the end,
though, he was showing up at the group meetings, even if he rarely
spoke. Once in a while he even went to arts and crafts. Mr. Reston
did not become an effusive, energetic person, but according to the
psychiatrist he no longer actively expressed the wish to die. That
was considered a major success. And once he was no longer suicidal, there was no justification for keeping him involuntarily hos-
pitalized. He could go home to his wife and continue with his regular outpatient therapy.

    The psychiatrist commiserated with me over the many painful
but immutable realities of Mr. Reston's life. A social worker was trying to help Mr. Reston get a new dog — that was about the only
thing they could remedy.

    I flew to Mexico the following week. In the end I'd decided to fly
directly to Oaxaca for a month of Spanish lessons. Afterward I'd
trek to Chiapas to see the Mayan ruins. I plunged into my classes,
determined not to speak a word of English for six weeks, if that was
possible. I rented a room from a family that spoke no English; I

purchased Spanish editions of *Jonathan Livingston Seagull* and *The Little Prince* as my reading material; I tried to minimize my social contacts with the other foreigners in my classes and instead hang out at local cafés.

But I still thought about Wilbur Reston and wondered how he was doing. Those thoughts could only be in English. I imagined that he was sitting alone in his house, his wife at yet another volunteer function, his bones still aching, his weak heart preventing him from even getting the mail. But maybe there was now a puppy yapping at his feet, freely dispensing and demanding love. When the headaches and joint pains became overwhelming, maybe Mr. Reston would again consider ending his life. But then he might stop and think: Who would feed the puppy?

SAM PICKERING

Dog Days

FROM RIVER TEETH

AN AGING MAN should not own an old dog. George turned thirteen in July. His dog days foreshadowed the doldrums into which I am slowly nodding. In past summers George loped down the lane behind the barn, air currents spinning salty fragrances around him, pulling his nose right and left. This summer George wallowed through troughs of grass, his hull slipping warped, no longer scudding in the bright sun. His head hung down, and the skin under his jaw looked like a flying jib stripped of wings. During days he wandered without purpose, one moment hunching by the steps leading to the backhouse, appearing to want to go outside, the next scratching the screen door on the porch, asking to come in. Time has swept his helmsman overboard, and his tiller swung directionless. When not pitching and yawing, he clung to me, seeming to need assurance and affection. Occasionally I became exasperated and shouted, "Go to your bed." Immediately thereafter I imagined myself tottering toward the kitchen in slippers and bathrobe, weary children saying, "Go back to bed, Dad." At nine o'clock every night I carried George upstairs. I set him atop a pillow on the floor next to my bed, then I covered him with a blanket. At a quarter after eleven I lugged him back downstairs and took him outside so he could pump himself dry for the voyage through the night. Afterward I carted him back upstairs. Shortly before six in the morning, he stood and flapped his ears to awaken me. I took him back outside, after which I built a fire in the kitchen stove and he fell asleep on a pad beside my rocking chair.

"You live a dog's life," Vicki said one night.

"Not yet," I answered, "not quite yet."

In the past George resembled a trim bark. This summer he became a lugger. Heavily laden and lumbering, he bolted meals and lived, Vicki said, to eat. Like me, I thought. Once a week I went to Tim Hortons, a doughnut shop in Yarmouth. I drank a medium-sized cup of coffee, always in a ceramic cup, and ate a Dutchie, a rectangular wad of glazed dough spotted with raisins and fat. Trips to Tim Hortons were the high points of weeks in Nova Scotia, and I looked forward to them eagerly. One Wednesday an old man sat across the aisle from me, a worn version of myself, I thought. The man's back curled like the upper half of a question mark. He wore a green-and-white-checked shirt, a red baseball cap, "Canadian Tire" sewed above the bill, boots, and dark khaki trousers held up by red suspenders. Time had shrunk the man's hips into coat hangers, and the trousers hung loosely from his waist, wrinkled like laundry bags. His two middle-aged daughters accompanied him, one sitting on his right, the other on the left. That morning they had signed him out of "the home" for an outing, and for a treat brought him to Tim Hortons. The man was deaf, and while he ate a sugar doughnut, the women leaned toward each other and talked over his shoulders. The man paid no attention to them and concentrated on eating. He held the doughnut tightly in both hands, head pushed up looking like that of a turtle sticking out of its shell. His eyes gleamed alertly, as if he thought someone might snatch the treat away. No more Dutchies for me, I resolved. The resolution lasted only until the following week.

July was flush with beginnings. Four newly hatched red-bellied snakes lay under a slab of plywood near the bluff overlooking the Gulf of Maine. Tadpoles, big as thumbs, roiled the cow pond. A young muskrat swirled through rushes growing beside the bridge spanning the Beaver River outlet. Seventy yards above the bridge six ermine bundled across the gravel road. A robin lured a fledgling from its nest in the golden elder behind the backhouse. Hares no bigger than fists crouched under canes of rugosa roses. Some mornings I got up at three-thirty and, after brewing a pot of tea, wrote in the study, sitting at the desk in the bay window. One morning I watched a young hare thrust through periwinkle under the window. On reaching the front entrance, he tried to hop up the steps. The hare was so young that he moved awkwardly. Instead of forward, its big feet pushed its body sideways, and the hare tumbled over four times before he reached the top step.

Often while the green extravagance of summer nourished my eyes, my thoughts drifted to endings. Two days before watching the hare climb steps, I'd found tufts of brown fur on the headland, sweepings from the meal of a marsh hawk. I chased the hare off the porch into roses bearded with ferns. "Stay there," I said, "and maybe the hawk won't get you." Life, alas, is beaked. That morning I received a letter informing me that two days before his retirement party, a friend died in a car wreck. That night cirrus clouds curled fruity overhead, orange then pink and purple. Instead of imagining fair seedtimes, I thought about sad old women, dyeing and baking thin locks in hopes of disguising age, hiding not so much from others but from the people who stared at them from mirrors.

"More than two score years and ten have come and gone since that day when I, Benjamin Lathrop, put out from Salem harbor, a green hand on the ship *Island Princess*," Charles Boardman Hawes wrote at the beginning of *The Mutineers* (1920). Almost as much time had passed since I read such books. Late in life, though, a man returns to childhood reading, when tales of butchery and cowardice on the high seas, of bravery and the improbable survival of virtue, appeal more than great books in which meaning gapes like a bog, pages scratchy with leatherleaf. After dinner, between journeying up and down stairs with George, I read three of Hawes's books: *The Mutineers, The Great Quest,* and *The Dark Frigate.* No matter the guttural cough of the foghorn at Port Maitland, I steered a straight course under blue skies to enjoyment.

"What do those books make you think about?" Vicki asked.

"Nothing," I said, "just the subject people my age should think about."

Returning to Nova Scotia every summer contributes to the illusion of smooth continuance, each summer not the first thread in a new fabric but another button on a cardigan, perhaps looser than buttons below but still familiar and comfortable. Every summer the songs of white-throated sparrows bounce from scrub like novelty tunes from the fifties. Early in the morning ravens grind woodenly. In the evening verries perch in damp ruffs of spruce, their songs refracting and piercing the fog in beams of color, blue,

green, and pale pink. Every summer I scythe Japanese knotweed
growing at the edge of the side meadow. In the barn I split
firewood. Early in July Vicki buys beet greens and strawberries at
roadside stands. After a flick of time she buys potatoes, peas, rasp-
berries, and Swiss chard. No matter how slowly I jog, on the headland butterflies spring from my feet in clumps, first azures and orange crescents, then wood nymphs, and finally, over the lowlands
near the outlet, cabbage whites spiraling, dizzy with mating. Although the children now spend summers far from Beaver River
and the arms that carried them down the sharp headland to the
beach, occasionally a child telephones and memory lifts me. Late
in July Eliza called from Minnesota, where she was teaching Russian. She was weeping. Francis, her brother, sent her an e-mail
from Storrs. He said Harvard had written her. Because of an unan-
ticipated high rate of acceptance, some freshmen, including Eliza,
would have to live off campus.

"The university," Francis wrote, "will help you find an apartment."

"Daddy," Eliza sobbed, "I want to meet other freshmen. I have
been so lonely in high school. I want to make friends and be part
of college."

Francis's e-mail was a joke. "I must have forgotten to write 'ha,
ha' at the end," he said. I explained that good jokes did not upset
or create anxiety; they provoked warm laughter, making people appreciate life.

Vicki and I do not agree on humor; the disagreement, however,
is long-standing. This summer we didn't watch television. Instead
we listened to the radio, on Saturday nights tuning in the CBC
and *Finkleman's 45s*. For two hours Danny Finkleman played pop
songs from the fities, sixties, and seventies, lining each record with
quirky commentary, suggesting, for example, that the CBC construct a bowling ally in the basement of its building in Toronto.
One Saturday while Vicki was outside emptying the slop dish,
Finkleman told a joke. Normally I don't like jokes, but I enjoyed
this one so much I was gasping for breath when Vicki returned
from the compost pile. Golf provided the frame for the joke, any
discussion of which makes me dream of holing out. Moreover, the
pesticides and weed killers slathered over courses have turned fair-
ways into toxic dumps.

"The poisons pit even steel-plated shoes," my friend Josh told me, stepping forward to address an idea. "The only safe way to indulge in golf is on stilts. Even so, eighteen holes can reduce a pair of sixteen-foot titanium stilts to six inches."

"If sprays shrink stilts that much," I said, swinging my niblick at the idea, "a real sportsman would need several bags of clubs for a single round, the lengths of the clubs in one bag different from those in another. Caddy fees would be enormous. The game is doomed."

"No," Josh said, always up for the short game, "all a duffer needs is a set of clubs with adjustable shafts, the length of a driver at the top end, say, twenty-one feet. Of course bags would be expensive, and giants could charge monstrous fees for caddying."

Finkleman's joke hooked less than Josh's musings. At the bar on the nineteenth hole, a man described his new golf ball to a friend. "If topped into water, the ball floats," he said. "If sliced out of sight into deep rough, it beeps, and at dusk a light beneath the gutta-percha blinks automatically." "Goodbye, double bogies," the friend exclaimed. "That's fabulous. Where did you get the ball?" "I found it," the man said. I laughed uncontrollably after telling the story, belly rising like a bunker, then sinking into a divot. Vicki looked, as scratch narrators put it, teed off, her expression grittier than a sand wedge.

I expected silence, that being par for a 7,200-yard course of marriage. Often I don't respond to Vicki's remarks, and if I answer, frequently I chip only a word or two her way. Unlike Vicki, I eschew fashionable discussion on the radio, particularly boutique programs that pander to the salacious. One chilly July afternoon Vicki sat in the rocking chair by the stove, sipping Earl Grey tea, feet raised, resting on the seat of a kitchen chair. From the radio atop the table to her right a feline voice purred.

"Do you think," Vicki said as I strolled into the room, "our marriage could survive a sex change?"

"Yes," I said, striding out to the barn to split wood.

Next spring Michigan will publish two books I wrote. "I wonder if I will make a half million on the books," I said in the kitchen that night.

"I want to win the lottery," Vicki replied.

"I'm talking about the sales of my books," I said.

"I prefer to talk about something more realistic," Vicki said, "like winning the lottery." Years ago, Vicki would have allowed me a handicap and not responded to my musings. The most any of my books has earned is four thousand dollars, the half million simply the dream of a buccaneering reader.

Not all summer's doings dragged like anchors, stirring silt. I thought of titles for two essays, both from songs, the first, "Precious Memories," susceptible, I am afraid, to waterlogged melancholy. The second song, "Give My Love to Nell," told a story. Two close friends, Jack and Bill, left home arm in arm and sailed across the ocean seeking to better their lot in life. Besides home and family, Bill left his girlfriend, Nell. Jack made his fortune first. "Give my love to Nell," Bill requested before Jack returned home. Jack obeyed his friend, and later, when Bill arrived home, he discovered that Nell and Jack had married. Instead of pining or behaving badly, as characters often do in sentimental songs, Bill wished the couple well and got on with living. Rather than mulling connection or opportunity missed, my essay would celebrate actual happenings. "In other words," Vicki said, "whatever is, is," adding, "that's a wallet stuffer."

Although the titles now look hackneyed, other summer doings seemed practically new. A boreal chickadee foraged alders around the cow pond, the second boreal chickadee I've seen. At my age sights and sounds are suspect. Not until a second sighting confirms the first do I claim seeing a bird. At the Beaver River outlet I found a dead loon. Salt had cured and sun had dried the body. The loon had died during winter, the feathers on its head dark gray and a white patch under its bill. I snapped the loon's spine at the base of the neck. The neck was long, resembling the butt of a pistol. When school starts in August, I'll take the head to class and use it as a pointer. "Students will think you insane," Vicki said.

"Exactly," I said, "a lunatic."

"Is everything a joke with you?" Vicki asked.

"Very little," I said, lifting George into my lap and rubbing him behind the ears.

Not every animal I held was dead or declining. "What's that?" Vicki said one night, switching on the lamp on her bedside table. A little brown bat whirled overhead, then, swooping low, flew out of the bedroom into the upstairs hall. The house resembles a barn.

Ceilings are high, that of Vicki's and my bedroom being the highest, beyond my fingertips even when I stand on a stool. I closed the bedroom door so the bat could not return and hang himself high above my reach.

"I will find him in the morning," I told Vicki.

"I hope so," she said. "I'd feel terrible if the bat starved to death." Before breakfast the next morning I searched the house. I began upstairs, scouring the long hall and the other four bedrooms. I peered under beds and looked behind headboards. I pushed chests away from walls and shifted clothes in closets. Downstairs I searched the hall and the study. I lay on the floor trying to spot droppings. I almost gave up and told Vicki the bat must have flown into the chimney in the study and escaped. But then I found it behind the door to the front parlor. The bat looked like a furry Mars bar. While Vicki peeled the bat's legs off the top of the door, I held a butterfly net over and below the animal. The bat clicked, then slipped into the net. I carried the bat into the barn and set it atop the old sleigh, placing it on the rear seat, making sure it couldn't slip off. Eight minutes later, when I returned to the barn, the bat was gone.

"We should have named it," Vicki said.

"Yes," I said, "it is our first house bat. What a thrill!"

This summer I spent more time than ever before stirring about purposelessly. "Like George," Vicki said. I wandered outside throughout the day, hoping to glimpse an unfamiliar insect. I had spent fourteen summers in Beaver River. The chances of my spotting a creature not seen before were small, and so like those of George, my excursions were short, and I quickly returned to the kitchen and munched on cheese and crackers, prunes and peanut butter, muffins, and rhubarb flummery, in the middle of this last a mound of whipped cream as alluring as Treasure Island. To prevent myself from dozing the summer away, I did things I had not done before. The first Saturday in August Vicki and I went to the Quilt Show and Tea, sponsored by the Patchwork Pals Quilters Guild and held at Beacon United Church in Yarmouth. More than 150 quilts hung from railings or were draped over the backs of chairs. The chairs stood in double rows on the tops of tables, eight, six, four, or two chairs to a table. For an hour and a half I roamed the hall studying patterns: bow tie, double wedding ring, flying geese, Dresden plate, city streets, winning hand, postage stamp, Ohio rose, Lady of the Lake, and bargello rippling in waves. Color spilled from vases of trapunto flowers. From the center of a radiant star, eleven pink and red eight-pointed stars shimmered outward. My favorite quilts were old, in particular grandmother's flower garden, its bright bouquets washed into pale delicacy. The three-dollar ticket not only admitted me to the show but also let me drink tea or coffee and eat as many homemade confections as I wanted. I sampled six. Culinary memory deteriorating almost as fast as nominal, I recall only two, a devil's food cake muddy with icing and cheesecake, a bush laden with blueberries drooping over the top. Few men attended the exhibition. On entering the auditorium I counted six men and forty-four women; on leaving, seven men and seventy-four women.

Pasted to a wall in the men's lavatory was a yellow sign, black letters printed on it: "Please wrap your gum in a piece of paper towel and throw it in the garbage not in the urinal." Under the request, someone had scribbled, "as it tastes bad then." The impulse toward disorder runs deep in me, as in society itself, and I admired the person who wrote on the sign, in the act not marring cardboard but making it reflect human nature. In contrast, the quilts fostered the pleasant falsehood that life radiated design, or at least that order could be imposed upon living, transforming chaos into the beautiful and the functional. In the house at Beaver River clocks tick like balm, generating the illusion that time is regular. In the attempt to control living, man created time. Now man deludes himself into believing he controls time, when the truth is that man never masters his creations. They master him, binding him and his offspring like serfs to ways of living. Studying the quilts led me to ponder education. Instead of attending university for four years and coming to believe that learning prepares people for life, wouldn't children fare better, I thought, if they mastered quilting? Although sewing might foster wrong-headed ideas about order and disorder, at least the children would belong to a community. Society has accepted the exaggerated claims of education for so long that place and family no longer provide identity. Now schools furnish pedigrees; the bluer the educational lines, the more admirable the person. Rarely do people mention family or birthplace when they introduce me. They cite the schools I attended, almost never referring to Sewanee but not failing to mention Cambridge and Princeton.

Such ponderings are not for young but old dogs who have ground teeth away chewing at life. That aside, one Sunday Vicki and I drove to Salmon River and watched the stock-car races at Lake Doucette, a clay triangle sunk into a hilltop and bound on three sides by spruce. Berms, buttressed curbs of tires, and wire fences surrounded the track. We sat at the base of the triangle, just beyond the end of the straightaway below the start. Protection seemed flimsy.

"That fence couldn't restrain a sleepy cow, much less an automobile," Vicki said after a car cartwheeled toward the grandstand, trunk over engine, at the start of the first race.

"Right," I said, brushing clods of dirt from my shirt and trousers. Throughout the afternoon dirt rained on us. When Vicki bit into a slice of pizza, she got "the works." Gravel had drizzled over us and covered her pizza, resembling nubs of hamburger. The cars looked like boxes wrapped in crumpled foil. Trucks towed them into the infield: dump, pickup, tow, and a pink and white Firestone repair truck. During races people sat in white plastic chairs on the roof of the Firestone truck. All afternoon tires smashed into berms, and the cars themselves whirled about like water beetles. I scanned the infield looking for an ambulance but did not discover one.

"What happens if someone in the stands is hurt?" Vicki asked.

"I don't know," I said. "The best you can do is learn from that woman in front of us." I pointed down to the right. Tattooed on the woman's left shoulder were two hands, palms pressed together in prayer.

Just after the start of the first race, three cars flipped. At the first turn following the restart, five cars spun out, smacking the berm beneath us. "Oh, shit!" Vicki said when a tire flew over the grandstand. Vicki said the word so many times during the first three races that I suggested she emend her exclamations.

"'Sugar' would sound more like a lady."

"Fudge you," she said.

The cars raced in categories: those with four-cylinder engines, six-cylinder, then eights, followed by cars whose eight-cylinder engines had been modified. To muffle the storm of noise, we stuffed cotton balls into our ears. Still, by afternoon's end I recognized cat-

egories by the noises engines made: the heavy thrum of modifieds
and the thin popping of four-cylinders. Individual cars stood out,
one with "Welcome to the Swamp" printed on a mud flap and a
1989 Volkswagen Fox painted white and black like a Holstein. Rubber udders hung beneath rear doors on both sides of the car.
Unfortunately the car needed freshening and did not finish a single race. Local businesses sponsored racers, and their names appeared on doors and hoods, often sprayed on: Nighttime Auto Sal-
vage, Howard Andrews Electrical, S & H Newell Trucking & Bait,
Bishara's Garage, Waterview Machine Works, Andrew LeBlanc's
Excavating, and D. J.'s Corner Store, this last in Salmon River,
where we bought newspapers and ice cream cones. Between races
the "Water Buffalo," an old tanker that once hauled milk, sprinkled water over the track. The announcer discussed cars and drivers. Sometimes he addressed the crowd, wishing Gerald and Chris-
tine a happy anniversary. At the entrance to the track, the Lions
Club sold tickets for the half-and-half. Tickets cost a dollar, fifty
cents going to the Lions, fifty cents to a winner-take-all pot. I
bought three tickets, and we stayed until the draw. We arrived at
the track at 11:20; the drawing took place at 3:15, the winner receiving $954. "We must go now," I said to Vicki. "I have to let
George out."

"I know. I know," Vicki said. "But we are coming back next week.
This is the real stuff."

"Perhaps," I said, "but maybe you have been brainwashed."

"Washed!" Vicki exclaimed, brushing off her trousers. "I look
like I have spent the day on my hands and knees in a garden."

"I read an article that accused the government of experimenting
with mind control," I continued, ignoring the interruption.

"What proof did the article cite?" Vicki asked.

"The number of yellow cars in New York City," I said. "Mind control provides the only reasonable explanation for so many people
driving yellow cars."

"Sugar," Vicki said.

On the way home, Vicki didn't talk. She stared at the dunes behind Bartlett's Beach. George moved so slowly when I let him out
that I picked him up and carried him into the yard. "You're a good
old fellow, my good old fellow," I said, suddenly unutterably sad.

OLIVER SACKS

Speed

FROM THE NEW YORKER

As A BOY, I was fascinated by speed, the wild range of speeds in
the world around me. People moved at different speeds; animals
much more so. The wings of insects moved too fast to see, though
one could judge their frequency by the tone they emitted — a
hateful noise, a high E, with mosquitoes, or a lovely bass hum with
the fat bumblebees that flew around the hollyhocks each summer.
Our pet tortoise, which could take an entire day to cross the lawn,
seemed to live in a different time frame altogether. But what then
of the movement of plants? I would come down to the garden in
the morning and find the hollyhocks a little higher, the roses more
entwined around their trellis, but, however patient I was, I could
never catch them moving.

Experiences like this played a part in turning me to photography, because it allowed me to alter the rate of motion, speed it up,
slow it down, so I could see, adjusted to a human perceptual rate,
the details of movement or change otherwise beyond the power of
the eye to register. Being fond of microscopes and telescopes —
my older brothers, medical students and birdwatchers, kept theirs
in the house — I thought of the slowing down or the speeding up
of motion as a sort of temporal equivalent: slow motion as an en-
largement, a microscopy of time, and speeded-up motion as a fore-
shortening, a telescopy of time.

I experimented with photographing plants. Ferns, in particular,
had many attractions for me — not least in their tightly wound cro-
siers or fiddleheads, tense with contained time, like watch springs,
with the future all rolled up in them. So I would set my camera on

a tripod in the garden and take photographs of fiddleheads at intervals of an hour; I would develop the negatives, print them up, and bind a dozen or so prints together in a little flick-book. And then, as if by magic, I could see the fiddleheads unfurl like the curled-up paper trumpets one blew into at parties, taking a second or two for what, in real time, took a couple of days.

Slowing down motion was not so easy as speeding it up, and here I depended on my cousin, a photographer, who had a cinecamera capable of taking more than a hundred frames per second. With this, I was able to catch the bumblebees at work as they hovered in the hollyhocks, and to slow down their time-blurred wing beats so that I could see each up-and-down movement distinctly.

My interest in speed and movement and time, and in possible ways to make them appear faster or slower, made me take a special pleasure in two of H. G. Wells's stories, *The Time Machine* and "The New Accelerator," with their vividly imagined, almost cinematic descriptions of altered time.

"As I put on pace, night followed day like the flapping of a black wing," Wells's Time Traveller relates:

> I saw the sun hopping swiftly across the sky, leaping it every minute, and every minute marking a day . . . The slowest snail that ever crawled dashed by too fast for me . . . Presently, as I went on, still gaining velocity, the palpitation of day and night merged into one continuous greyness . . . the jerking sun became a streak of fire . . . the moon a fainter fluctuating band . . . I saw trees growing and changing like puffs of vapour . . . huge buildings rise up faint and fair, and pass like dreams. The whole surface of the earth seemed changed — melting and flowing under my eyes.

The opposite of this occurs in "The New Accelerator," the story of a drug that accelerates one's perceptions, thoughts, and metabolism several thousand times or so. Its inventor and the narrator, who have taken the drug together, wander out into a glaciated world, watching

> people like ourselves and yet not like ourselves, frozen in careless attitudes, caught in mid-gesture . . . and sliding down the air with wings flapping slowly and at the speed of an exceptionally languid snail — was a bee.

The Time Machine was published in 1895, when there was intense interest in the new powers of photography and cinematography to reveal details of movements inaccessible to the unaided eye. Étienne-Jules Marey, a French physiologist, had been the first to show that a galloping horse at one point had all four hooves off the ground. His work, as the historian Marta Braun brings out, was instrumental in stimulating Eadweard Muybridge's famous photographic studies of motion. Marey, in turn stimulated by Muybridge, went on to develop high-speed cameras that could slow and almost arrest the movements of birds and insects in flight; and, at the opposite extreme, to use time-lapse photography to accelerate the otherwise almost imperceptible movements of sea urchins, starfish, and other marine animals.

I wondered sometimes whether the speeds of animals and plants could be very different from what they were: how much they were constrained by internal limits, how much by external — the gravity of the earth, the amount of energy received from the sun, the amount of oxygen in the atmosphere, and so on. So I was fascinated by yet another Wells story, *The First Men in the Moon,* with its beautiful description of how the growth of plants was dramatically accelerated on a celestial body with only a fraction of the earth's gravity:

> With a steady assurance, a swift deliberation, these amazing seeds thrust a rootlet downward to the earth and a queer little bundle-like bud into the air . . . The bundle-like buds swelled and strained and opened with a jerk, thrusting out a coronet of little sharp tips . . . that lengthened rapidly, lengthened visibly even as we watched. The movement was slower than any animal's, swifter than any plant's I have ever seen before. How can I suggest it to you — the way that growth went on? . . . Have you ever on a cold day taken a thermometer into your warm hand and watched the little thread of mercury creep up the tube? These moon plants grew like that.

Here, as in *The Time Machine* and "The New Accelerator," the description was irresistibly cinematic, and made me wonder if the young Wells had seen or experimented with time-lapse photography of plants, as I had.

A few years later, when I was a student at Oxford, I read William James's *Principles of Psychology,* and there, in a wonderful chapter on "The Perception of Time," I found this description:

> We have every reason to think that creatures may possibly differ enormously in the amounts of duration which they intuitively feel, and in the

fineness of the events that may fill it. Von Baer has indulged in some interesting computations of the effect of such differences in changing the
aspect of Nature. Suppose we were able, within the length of a second,
to note 10,000 events distinctly, instead of barely 10, as now; if our life
were then destined to hold the same number of impressions, it might be
1000 times as short. We should live less than a month, and personally
know nothing of the change of seasons. If born in winter, we should believe in summer as we now believe in the heats of the Carboniferous era.
The motions of organic beings would be so slow to our senses as to be
inferred, not seen. The sun would stand still in the sky, the moon be almost free from change, and so on. But now reverse the hypothesis and
suppose a being to get only one 1000th part of the sensations that we
get in a given time, and consequently live 1000 times as long. Winters
and summers will be to him like quarters of an hour. Mushrooms and
the swifter-growing plants will shoot into being so rapidly as to appear
instantaneous creations; annual shrubs will rise and fall from the earth
like restlessly boiling-water springs; the motions of animals will be as invisible as are to us the movements of bullets and cannon-balls; the sun
will scour through the sky like a meteor, leaving a fiery trail behind him,
etc. That such imaginary cases (barring the superhuman longevity) may
be realized somewhere in the animal kingdom, it would be rash to deny.

This was published in 1890, when Wells was a young biologist
(and writer of biology texts). Could he have read James, or, for that
matter, the original computations of Von Baer, from the 1860s? Indeed, one might say that a cinematographic model is implicit in all
these descriptions, for the business of registering larger or smaller
numbers of events in a given time is exactly what cinecameras do if
they are run faster or slower than the usual twenty-four or so
frames per second.

It is often said that time seems to go more quickly, the years rush
by, as one grows older — either because when one is young one's
days are packed with novel, exciting impressions or because as one
grows older a year becomes a smaller and smaller fraction of one's
life. But if the years appear to pass more quickly, the hours and
minutes do not — they are the same as they always were.

At least they seem so to me (in my seventies), although experiments have shown that while young people are remarkably accurate at estimating a span of three minutes by counting internally,
elderly subjects apparently count more slowly, so that their per-

ceived three minutes is closer to three and a half or four minutes. But it is still not clear that this phenomenon has anything to do with the existential or psychological feeling of time passing more quickly as one ages.

The hours and minutes still seem excruciatingly long when I am bored, and all too short when I am engaged. As a boy, I hated school, being forced to listen passively to droning teachers. When I looked at my watch surreptitiously, counting the minutes to my liberation, the minute hand, and even the second hand, seemed to move with infinite slowness. There is an exaggerated consciousness of time in such situations; indeed, when one is bored there may be no consciousness of anything *but* time.

In contrast were the delights of experimenting and thinking in the little chemical lab I set up at home, and here, on a weekend, I might spend an entire day in happy activity and absorption. Then I would have no consciousness of time at all, until I began to have difficulty seeing what I was doing, and realized that evening had come. When, years later, I read Hannah Arendt, writing in *The Life of the Mind* of "a timeless region, an eternal presence in complete quiet, lying beyond human clocks and calendars altogether . . . the quiet of the Now in the time-pressed, time-tossed existence of man . . . This small non-time space in the very heart of time," I knew exactly what she was talking about.

There have always been anecdotal accounts of people's perception of time when they are suddenly threatened with mortal danger, but the first systematic study was undertaken in 1892 by the Swiss geologist Albert Heim; he explored the mental states of thirty subjects who had survived falls in the Alps. "Mental activity became enormous, rising to a hundred-fold velocity," Heim noted. "Time became greatly expanded . . . In many cases there followed a sudden review of the individual's entire past." In this situation, he wrote, there was "no anxiety" but, rather, "profound acceptance."

Almost a century later, in the 1970s, Russell Noyes and Roy Kletti, of the University of Iowa, exhumed and translated Heim's study and went on to collect and analyze more than two hundred accounts of such experiences. Most of their subjects, like Heim's, described an increased speed of thought and an apparent slowing of time during what they thought to be their last moments.

A racecar driver who was thrown thirty feet into the air in a crash said, "It seemed like the whole thing took forever. Everything was in slow motion, and it seemed to me like I was a player on a stage and could see myself tumbling over and over . . . as though I sat in the stands and saw it all happening . . . but I was not frightened." Another driver, cresting a hill at high speed and finding himself a hundred feet from a train that he was sure would kill him, observed, "As the train went by, I saw the engineer's face. It was like a movie run slowly, so that the frames progress with a jerky motion. That was how I saw his face."

While some of these near-death experiences are marked by a sense of helplessness and passivity, even dissociation, in others there is an intense sense of immediacy and reality, and a dramatic acceleration of thought and perception and reaction, which allow one to negotiate danger successfully. Noyes and Kletti describe a jet pilot who faced almost certain death when his plane was improperly launched from its carrier: "I vividly recalled, in a matter of about three seconds, over a dozen actions necessary to successful recovery of flight attitude. The procedures I needed were readily available. I had almost total recall and felt in complete control."

Many of their subjects, Noyes and Kletti said, felt that "they performed feats, both mental and physical, of which they would ordinarily have been incapable."

It may be similar, in a way, with trained athletes, especially those in games demanding fast reaction times. A baseball may be approaching at close to a hundred miles per hour, and yet, as many people have described, the ball may seem to be almost immobile in the air, its very seams strikingly visible, and the batter finds himself in a suddenly enlarged and spacious timescape, where he has all the time he needs to hit the ball.

In a bicycle race, cyclists may be moving at nearly forty miles per hour, separated only by inches. The situation, to an onlooker, looks precarious in the extreme, and indeed the cyclists may be mere milliseconds away from each other. The slightest error may lead to a multiple crash. But to the cyclists themselves, concentrating intensely, everything seems to be moving in relatively slow motion, and there is ample room and time, enough to allow improvisation and intricate maneuverings.

The dazzling speed of martial-arts masters, the movements too fast for the untrained eye to follow, may be executed, in the performer's mind, with an almost balletic deliberation and grace, what trainers and coaches like to call "relaxed concentration." This alteration in the perception of speed is often conveyed in movies like *The Matrix* by alternating accelerated and slowed-down versions of the action.

The expertise of athletes (whatever their innate gifts) is only to be acquired by years of dedicated practice and training. At first, an intense conscious effort and attention are necessary to learn every nuance of technique and timing. But at some point the basic skills and their neural representation become so ingrained in the nervous system as to be almost second nature, no longer in need of conscious effort or decision. One level of brain activity may be working automatically, while another, the conscious level, is fashioning a perception of time, a perception that is elastic and can be compressed or expanded.

In the 1960s, the American neurophysiologist Benjamin Libet, investigating how simple motor decisions were made, found that brain signals indicating an act of decision could be detected several hundred milliseconds *before* there was any conscious awareness of it. A champion sprinter may be up and running and already sixteen or eighteen feet into the race before he is consciously aware that the starting gun has fired. (He can be off the blocks in 130 milliseconds, whereas the conscious registration of the gunshot requires 400 milliseconds or more.) The runner's belief that he consciously heard the gun and then, immediately, exploded off the blocks is an illusion made possible, Libet would suggest, because the mind "antedates" the sound of the gun by almost half a second.

Such a reordering of time, like the apparent compression or expansion of time, raises the question of how we normally perceive time. William James speculated that our judgment of time, our speed of perception, depends on how many "events" we can perceive in a given unit of time.

There is much to suggest that conscious perception (at least visual perception) is not continuous but consists of discrete moments, like the frames of a movie, which are then blended to give an appearance of continuity. No such partitioning of time, it would seem, occurs in rapid, automatic actions, such as returning a tennis shot or hitting a baseball. Christof Koch, a neuroscientist at Caltech, distinguishes between "behavior" and "experience," and proposes that "behavior may be executed in a smooth fashion, while experience may be structured in discrete intervals, as in a movie." This model of consciousness would allow a Jamesian mechanism by which the perception of time could be speeded up or slowed down. Koch speculates that the apparent slowing of time in emergencies and athletic performances (at least when athletes find themselves "in the zone") may come from the power of intense attention to reduce the duration of individual frames.

The subject of space and time perception is becoming a popular topic in sensory psychology, and the reactions and perceptions of athletes, and of people facing sudden demands and emergencies, would seem to be an obvious field for further experiment, especially now that virtual reality gives us the power to simulate action under controlled conditions and at ever more taxing speeds.

For William James, the most striking departures from "normal" time were provided by the effects of certain drugs. He tried a number of them himself, from nitrous oxide to peyote, and in his chapter on the perception of time he immediately followed his meditation on Von Baer with a reference to hashish. "In hashish-intoxication," he writes, "there is a curious increase in the apparent time-perspective. We utter a sentence, and ere the end is reached the beginning seems already to date from indefinitely long ago. We enter a short street, and it is as if we should never get to the end of it."

James's observations are an almost exact echo of Jacques-Joseph Moreau's, fifty years earlier. Moreau, a physician, was one of the first to make hashish fashionable in the Paris of the 1840s — indeed, he was a member, along with Gautier, Baudelaire, Balzac, and other savants and artists, of Le Club des Hachichins. Moreau wrote:

> Crossing the covered passage in the Place de l'Opéra one night, I was struck by the length of time it took to get to the other side. I had taken a few steps at most, but it seemed to me that I had been there two or three hours . . . I hastened my step, but time did not pass more rapidly . . . It seemed to me . . . that the walk was endlessly long and that the exit to-

wards which I walked was retreating into the distance at the same rate as my speed of walking.

Going along with the sense that a few words, a few steps, may last an unconscionable time, there may be the sense of a world profoundly slowed, even suspended. L. J. West, in the 1970 book *Psychotomimetic Drugs*, relates this anecdote: "Two hippies, high on pot, are sitting in the Golden Gate Park in San Francisco. A jet aircraft goes zooming overhead and is gone; whereupon one hippie turns to the other and says, 'Man, I thought he'd never leave.'"

But while the external world may appear slowed, an inner world of images and thoughts may take off with great speed. One may set out on an elaborate mental journey, visiting different countries and cultures, or compose a book or a symphony, or live through a whole life or an epoch of history, only to find that mere minutes or seconds have passed. Gautier described how he entered a hashish trance in which "sensations followed one another so numerous and so hurried that true appreciation of time was impossible." It seemed to him, subjectively, that the spell had lasted "three hundred years," but he found, on awakening, that it had lasted no more than a quarter of an hour.

The word "awakening" may be more than a figure of speech here, for such "trips" have surely to be compared with dreams. I have occasionally, it seems to me, lived a whole life between my first alarm, at 5 A.M., and my second alarm, five minutes later.

Sometimes, as one is falling asleep, there may be a massive, involuntary jerk — a myoclonic jerk — of the body. Though such jerks are generated by primitive parts of the brain stem (they are, so to speak, brain-stem reflexes), and as such are without any intrinsic meaning or motive, they may be given meaning and context, turned into acts, by an instantly improvised dream. Thus the jerk may be associated with a dream of tripping, or stepping over a precipice, lunging forward to catch a ball, and so on. Such dreams may be extremely vivid and have several "scenes." Subjectively, they appear to start *before* the jerk, and yet presumably the entire dream mechanism is stimulated by the first, preconscious perception of the jerk. All of this elaborate restructuring of time occurs in a second or less.

There are certain epileptic seizures, sometimes called "experiential seizures," when a detailed recollection or hallucination of the past suddenly imposes itself upon a patient's consciousness, and pursues a subjectively lengthy and unhurried course, to complete itself in what, objectively, is only a few seconds. These seizures are typically associated with convulsive activity in the brain's temporal lobes, and can be induced, in some patients, by electrical stimulation of certain trigger points on the surface of the lobes. Sometimes such epileptic experiences are suffused with a sense of metaphysical significance along with their subjectively enormous duration. Dostoyevsky wrote of such seizures:

> There are moments, and it is only a matter of a few seconds, when you feel the presence of the eternal harmony . . . A terrible thing is the frightful clearness with which it manifests itself and the rapture with which it fills you . . . During these five seconds I live a whole human existence, and for that I would give my whole life and not think that I was paying too dearly.

There may be no inner sense of speed at such times, but at other times — especially with mescaline or LSD — one may feel hurtled through thought-universes at uncontrollable, supraluminal speeds. In *The Major Ordeals of the Mind,* the French poet and painter Henri Michaux writes, "Persons returning from the speed of mescaline speak of an acceleration of a hundred or two hundred times, or even of five hundred times that of normal speed." He comments that this is probably an illusion, but that even if the acceleration were much more modest — "even only six times" the normal — the increase would still feel overwhelming. What is experienced, Michaux feels, is not so much a huge accumulation of exact literal details as a series of overall impressions, dramatic highlights, as in a dream.

But, this said, if the speed of thought could be significantly heightened, the increase would readily show up (if we had the experimental means to examine it) in physiological recordings of the brain, and would perhaps illustrate the limits of what is neurally possible. We would need, however, the right level of cellular activity to record from, and this would be not the level of individual nerve cells but a higher level, the level of interaction between *groups* of neurons in the cerebral cortex, which, in their tens or hundreds of thousands, form the neural correlate of consciousness.

The speed of such neural interactions is normally regulated by a delicate balance of excitatory and inhibitory forces, but there are certain conditions in which inhibitions may be relaxed. Dreams can take wing, move freely and swiftly, precisely because the activity of the cerebral cortex is not constrained by external perception or reality. Similar considerations, perhaps, apply to the trances induced by mescaline or hashish.

Other drugs — depressants, by and large, like opiates and barbiturates — may have the opposite effect, producing an opaque, dense inhibition of thought and movement, so that one may enter a state in which scarcely anything seems to happen, and then come to, after what seems to have been a few minutes, to find that an entire day has been consumed. Such effects resemble the action of the Retarder, a drug that Wells imagined as the opposite of the Accelerator:

> The Retarder . . . should enable the patient to spread a few seconds over many hours of ordinary time, and so to maintain an apathetic inaction, a glacier-like absence of alacrity, amidst the most animated or irritating surroundings.

That there could be profound and persistent disorders of neural speed lasting for years or decades first hit me when, in 1966, I went to work in the Bronx at Beth Abraham, a hospital for chronic illness, and saw the patients whom I was later to write about in my book *Awakenings*. There were dozens of these patients in the lobby and corridors, all moving at different tempos — some violently accelerated, some in slow motion, some almost glaciated. As I looked at this landscape of disordered time, memories of Wells's Accelerator and Retarder suddenly came back to me. All of these patients, I learned, were survivors of the great pandemic of encephalitis lethargica that swept the world from 1917 to 1928. Of the millions who contracted this "sleepy sickness," about a third died in the acute stages, in states of coma sleep so deep as to preclude arousal, or in states of sleeplessness so intense as to preclude sedation. Some of the survivors, though often accelerated and excited in the early days, had later developed an extreme form of Parkinsonism that had slowed or even frozen them, sometimes for decades. A few of the patients at Beth Abraham continued to be accelerated, and one, Ed M., was actually accelerated on one side of his body and slowed on the other.

Dopamine, a neurotransmitter essential for the normal flow of movement and thought, is drastically reduced in ordinary Parkinson's disease, to less than fifteen percent of normal levels. In post-encephalitic Parkinsonism, dopamine levels may become almost undetectable. In ordinary Parkinson's disease, in addition to tremor or rigidity, one sees moderate slowings and speedings; in post-encephalitic Parkinsonism, where the damage in the brain is usually far greater, there may be slowings and speedings to the utmost physiological and mechanical limits of the brain and body.

The very vocabulary of Parkinsonism is couched in terms of speed. Neurologists have an array of terms to denote this: if movement is slowed, they talk about "bradykinesia"; if brought to a halt, "akinesia"; if excessively rapid, "tachykinesia." Similarly, one can have bradyphrenia or tachyphrenia — a slowing or accelerating of thought.

In 1969, I was able to start most of these frozen patients on the drug L-dopa, which had recently been shown to be effective in raising dopamine levels in the brain. At first, this restored a normal speed and freedom of movement to many of the patients. But then, especially in the most severely affected, it pushed them in the opposite direction. One patient, Hester Y., I observed in my journal, showed such acceleration of movement and speech after five days on L-dopa that "if she had previously resembled a slow-motion film, or a persistent film frame stuck in the projector, she now gave the impression of a speeded-up film, so much so that my colleagues, looking at a film of Mrs. Y. which I took at the time, insisted that the projector was running too fast."

I assumed at first that Hester and other patients realized the unusual rates at which they were moving or speaking or thinking but were simply unable to control themselves. I soon found that this was by no means the case. Nor is it the case in patients with ordinary Parkinson's disease, as William Gooddy, a neurologist in England, remarks at the beginning of his book *Time and the Nervous System*. An observer may note, he says, how slowed a Parkinsonian's movements are, but "the patient will say, 'My own movements . . .

seem normal unless I see how long they take by looking at a clock. The clock on the wall of the ward seems to be going exceptionally fast.'"

Gooddy refers here to "personal" time, as contrasted with "clock" time, and the extent to which personal time departs from clock time may become almost unbridgeable with the extreme bradykinesia common in post-encephalitic Parkinsonism. I would often see my patient Miron V. sitting in the hallway outside my office. He would appear motionless, with his right arm often lifted, sometimes an inch or two above his knee, sometimes near his face. When I questioned him about these frozen poses, he asked indignantly, "What do you mean, 'frozen poses'? I was just wiping my nose."

I wondered if he was putting me on. One morning, over a period of hours, I took a series of twenty or so photos and stapled them together to make a flick-book, like the ones I used to make to show the unfurling of fiddleheads. With this, I could see that Miron actually *was* wiping his nose but was doing so a thousand times more slowly than normal.

Hester, too, seemed unaware of the degree to which her personal time diverged from clock time. I once asked my students to play ball with her, and they found it impossible to catch her lightning-quick throws. Hester returned the ball so rapidly that their hands, still outstretched from the throw, might be hit smartly by the returning ball. "You see how quick she is," I said. "Don't underestimate her — you'd better be ready." But they could not be ready, since their best reaction times approached a seventh of a second, whereas Hester's was scarcely more than a tenth of a second.

It was only when Miron and Hester were in normal states, neither excessively retarded nor accelerated, that they could judge how startling their speed or slowness had been, and it was sometimes necessary to show them a film or a tape to convince them.

(Disorders of spatial scale are as common in Parkinsonism as disorders of time scale. An almost diagnostic sign of Parkinsonism is micrographia — minute, and often diminishingly small, handwriting. Typically, patients are not aware of this at the time; it is only later, when they are back in a normal spatial frame of reference, that they are able to judge that their writing was smaller than usual.

Thus there may be, for some patients, a compression of space that is comparable to the compression of time. One of my patients, a post-encephalitic woman, used to say, "My space, our space, is nothing like your space.")

With disorders of time scale, there seems almost no limit to the degree of slowing that can occur, and the speeding up of movement sometimes seems constrained only by the physical limits of articulation. If Hester tried to speak or count aloud in one of her very accelerated states, the words or numbers would clash and run into each other. Such physical limitations were less evident with thought and perception. If she was shown a perspective drawing of the Necker cube — an ambiguous drawing that normally seems to switch perspective every few seconds — she might, when slowed, see switches every minute or two (or not at all, if she was "frozen"), but when speeded up she would see the cube "flashing," changing its perspective several times a second.

Striking accelerations may also occur in Tourette's syndrome, a condition characterized by compulsions, tics, and involuntary movements and noises. Some people with Tourette's are able to catch flies on the wing. When I asked one man with Tourette's how he managed this, he said that he had no sense of moving especially fast but, rather, that to him the flies moved slowly.

If one reaches out a hand to touch or grasp something, the normal rate is about 1 meter per second. Normal experimental subjects, when asked to do this as quickly as possible, reach at about 4.5 meters per second. But when I asked Shane F., an artist with Tourette's, to reach as quickly as he could, he was able to achieve a rate of 7 meters per second with ease, without any sacrifice of smoothness or accuracy. When I asked him to stick to normal speeds, his movements became constrained, awkward, inaccurate, and tic-filled.

Another patient with severe Tourette's and very rapid speech told me that, in addition to the tics and vocalizations I could see and hear, there were others of which — with my "slow" eyes and ears — I might be unaware. It was only with videotaping and frame-by-frame analysis that the great range of these "micro-tics" could be seen. In fact, there could be several trains of micro- tics proceeding simultaneously, apparently in complete dissociation from one another, adding up to, perhaps, dozens of micro-tics in a single second. The complexity of all this was as astonishing as its speed, and I thought that one could write an entire book, an atlas of tics, based on a mere five seconds of videotape. Such an atlas, I felt, would provide a sort of microscopy of the brain-mind, for all tics have determinants, whether inner or outer, and every patient's repertoire of tics is unique.

The blurted-out tics that may occur in Tourette's resemble what the great British neurologist John Hughlings Jackson called "emotional" or ejaculate speech (as opposed to complex, syntactically elaborate "propositional" speech). Ejaculate speech is essentially reactive, preconscious, and impulsive; it eludes the monitoring of the frontal lobes, of consciousness, and of ego, and it escapes from the mouth before it can be inhibited.

Not just the speed but the quality of movement and thought is altered in Tourettism and Parkinsonism. The accelerated state tends to be exuberant in invention and fancy, leaping rapidly from one association to the next, carried along by the force of its own impetus. Slowness, in contrast, tends to go with care and caution, a sober and critical stance, which has its uses no less than the "go" of effusion. This was brought out by Ivan Vaughan, a psychologist with Parkinson's disease, who wrote a memoir about his experiences (*Ivan: Living with Parkinson's Disease,* 1986). He sought to do all his writing, he told me, while he was under the influence of L-dopa, for at such times his imagination and his mental processes seemed to flow more freely and rapidly, and he had rich, unexpected associations of every sort (though if he was too accelerated, this might impair his focus and lead him to tangents in all directions). But when the effects of L-dopa wore off, he turned to editing, and would find himself in a perfect state to prune the sometimes too exuberant prose he had written while he was "on."

My Tourettic patient Ray, while often beleaguered and bullied by his Tourette's, also managed to exploit it in various ways. The rapidity (and sometimes oddness) of his associations made him quick-witted — he spoke of his "ticcy witticisms" and his "witty ticcicisms" and referred to himself as Witty Ticcy Ray. This quickness and wittiness, when combined with his musical talents, made him a formidable improviser on the drums. He was almost unbeatable at Ping-Pong, partly because of his sheer speed of reaction and partly because his shots, though not technically illegal, were so unpredictable (even to himself) that his opponents were flummoxed and unable to answer them.

People with extremely severe Tourette's syndrome may be our closest approximation to the sorts of speeded-up beings imagined by Von Baer and James, and people with Tourette's sometimes describe themselves as being "supercharged." "It's like having a five-hundred-horsepower engine under the hood," one of my patients says. Indeed, there are a number of world-class athletes with Tourette's — among them Jim Eisenreich and Mike Johnston in baseball, Mahmoud Abdul-Rauf in basketball, and Tim Howard in soccer.

If the speed of Tourette's can be so adaptive — a neurological gift of sorts — then what is the sense of being relatively sluggish, staid, and "normal"? Why has natural selection not served to increase the number of "speeders" in our midst? The disadvantages of excessive slowness are obvious, but it may be necessary (since we sometimes think of speed as unreservedly good) to point out that excessive speed is equally freighted with problems. Tourettic or post-encephalitic speed goes with disinhibition, an impulsiveness and impetuosity that allow "inappropriate" movements and impulses to emerge precipitately. In such conditions, then, dangerous impulses such as putting a finger in a flame or darting in front of traffic, usually inhibited in the rest of us, may be released and acted on before consciousness can intervene.

And in extreme cases, if the stream of thought is too fast, it may lose itself, break into a torrent of superficial distractions and tangents, dissolve into a brilliant incoherence, a phantasmagoric, almost dreamlike delirium. People with severe Tourette's, like Shane, may find the movements and thoughts and reactions of other people unbearably slow for them, and we "neuro-normals" may at times find the Shanes of this world disconcertingly fast. "Monkeys these people seem to us," James wrote in another context, "whilst we seem to them reptilian."

In the famous chapter in *The Principles of Psychology* on "Will," James speaks of what he calls the "perverse" or pathological will, and of its having two opposite forms: the "explosive" and the "obstructed." He used these terms in relation to psychological dispositions and temperaments, but they seem equally apposite in speaking of such physiological disorders as Parkinsonism, Tourette's syndrome, and catatonia. It seems strange that James never speaks of these opposites, the "explosive" and "obstructed" wills, as having, at least sometimes, a relation with each other, for he must have seen people with what we now call manic-depressive or bipolar disorder being thrown, every few weeks or months, from one extreme to the other.

One Parkinsonian friend of mine says that being in a slowed state is like being stuck in a vat of peanut butter, while being in an accelerated state is like being on ice, frictionless, slipping down an ever-steeper hill, or on a tiny planet, gravityless, with no force to hold or moor him.

Though such jammed, impacted states would seem to be at the opposite pole from accelerated, explosive ones, patients can move almost instantaneously from one to the other. The term "kinesia paradoxa" was introduced by French neurologists in the 1920s to describe these remarkable if rare transitions in post-encephalitic patients, who had scarcely moved for years but might suddenly be "released" and move with great energy and force, only to return, after a few minutes, to their previously motionless states. When Hester Y. was put on L-dopa, such alternations reached an extraordinary degree, and she was apt to make dozens of abrupt reversals a day.

Similar reversals may be seen in patients with extremely severe Tourette's syndrome, who can be brought to an almost stuporous halt by the most minute dose of certain drugs. Even without medication, states of motionless and almost hypnotic concentration tend to occur in Touretters, and these represent the other side, so to speak, of the hyperactive and distractible state.

In catatonia there may also be dramatic, instantaneous transformations from immobile, stuporous states to wildly active, frenzied ones. The great psychiatrist Eugen Bleuler described this in 1911:

> At times the peace and quiet is broken by the appearance of a catatonic raptus. Suddenly the patient springs up, smashes something, seizes someone with extraordinary power and dexterity . . . A catatonic arouses himself from his rigidity, runs around the streets in his nightshirt for three hours, and finally falls down and remains lying in a cataleptic state in the gutter. The movements are often executed with great strength, and nearly always involve unnecessary muscle groups . . . They seem to have lost control of measure and power of their movements.

Catatonia is rarely seen, especially in our present, tranquilized age, but some of the fear and bewilderment inspired by the insane must have come from these sudden, unpredictable transformations.

Catatonia, Parkinsonism, and Tourette's, no less than manic depression, may all be thought of as "bipolar" disorders. All of them, to use the nineteenth-century French term, are disorders *à double forme* — Janus-faced disorders, which can switch, incontinently, from one face, one form, to the other. The possibility of any neutral state, any unpolarized state, any "normality," is so reduced in such disorders that we must envisage a dumbbell- or hourglass-shaped "surface" of disease, with only a thin neck or isthmus of neutrality between the two ends.

It is common in neurology to speak of "deficits" — the knocking out of a physiological (and perhaps psychological) function by a lesion, or area of damage, in the brain. Lesions in the cortex tend to produce "simple" deficits, like loss of color vision or the ability to recognize letters or numbers. In contrast, lesions in the regulatory systems of the subcortex — which control movement, tempo, emotion, appetite, level of consciousness, etc. — undermine control and stability, so that patients lose the normal broad base of resilience, the middle ground, and may then be, like puppets, thrown almost helplessly from one extreme to another.

Doris Lessing once wrote of the situation of my post-encephalitic patients, "It makes you aware of what a knife-edge we live on," yet we do not, in health, live on a knife edge but on a broad and stable saddleback of normality. Physiologically, neural normality reflects a balance between excitatory and inhibitory systems in the brain, a balance that, in the absence of drugs or damage, has a remarkable latitude and resilience.

We, as human beings, have relatively constant and characteristic rates of movement, though some people are a bit faster, some a bit slower, and there may be variations in our levels of energy and engagement throughout the day. We are livelier, we move a little faster, we live faster when we are young; we slow down a little, at least in terms of bodily movement and reaction times, as we age. But the range of all these rates, at least in ordinary people, under normal circumstances, is quite limited. There is not that much difference in reaction times between the old and the young, or between the world's best athletes and the least athletic among us. This seems to be the case with basic mental operations, too — the maximum speed at which one can perform serial computations, recognition, visual associations, and so on. The dazzling performances of chess masters, lightning-speed calculators, musical improvisers, and other virtuosos may have less to do with basic neural speed than with the vast range of knowledge, memorized patterns and strategies, and hugely sophisticated skills they can call upon.

And yet there are those who seem to reach almost superhuman speeds of thought. Robert Oppenheimer, famously, when young physicists came to explain their ideas to him, would grasp the gist and implications of their thoughts within seconds, and interrupt them, extend their thoughts, almost as soon as they opened their mouths. Virtually everyone who heard Isaiah Berlin improvise in his torrentially rapid speech, piling image upon image, idea upon idea, building enormous mental structures that evolved and dissolved before one's eyes, felt they were privy to an astonishing mental phenomenon. And this is equally so of a comic genius like Robin Williams, whose explosive, incandescent flights of association and wit seem to take off and hurtle along at rocketlike speeds. Yet here, presumably, one is dealing not with the speeds of individual nerve cells and simple circuits but with neural networks of a much higher order, exceeding the complexity of the largest supercomputer.

Nevertheless, we humans, even the fastest among us, are limited in speed by basic neural determinants, by cells with limited rates of firing, and by limited speeds of conduction between different cells and cell groups. And if somehow we could accelerate ourselves a dozen or fifty times, we would find ourselves wholly out of sync with the world around us, and in a situation as bizarre as that of the narrator in Wells's story.

But we can make up for the limitations of our bodies, our senses, by using instruments of various kinds. We have unlocked time, as in the seventeenth century we unlocked space, and now have at our disposal what are, in effect, temporal microscopes and temporal telescopes of prodigious power. With these, we can achieve a quadrillionfold acceleration or retardation, so that we can watch, at leisure, by laser stroboscopy, the femtosecond-quick formation and dissolution of chemical bonds; or observe, contracted to a few minutes through computer simulation, the thirteen-billion-year history of the universe from the Big Bang to the present, or (at even higher temporal compression) its projected future to the end of time. Through such instrumentalities, we can enhance our perceptions, speed or slow them, in effect, to a degree infinitely beyond what any living process could match. In this way, stuck though we are in our own speed and time, we can, in imagination, enter all speeds, all time.

CATHLEEN SCHINE

Dog Trouble

FROM THE NEW YORKER

FOUR YEARS AGO, I was in a relationship that everyone who cared about me considered abusive. I was covered with bruises and scars. When my older son came home from college, he was greeted with a scene of loud, belligerent menace. My younger son, who still lived with us, tried to reach out, but more often than not his kindness was met by violence. My mother was terrified and refused to set foot in our house. In fact, no one came to visit us anymore. Nor were we welcome at anyone else's house. Even a short walk on the street held the threat of an ugly brawl. At night, I lay in bed, felt the warmth of his body beside me, and tried not to move. I didn't want to set him off. He was volatile, unpredictable. But I felt responsible for him. And, against all odds, I loved him.

He was not my husband, with whom I had just split up. Nor was he my boyfriend. (I had made one of those unforeseen middle-aged discoveries and was living with a woman.) My looming, destructive, desperate, and compelling companion was not even a human being. He was a dog. Or, as my friends and family pointed out, he was "just" a dog.

He appeared to be a lovely little dog, about two and half years old, when we first saw him. It was a spring day, and he stood at the end of a long line of caged dogs in a Los Angeles pet-supply store, all strays to be adopted, all barking and yapping and hurling themselves against their wire enclosures. But he neither barked nor yapped. He stood politely, his head cocked expectantly. He wagged his tail in vigorous anticipation. When I picked him up, he squirmed with joy and lunged, ecstatic, licking my face, overwhelming me with a wave of urgent, instant love.

"Why do you want a dog?" my mother asked me. "I know why you want a dog. Because your son is going to college." She looked at me pityingly. "When you went to college, I got a geranium."

Buster, which is what we named him, was a seventeen-pound bowlegged mutt with a nondescript coat of short brown hair and a bulldog chest. His tail was far too long for his body, a dachshund's tail. One ear stood up, the other flopped down. His face had the big, worried eyes of a Chihuahua, the anxious furrowed brow of a pug, and the markings of a German shepherd. He yodeled like a beagle and shook his toys with the neck-wrenching vigor of a pit bull terrier. A tough stray missing two toes on his left hind foot, he had been picked up in South L.A. and dumped in the city pound, where, we were told, larger dogs stole his food until, the day before he was to be euthanized, he was saved by a private rescue group that tried to find a home for him. After we discovered Buster, a representative of the group came to our house to make sure it was safe for the dog. She neglected to tell us that the dog was not safe for us. Perhaps the rescuers were blinded by hope, since we had lifted the dog from his crate and hugged and kissed him with no ill effect. Perhaps they were confused. They had so many dogs to place in homes. Perhaps they were simply desperate.

I grew up reading books about heroic collies. It was from the novels of the popular writer Albert Payson Terhune, treasured by my father before me, that I learned the word "puttee." Terhune would don a pair to walk through the grounds of Sunnybank. I also learned about "carrion," in which his dogs would roll luxuriously, and a "veranda," on which they would sit of an evening, curled contentedly at the feet of their god. Sunnybank was two generations and several classes and ethnic groups away from my world. Terhune, who in the books referred to himself as the Master, raised collies on a sprawling estate in northern New Jersey, which in his novels was called The Place. As impeccably bred as Sunnybank Lad, the Master claimed ancestors who had come to the New World from Holland and England in the seventeenth century. Terhune heatedly defended the rights of dogs and trees, but he was not a man of the people. There is a wonderful story by James Thurber describing the Master's highborn rage ("like summer thunder") when a Mr. Jacob R. Ellis and family, midwestern tourists come to take a gander at Sunnybank in their Ford sedan, ran over the beloved champion Sunnybank Jean. And the Master's disgust for Negroes and the "rich city dweller of sweatshop origin" was virulent and unashamed. But I noticed none of that as a child, for we had collies too. Our patient, plodding dogs with their matted ruffs in no way resembled the grand animals of the novels, but they did follow my brother and me protectively around the neighborhood. Would they have leaped at the throat of an attacker, like Buff of "Buff: A Collie" or Lad in "The Juggernaut"? Would they have instinctively guided stolen sheep back into their proper herd? Or wandered for months, living on squirrels, looking for me, their only true Mistress? One of them took long walks every day with an inmate from the sanitarium just down the road. They herded children during recess at an elementary school nearby. They wandered for miles until someone from several towns away would check their tags and call us to come get them, at which point they would greet us with unalloyed, and unsurprised, joy. This was my background with dogs: they were in the background. Or they were in books.

Then one afternoon when I was eight, and unaccountably home alone, sitting in front of the Admiral TV with its big round knobs, watching *The Mickey Mouse Club,* my chin resting on my knees, Laurie, our small mahogany-colored collie, poked her nose in my face. I pushed her away. She whined and whimpered. I ignored her. She pushed my shoulder, hard. She licked my face, pushed again, barked, ran frantically to the door and back, whining, licking, nudging, until I tore myself away from the television and allowed myself to be herded through the kitchen and to the front door, where the dog planted her feet, barking and wagging her tail, until I understood. Smoke and flames were billowing from the bedroom hallway. Our squat little collie had saved my life.

Devotion to a dog like that is not hard for anyone to understand. But how do you explain your devotion to a dog who is not man's best friend? Who is neither noble nor loyal? There is a popular training book called *No Bad Dogs,* but what happens when one is indeed bad and he belongs to you? What happens when bad dogs happen to good, or at least conscientious, people? When an animal defies kindness, defies the culture of therapy, and refuses to be redeemed?

On our very first evening with the little stray, we proudly placed his bowl of food on the kitchen floor. He rushed toward it, poking his muzzle eagerly into the organic human-grade kibble. We watched him, happy that we had rescued him from his hard, hungry life. There is something profoundly satisfying about taking in a creature no one else wants, a delicious flicker of moral superiority and the surprisingly powerful pleasure of generosity. We watched our dog, a bit smug, perhaps, but as I look back at the two of us, a new couple opening our lives to a needy dog, I feel only compassion. We had no idea what lay in store. Suddenly, Buster lifted his Chihuahua head. He jerked his pug face back toward his dachshund tail. He bared his pit bull fangs, and — this all happened in seconds — savagely growling, as if another dog were threatening to move in on his meal, he lunged for his own tail, for his own flank, for his back foot. He whirled, a blur of snarling and slashing. It was a full-blown dogfight, the worst I had ever seen, and he was having it with himself.

That night, Buster jumped up on the bed, crawled under the covers, rested his head on the pillow like a little man, and fell asleep. Around three o'clock, I sat up, terrified. A deep angry roar swept over my face. It was Buster, his eyes rolling, pursuing something that wasn't there. Sleeping with Buster, we soon discovered, was like sleeping with a Vietnam vet who suffers from post-traumatic stress disorder. Demons haunted Buster's sleep. The first time we left him alone in the house, we returned half an hour later to find him panting, foaming at the mouth, licking his new, self-inflicted wounds on a sofa covered with blood. And so, almost as soon as we got Buster, we began the quest to save him.

Over the next year and a half, we had Buster's legs and spine and tail x-rayed; we had him tested for every conceivable kind of worm and fed him a hypoallergenic diet of pure venison and sweet potatoes. We consulted a chiropractor and an acupuncturist. We took him to The BodyWorks with Veronica for Alexander technique and Feldenkrais. I searched the Internet for dog behaviorists and tried spray bottles of water and jars of noisy coins, clickers, herbal remedies, even aromatherapy. I typed "selfmutilation + dog" into Google, and articles in veterinary journals about paw licking and scratching came up. If only that were the problem, I thought. I typed in "Obsessive-compulsive disorder + dog" and consulted, by e-mail and phone, vets and animal behaviorists from all over the country. We watched *Emergency Vets* on Animal Planet, hoping we'd see some clue to Buster's problems. We watched *Animal Precinct,* both heartened by and envious of all the bony, beaten, scarred, one-eyed dogs who caressed the hands of strangers and frolicked tenderly with babies when given half a chance. The only thing we didn't try was a pet psychic. But sometimes, late at night, even that seemed plausible.

We couldn't leave Buster at home, but when we took him with us in the car he threw himself against the window in an attempt to attack every bicycle, motorcycle, Rollerblade, and shopping cart we passed. If it rained, he tried to subdue the windshield wipers. Parking-garage attendants pulled back when one of us handed them our ticket through the window while the other hung on to the snarling cur. When we fed Buster, we had to stand with a leg on either side, touching his flanks, to reassure him, we hoped, that no one was lurking behind his tail waiting to steal his food. But when, after a while, that too failed, and we began feeding Buster one piece of kibble at a time, he bit the hand that fed him. He bit the hand that groomed him. He bit the hand that petted him. After each attack, he would whimper and grovel, licking our faces. If you said "Kisses" to Buster, he would hurl himself at you to lick your face. When you whistled, he sang along, yodeling comically. He was terrified of men, especially men with hats and, embarrassingly, black men, but he was also afraid of women and children, and he hated other dogs.

Buster slept splayed companionably across your torso if you lay on the couch reading. I thought he was beautiful. He had filled out. His chest was smooth and muscular, his coat shining. When he slept on me like that, momentarily calm, I was momentarily full of hope. One day, the young woman who lived next door reached in the car window to pet him, and he lunged at her, tearing a deep gash in her hand. She was unbelievably understanding, the wound did not require stitches, there was no lawsuit. But we were frantic, and ashamed.

A new vet told us he could tell by the dog's teeth that he had had distemper when he was a puppy. Perhaps this had caused neurological damage. He couldn't be sure. But he was sure about one thing. "Your dog bites," the vet said. "Dogs that bite almost always continue to bite." Then he said, "If this were my dog, I would put him to sleep."

In the waiting room the day the vet told us to euthanize Buster, I saw an ad for a trainer in a local pet newsletter. Her name was Cinimon and she worked with rescued, hopeless, vicious pit bulls. We called her as soon as we got home.

Cinimon, a tan blonde with a pierced tongue, arrived with short-short cutoff jeans, an exposed midriff, and combat boots. She talked to us for hours, purposely ignoring Buster until he approached her, then handling him with incredible gentleness. She said we had to establish dominance over Buster now that he was in our pack. Her approach was not radical. We should put him in a crate at night and make him earn his treats by doing something, anything, even if it was as simple as sitting when told. Cinimon was full of hope and enthusiasm. I could not help seeing Cinimon, her delicious, oddly spelled name, and her own blooming California good health, as a promise of what Buster could hope for. The vet was probably right, but Buster would be the exception. Cinimon, a Valkyrie from the Valley, a girl with a household full of docile monsters, would make it so. Her training program was a reasonable behavior-modification approach. It made sense. To Cinimon. To us. Just not to Buster.

Buster was becoming a full-time job, or, more precisely, a whole life. We went to bed at night worrying about him. Had he got enough exercise? Did exercise tire him out and calm him down, as it was supposed to, or did it hurt his damaged foot and stress his awkward anatomy? Would he sleep through the night, or would he wake and chase his demons and slash my calf in his confused fury? If we put him in his bed on the floor, would he fall asleep this time, or would he spin and spin and spin, tearing wildly at himself? We had an obligation to him. We had an obligation to innocent bystanders. Had we pursued every possible road to recovery? Did our umbrella insurance cover liability for dog bites? Should we put him to sleep?

In the morning, he would snuggle up and lay his head across my neck, snoring gently, his breath soft and sweet. He played in the morning, too, chasing toys and shaking them like dying rats. During the day, he snoozed, threw himself angrily against the glass doors to the front garden when the mailman walked by, threw himself angrily at his own back legs, at his long tail, at his deformed foot, at his good feet, at our feet. He sat when we told him to, looking up innocently. He was innocent: that was the most painful part.

He was a vicious dog; even we would have to agree. He was destructive and dangerous, and if he had been a larger dog, we would have had no choice but to put him down. But he was as innocent as a babe, baffled by his own behavior, terrified of everything that moved. He had been a lost dog. He was still a lost dog.

Then Cinimon suggested Prozac. In the months that followed, we consulted three vets, two psychopharmacologists, and a psychiatrist. We slapped peanut butter around Prozac, Buspar, Elavil, Effexor, Xanax, and Clomicalm, feeding the pills to Buster in a variety of doses and combinations. Even when they seemed to have some positive effect, it would last only a little while. Eventually, the violent behavior would return, worse than ever.

In September, we returned to New York. On the plane, the man in front of me tapped his headphones. Static? Up and down the aisle, people jiggled their headphones, wondering where the strange, ominous rumble came from. It came from under my seat, where a five-hour unilateral dogfight was taking place. At the airport, I put Buster's case on the floor while we waited for the luggage. Someone screamed. I looked back. The case was whirling across the floor, unguided, an eerie missile of snarling desperation.

There are a million or so dogs in New York City. About thirty of them live on our block on the Upper West Side of Manhattan. We have a laundromat, two dry cleaners, two churches, two dentists, a senior center, a Malaysian restaurant, a Korean market, a bakery, and a store that sells cheap leather jackets. A homeless man of regular habits lives in the doorway of the Lutheran church. He does not have a dog. But the gay men who live in the brownstone next door with their five children have two beagles. A woman down the block has a West Highland terrier, a retired champion, whom she took in when the dog's owner, a close friend, died suddenly, though she lives in one room and already had a shepherd mix named Tulip, after the heroine of J. R. Ackerley's obsessively brilliant *My Dog Tulip*. There is an Afghan and an Italian greyhound with legs as spindly as pipe cleaners whose owner rides a bicycle to work. There is a blind miniature schnauzer who wobbles down the sidewalk without leash or supervision until, from a doorway, his owner hollers "Henry!" and he totters home. There is a man who is in thrall to his young golden retriever; a three-legged yellow lab;

two handsome young men with a Brussels griffon puppy; a man who lives with his mother and three tiny scruffy mutts; and a heavily tattooed window washer with a racing bike whose shepherd mix just died. One woman who leans carefully on a cane and smiles beatifically from beneath pure-white hair gives gentle advice in a soft Irish brogue while Waldo, her Boston terrier, waits patiently, staring with his round bug eyes. And there is a woman with a warm and generous smile and a rich, cultured German accent who walks her aging Pekingese, Lord Byron, four times a day no matter how terrible the weather, a Holocaust survivor whose view of life is so beneficent I sometimes wait outside her building hoping she will materialize and provide wise counsel.

I don't know the names of all our neighbors, but I know the names of their dogs. I do not go out to dinner or to the movies with the neighbors, as I do with my friends. I don't make dates with them. I don't have to. I know I will see one or two or more of them every day. The dogs on the block gambol happily toward a puddle of urine to sniff and amplify, then sniff and be sniffed, twisting until their leashes are laced like ribbons on a Maypole. Towering above them in choking humidity or cutting wind or hushed snow, the owners say hello, comment on the humidity or the wind or the snow, discuss the latest catastrophe in the city, admire each other's animals, occasionally drop some highly personal remark about physical illness, a child, a parent, a divorce, nod sympathetically, and move on to scrape up a small, neat coil of excrement into an inside-out Fairway bag. New York City, on my block, is as small a town as Andy and Opie's Mayberry. And it was Buster who introduced me to its citizens, lunging at saintly old ladies, storming wheelchairs and strollers, his hair bristling and his teeth bared. Everyone knew him. Everyone had advice. But mostly, everyone had sympathy. When I saw Waldo or Lord Byron coming down the street, my heart beat faster and I felt tears of gratitude forming, for their owners, women who have seen hardship and evil, would reassure me that there was hope. With patience, they said softly, there was hope.

But Buster was not getting better. We contacted an animal behaviorist recommended to us by the New York Animal Hospital. He arrived with a Snoot Loop, a contraption he was marketing that was very similar to the better known Gentle Leader, a kind of bridle with a strap that tightens around the muzzle of a dog when he pulls. He charged us hundreds of dollars, the Snoot Loop cut into Buster's nose, leaving a bloody welt, and the issue of self-mutilation was not addressed. My girlfriend, Janet, and I, outcasts everywhere but our one little block, began to argue about what to do, how to train Buster, what to feed him, when to feed him. Exhausted, discouraged, we resorted to the wisdom of our forebears, smacking the dog with a rolled-up newspaper when he attacked himself or us. It was not effective.

One day, I took Buster to the dog run in Riverside Park near Eighty-second Street. We could let him loose there only when no other dogs were around. On this particular fall day, when the sky was a solemn gray and the leaves were dead on the ground around us, as brown as the dirt, I sat on a bench in the section reserved for small dogs and threw a hard red rubber ball for Buster. We had spent a disastrous Thanksgiving at my aunt's house in Massachusetts. Buster had come with us. Whom could we have left him with? We were assigned a bedroom, and a large sign was taped to our door warning anyone who dared to enter not to let the dog exit. The day we left, we walked out of the room, loaded down with our bags and with Buster on his leash. We had been vigilant and tense for three days and had been rewarded with a Thanksgiving free of bloodshed. There was a great flurry of relieved family hugs and kisses, my two-year-old nephew waddled bumpily toward us, squealing, Buster lunged for him, leaped back with a mouthful of soggy diaper, whimpered while my nephew wailed, and we skulked off in disgrace.

Now I sat on the park bench and watched Buster. My sister-in-law and brother were barely speaking to me. My mother thought I was disturbed. My nephew was terrified of dogs. Janet and I were squabbling. My children were disgusted. Buster chased the ball happily, brought it back, waited until I threw it again, and again, just like a normal, healthy dog. With his grinning face, one ear up and one flopped jauntily over his eye, his wriggling body and wagging tail, you would never know. That was one of the problems. People saw him and rushed over, cooing and crowing, hands stretched out to pet the adorable little dog. He would stiffen, growl, bare his teeth and lunge, all in a sickening second. When someone came within five feet, I would say something. At first, I struggled with the right wording. "He's unpredictable," I said. Or, "He's afraid of strangers." Sometimes, "He's aggressive." But all of these warnings seemed to leave an opportunity for people to test whether they might be the one special person he was not afraid of or aggressive toward, the unpredicted friend. Finally, I started saying, simply, "He bites."

"He bites," I said when a young woman came into the dog run with a bichon puppy, a cottony ball who bounced around her feet. Then I got up to leash Buster and take him away. But she put the bichon on her lap and told me not to worry about it. She was benevolent, awash with the joy of a merry new puppy. I thanked her. And then I felt it coming. I tried to stop myself, but I knew I was helpless. And, as I had done so many times before to so many unsuspecting strangers, I began to tell her the tale of Buster. I could hear the high note of panic, the rhythm of hysteria and desperation in my voice. I had heard something like it at playgrounds and bus stops from parents whose children threw sand or tantrums or took drugs or shoplifted or were flunking out of school. But the pitch, the speed of the chatter, the insistence on detail — I recognized that from somewhere else, from strangers approaching me on the street to tell me their life stories: from crazy people. I listened to myself and I heard a crazy woman.

Once again, a vet, this time our New York vet, told us to put the dog to sleep. "Your dog," said Dr. Raclyn, a holistic practitioner who does not give up easily, "is deeply disturbed." One evening when I brought Buster back into the building from his walk, I bumped into one of my neighbors, Virginia Hoffmann, a dog trainer. I blurted out that the dog was miserable, we were miserable, there was no hope. Virginia, who started out as an English teacher, became a trainer after having to deal with her own unhappy puppy. She had become more and more interested, more and more skilled, until one day she quit her day job. Here was someone, I thought, who could understand what we were going through. I asked her if she would help us. I wanted to give it one last try, to spend six months working seriously and consistently with Buster. He would never be sane, I recognized that. But maybe, just maybe, we could reduce the threshold of his suffering to make it bearable for him, and for us. Virginia took pity on us and agreed.

She wanted to help us, she said, to help Buster, and she would learn from the experience. But she was very clear about one thing. She offered no guarantees.

"I found a trainer for Buster," I said to my mother.

"Who? Clyde Beatty?"

Trim and neat, straightforward and calm, Virginia had a soothing effect on me. Perhaps she would on Buster, too. I had already considered another dog trainer who lived on the block. He had written several books and had a Catskill-comedian spiel that I found very engaging. His fee was so high that I tried one of his books first and discovered that his system required throwing things at your dog, to which approach Buster responded by attacking the suggested keys or wallet or paperback book that was launched at him and then cowering in confusion. Another dog trainer I once ran into on the East Side told me she knew just what to do: lift Buster by the back legs and whack him across the jaw hard enough so it rattled. Then she gave me her card and walked on. I gratefully turned to Virginia, with her soft, firm voice and endless sympathy. She came three or four times a week.

Janet was in L.A. a lot then, and my day was centered on the dog. I approached him with a glove attached to a wooden spoon, rewarding him when he didn't bite it. I used toys as a reward instead of food. I let him carry his toys in his mouth when we went outside, on the theory that he would be hard-pressed to bite with his mouth full. He learned the commands "touch" and "leave it." I taught him to go to his bed, to stay, to heel, to jump through a yellow hula hoop. Clyde Beatty, indeed. All of this training had a goal — to give the dog something better to think about than his own fear. To give him confidence. To give him a better sense of his own deformed body. And to give us authority and control. I learned how to break up each task into tiny parts. We tried to get him used to wearing a muzzle, which he hated and would trigger one of his fits, by leaving it on for seconds at a time and rewarding him with a squirt of Cheese Whiz. I wished I had employed Virginia to help in child rearing. For, in addition to training, she taught me not simply to impose or demand but to observe. Virginia suggested that I keep a journal, noting the frequency and intensity of Buster's fits: the details of his misery. Which side of himself did he attack? What might have provoked it? A noise? A touch? A smell? I timed the violent fits. I noted the weather, the time of the day, his position. How long since he'd eaten? Drunk? And then I made him come to me, or stay sitting as I walked away, or jump through a hoop. Buster was a wonderful pupil, smart and willing and obedient. He was an exceptionally well-trained mad dog.

I couldn't wait until Virginia arrived for a lesson. When she walked through the door, my real day began. She brought me articles from veterinary behavioral journals. She relayed relevant anecdotes from friends and colleagues. I loved meeting Buster's big, alert dark eyes and recognizing a quick, happy understanding. Buster bit Virginia on the first visit. I had my Buster kit of butterfly bandages and Neosporin handy. Though he seemed to sense that here was someone sent to help him, he could never tolerate more than about twenty minutes of work. So the rest of the time we went over the behavior charts like sailors checking the stars.

Janet and I began going out only to places where we could take Buster with us, eating at outdoor cafés in the rain and the bitter wind. But then Buster bit the waiter at Señor Swanky's, and we stopped. We resorted to placing a large plastic collar shaped like an ice cream cone around his neck when we left him alone. Used by vets to keep dogs from licking their wounds, the plastic cone worked more like blinkers for Buster: he was unable to see, much less bite, his hindquarters. One night, when I had brought Buster to my mother's house in Connecticut (tolerated out of motherly pity and because it was the only way she would get to see me), I put him in his collar and went to visit an old friend. Ten minutes later, my cell phone rang.

"I'm locked in my room with the door closed," my mother said. "Your dog is in the living room having a fit." She sounded terrified.

When I got home, the dog was a blur of foam and fur. I ended up wrapping him in a blanket, the only way I could get near him without being bitten, and holding him on my chest in bed for four hours, trying to soothe him while he panted and trembled. I held him and I cried.

We could no longer leave Buster in his Elizabethan collar. He had another episode that required the blanket wrapped around him, the hours of trembling and rolling eyes. Virginia pointed me to an experiment that had been done with autistic children in which they were wrapped tightly to help them regain awareness of their own bodies. She found an unlikely product called Anxiety Wrap, a suit for dogs, which worked on the same principle. She said that really the next step would be contacting a research veterinary school and handing Buster over for brain scans and further study. "Would you be doing that for his sake?" she asked. "Or your own? That's always the hard question."

It was a good question. Buster had become an intellectual puzzle, a challenge I could not let go of. He was my companion, certainly. The intensity of his need made the bond between us urgent and powerful. And I felt a responsibility, it was true. You cannot throw away an animal because he is sick. But there was also a little pool of vanity involved, and that insistent, stubborn optimism, a cultural trait, I suppose, that demands constant improvement. I would save this dog because, in a just world, I ought to be able to save him. It was a kind of humanitarian hubris. My dog was miserable. I insisted he get better.

We euthanized Buster eighteen months after we'd got him. We petted him as he stood on the vet's stainless-steel examining table. He wagged his tail and licked our hands. After giving him an IV dose of valium, Dr. Raclyn added sodium pentobarbitol. Buster turned on him with one last snarl, looked back at us, wagged his tail again, crumpled into our arms, and was gone.

It took six months before we had either the heart or the courage to do it, but we decided to get another dog, a puppy this time. We searched Internet rescue sites and visited the ASPCA, the city pound, and the North Shore Animal League. There were enormous, sad-eyed shepherd mixes and venerable poodle mixes and hopeful bull terrier mixes. Lab mixes leaped and whippet mixes shivered. We should have taken them all. We should have taken every puppy, too, although their fat, gigantic paws foretold their gigantic futures. What we couldn't find was a puppy who would stay small enough for our bicoastal commute. Sometimes we took Virginia with us to guide us, to protect us from falling under the spell of another charismatic but impossible dog. All the best, sweetest dogs we know are rescued dogs; nevertheless — a little guiltily, a little nervously — we drove to Frederick, Maryland, and picked up a tiny ten-week-old Cairn terrier. We named him Hector. A few months later, on the coldest morning of the coldest winter in decades, I took Hector to Central Park. There was smooth, slick snow on the ground. We made our way to Hearnshead Rock, a scenic jog of boulders rolling out into the lake. In spring, deep-yellow irises rise up there. In winter, the cove lets ducks and swans escape the wind. On this dark, achingly cold morning, the lake was almost completely frozen. The silver ice and the silver sky were cut in two by the skyline, and only in the crook of the rocks, where hundreds of ducks swam in circles, had the gray water been prevented from freezing. There were buffleheads and scoters and coots and even a wood duck. There was a great blue heron standing, not a foot from shore, as still as the black trees. The dog and I had been watching this tableau for twenty minutes or so when suddenly the heron shot his head into the shallow water, then snapped his neck back into its looping posture, a large fish dangling from his beak. He swallowed it. We watched the fish, a protrusion inching slowly down the bird's elegant throat, and then we walked home through silent woods, catching each other's eye now and then, checking in, companionable and intimate, sharing the exhilarating quiet. Hector, trotting beside me in the snow, was, like Buster, just a dog. And if, at that moment, I didn't know exactly how to explain why people want to own dogs, with all the inconvenience and heartache attached, I felt that here, at least, was a clue.

Hector prances along the street Buster skulked, greeting neighbors and strangers and men in hats and toddlers in snowsuits. He loves everyone, and everyone loves him. I often think of Buster, and it breaks my heart. People say, "You did everything you could." But did we? What about phenobarbital, even though every vet recommended against it? What about the autism suit? We should have moved to the country or sent him to the man in San Diego who leads a pack of dogs through the hills. What *about* the pet psychic? Then Hector pounces on an empty forty-ounce Budweiser can, almost as big as he is, and carries it proudly home. He kisses babies like a politician. He comes in peace.

DAVID SEDARIS

Old Faithful

FROM THE NEW YORKER

OUT OF NOWHERE I developed this lump. I think it was a cyst or a boil, one of those words you associate with trolls, and it was right on my tailbone, like a peach pit. That's what it felt like, anyway. I was afraid to look. At first it was just this insignificant knot, but as it grew larger it started to hurt. Sitting became difficult, and forget about lying on my back or bending over. By day five my tailbone was throbbing and I told myself, just as I had the day before, that if this kept up I was going to see a doctor. "I mean it," I said. I even went so far as to pull out the phone book and turn my back on it, hoping that the boil would know that I meant business and go away on its own. But of course it didn't.

All of this took place in London, which is cruelly, insanely expensive. My boyfriend, Hugh, and I went to the movies one night, and our tickets cost a total of forty dollars, this after spending sixty dollars on pizzas. And these were mini-pizzas, not much bigger than pancakes. Given the price of a simple evening out, I figured that a doctor's visit would cost about the same as a customized van. More than the money, though, I was afraid of the diagnosis. "Lower-back cancer," the doctor would say. "It looks like we'll have to remove your entire bottom."

Actually, this being England, he'd probably have said "bum," a word I have never really cottoned to. The sad thing is that they could remove my ass and most people wouldn't even notice. It's so insubstantial that the boil was actually an improvement, something like a bustle but filled with poison. The only real drawback was the pain.

For the first few days I kept my discomfort to myself, thinking all the while of what a good example I was setting. When Hugh feels bad, you hear about it immediately. A tiny splinter works itself into his palm and he claims to know exactly how Jesus must have felt on the cross. He demands sympathy for insect bites and paper cuts, while I have to lose at least a quart of blood before I get so much as a pat on the hand.

One time in France we were lucky enough to catch an identical stomach virus. It was a twenty-four-hour bug, the kind that completely empties you out and takes away your will to live. You'd get a glass of water, but that would involve standing, and so instead you just sort of stare toward the kitchen, hoping that maybe one of the pipes will burst and the water will come to you. We had the exact same symptoms, yet he insisted that his virus was much more powerful than mine. I suspected the same thing, so there we were, competing over who was the sickest.

"You can at least move your hands," he said.

"No," I told him, "it was the wind that moved them. I have no muscle control whatsoever."

"Liar."

"Well, that's a nice thing to say to someone who'll probably die during the night. Thanks a lot, pal."

At such times you have to wonder how things got to this point. You meet someone and fall in love, then thirteen years later you're lying on the floor in a foreign country, promising, hoping, as a matter of principle, that you'll be dead by sunrise. "I'll show you," I moaned, and then I must have fallen back to sleep.

When Hugh and I bicker over who is in the most pain, I think back to my first boyfriend, whom I met while I was in my late twenties. Something about our combination was rotten, and as a result we competed over everything, no matter how petty. When someone laughed at one of his jokes, I would need to make that person laugh harder. If I found something at a yard sale, he would have to find something better — and so on. My boyfriend's mother was a handful, and every year, just before Christmas, she would schedule a mammogram, knowing she would not get the results until after the holidays. The remote possibility of cancer was something to hang over her children's heads, just out of reach, like mistletoe, and she took great pleasure in arranging it. The family would gather and she'd tear up, saying, "I don't want to spoil your happiness, but this may well be our last Christmas together." Other times, if somebody had something going on — a wedding, a graduation — she'd go in for exploratory surgery, anything to capture and hold attention. By the time I finally met her, she did not have a single organ that had not been touched by human hands. "Oh, my God," I thought, watching her cry on our living room sofa, "my boyfriend's family is more fucked up than my own." I mean, this actually bothered me.

We were together for six years, and when we broke up I felt like a failure, a divorced person. I now had what the self-help books called relationship baggage, which I would carry around for the rest of my life. The trick was to meet someone with similar baggage, and form a matching set, but how would one go about finding such a person? Bars were out; I knew that much. I'd met my first boyfriend at a place called the Man Hole — not the sort of name that suggests fidelity. It was like meeting someone at Fisticuffs and then complaining when he turned out to be violent. To be fair, he had never actually promised to be monogamous. That was my idea, and I tried my hardest to convert him, but the allure of other people was just too great.

Almost all of the gay couples I knew at that time had some sort of an arrangement. Boyfriend A could sleep with someone else as long as he didn't bring him home — or as long as he *did* bring him home. And boyfriend B was free to do the same. It was a good setup for those who enjoyed variety and the thrill of the hunt, but to me it was just scary, and way too much work — like having one job while applying for another. One boyfriend was all I could handle, all I wanted to handle, really, and while I found this to be perfectly natural, my friends saw it as a form of repression and came to view me as something of a puritan. Am I? I wondered. But there were buckles to polish and stones to kneel upon, and so I put the question out of my mind.

I needed a boyfriend as conventional as I was, and luckily I found one — just met him one evening through a mutual friend. I was thirty-three and Hugh had just turned thirty. Like me, he had recently broken up with someone, and had moved to New York to start over. His former boyfriend had been a lot like mine, and we spent our first few weeks comparing notes. "Did he ever say he was going out for a hamburger and then —"

"— up with someone he'd met that afternoon on a bus? Yes!"

We had a few practical things in common as well, but what really brought Hugh and me together was our mutual fear of abandonment and group sex. It was a foundation, and we built on it, adding our fears of AIDS and pierced nipples, of commitment ceremonies and the loss of self-control. In dreams sometimes I'll discover a handsome stranger waiting in my hotel room. He's usually someone I've seen earlier that day, on the street or in a television commercial, and now he's naked and beckoning me toward the bed. I look at my key, convinced that I have the wrong room, and when he springs forward and reaches for my zipper I run for the door, which is inevitably made of snakes or hot tar, one of those maddening, hard-to-clean building materials so often used in dreams. The handle moves this way and that, and while struggling to grab it I stammer an explanation as to why I can't go through with this. "I have a boyfriend, see, and, well, the thing is that he'd kill me if he ever found out I'd been, you know, unfaithful or anything."

Really, though, it's not the fear of Hugh's punishment that stops me. I remember once riding in the car with my dad. I was twelve, and it was just the two of us, coming home from the bank. We'd been silent for blocks, when out of nowhere he turned to me and said, "I want you to know that I've never once cheated on your mother."

"Um. OK," I said. And then he turned on the radio and listened to a football game.

Years later, I mentioned this incident to a friend, who speculated that my father had said this specifically because he *had* been unfaithful. "That was a guilty conscience talking," she said, but I knew that she was wrong. More likely my father was having some problem at work and needed to remind himself that he was not completely worthless. It sounds like something you'd read on a movie poster, but sometimes the sins you haven't committed are all you have to hold on to. If you're really desperate, you might find yourself groping, saying, for example, "I've never killed anyone *with a hammer*" or "I've never stolen from anyone *who didn't deserve it.*" But whatever his faults, my dad did not have to stoop quite that low.

I have never cheated on a boyfriend, and, as with my father, it's become part of my idea of myself. In my foiled wet dreams I can glimpse at what my life would be like without my perfect record, of how lost I'd feel without this scrap of integrity, and the fear is enough to wake me up. Once I'm awake, though, I tend to lie there wondering if I've made a terrible mistake.

In books and movies infidelity always looks so compelling, so right. Here are people who defy petty convention and are rewarded with only the tastiest bits of human experience. Never do they grow old or suffer the crippling panic I feel whenever Hugh gets spontaneous and suggests we go to a restaurant.

"A restaurant? But what will we talk about?"

"I don't know," he'll say. "What does it matter?"

Alone together, I enjoy our companionable silence, but it creeps me out to sit in public, propped in our chairs like a pair of mummies. At a nearby table there's always a couple in their late seventies, blinking at their menus from behind thick glasses.

"Soup's a good thing," the wife will say, and the man will nod or grunt or fool with the stem of his wineglass. Eventually he'll look my way, and I'll catch in his eyes a look of grim recognition. "We are your future," he seems to say. "Get used to it."

I'm so afraid that Hugh and I won't have anything to talk about that now, before leaving home, I'll comb the papers and jot down a half dozen topics that might keep a conversation going at least through the entrées. The last time we ate out, I prepared by reading both the *Herald Tribune* and the *Animal Finders' Guide,* a publication devoted to exotic pets and the nuts who keep them. The waiter took our orders, and as he walked away I turned to Hugh, saying, "So, anyway, I hear that monkeys can really become surly once they reach breeding age."

"Well, I could have told you that," he said. "It happened with my own monkey."

I tried to draw him out, but it saddens Hugh to discuss his childhood monkey. "Oh, Maxwell," he'll sigh, and within a minute he'll have started crying. Next on my list were the five warning signs of depression among captive camels, but I couldn't read my handwriting, and the topic crashed and burned after sign number two: an unwillingness to cush. At a nearby table an elderly woman arranged and rearranged the napkin in her lap. Her husband stared at a potted plant, and I resorted to the *Herald Tribune.* "Did you hear about those three Indian women who were burned as witches?"

"What?"

"Neighbors accused them of casting spells and burned them alive."

"Well, that's horrible," he said, slightly accusatory, as if I myself had had a hand in it. "You can't go around burning people alive, not in this day and age."

"I know it, but —"

"It's sick is what it is. I remember once when I was living in Somalia there was this woman . . ."

"Yes!" I whispered, and then I looked over at the elderly couple, thinking, "See, we're talking about witch burnings!" It's work, though, and it's always *my* work. If left up to Hugh, we'd just sit there acting like what we are: two people so familiar with one another they could scream. Sometimes, when I find it hard to sleep, I'll think of when we first met, of the newness of each other's body, and my impatience to know everything about this person. Looking back, I should have taken it more slowly, measured him out over the course of fifty years rather than cramming him in so quickly. By the end of our first month together, he'd been so thoroughly interrogated that all I had left was breaking news — what little had happened in the few hours since I'd last seen him. Were he a cop or an emergency room doctor, there might have been a lot to catch up on, but like me Hugh works alone, so there was never much to report. "I ate some potato chips," he might say, to which I'd reply, "What kind?" or "That's funny, so did I!" More often than not we'd just breathe into our separate receivers.

"Are you still there?"

"I'm here."

"Good. Don't hang up."

"I won't."

In New York we slept on a futon. I took the left side and would lie awake at night, looking at the closet door. In Paris we got a real bed in a room just big enough to contain it. Hugh would fall asleep immediately, the way he's always done, and I'd stare at the blank wall, wondering about all the people who had slept in this room before us. The building dated from the seventeenth century, and I envisioned musketeers in tall, soft boots, pleasuring the sorts of women who wouldn't complain when sword tips tore the sheets. I saw gentlemen in top hats and sleeping caps, women in bonnets and berets and beaded headbands, a swarm of phantom copulators all looking down and comparing my life with theirs.

After Paris came London, and a bedroom on the sixth floor with windows looking onto neat rows of Edwardian chimney tops. A friend characterized it as "a Peter Pan view," and now I can't see it any other way. I lie awake thinking of someone with a hook for a hand, and then, inevitably, of youth and whether I have wasted it. Twenty-five years ago I was twenty-two, a young man with his whole sexual life ahead of him. How had 9,125 relatively uneventful days passed so quickly, and how might I slow the days ahead? In another twenty-five years I'll be seventy-two, and twenty-five years after that I'll be one of the figures haunting my Paris bedroom. Is it morally permissible, I wonder, to cheat after death? Is it even called cheating at that point? What are the rules? Do I have to wait a certain amount of time, or can I just jump or, as the case may be, seep right in?

During the period that I had my boil, these questions seemed particularly relevant. The pain was always greater after dark, and by the sixth night I was fairly certain that I was dying. Hugh had gone to sleep hours earlier, and it startled me to hear his voice. "What do you say we lance that thing?" he said.

It's the sort of question that takes you off guard. "Did you just use the verb 'to lance'?" I asked.

He turned on the lights.

"Since when did you learn to lance boils?"

"I didn't," he said. "But I bet I could teach myself."

With anyone else I'd put up a fight, but Hugh can do just about anything he sets his mind to. This is a person who welded the plumbing pipes at his house in Normandy, then went into the cellar to make his own cheese. There's no one I trust more than him, and so I limped to the bathroom, that theater of home surgery, where I lowered my pajama bottoms and braced myself against the towel rack, waiting as he sterilized the needle.

"This is hurting me a lot more than it's hurting you," he said. It was his standard line, but I knew that this time he was right. Worse than the boil was the stuff that came out of it. What got to me, and got to him even worse, was the stench, which was unbearable and unlike anything I had come across before. It was, I thought, what evil must smell like — not an evil person but the wicked ideas that have made him that way. How could a person continue to live with something so rotten inside? And so much of it! "How are you doing back there?" I asked, but he was dry-heaving and couldn't answer.

When my boil was empty, he doused it with alcohol and put a bandage on it, as if it had been a minor injury, a shaving cut, a skinned knee, something normal he hadn't milked like a dead cow. And this, to me, was worth at least a hundred of the hundred and twenty nights of Sodom. Back in bed I referred to him as Sir Lance-a-Lot.

"Once is not a lot," he said.

This was true, but Sir Lance Occasionally lacks a certain ring. "Besides," I said, "I know you'll do it again if I need you to. We're an elderly monogamous couple, and this is all part of the bargain."

The thought of this kept Hugh awake that night, and still does. We go to bed and he stares toward the window as I sleep soundly beside him, my bandaged boil silently weeping onto the sheets.

PAULA SPECK

Six Seconds

FROM MERIDIAN

A FEW DAYS AFTER September 11, 2001, newspapers carried an interview with the wife of a passenger who died on the flight that lifted out of Boston for Los Angeles and, fifty-one minutes later, slammed into the World Trade Center. Her husband's business, she said, had led him to take this flight regularly, once or twice a month. His routine was to rise early, drive to the airport, check in, take his seat, and promptly fall asleep until nearing his destination. That day, his destination was a fireball ninety stories above lower Manhattan. The grieving wife told reporters: "I hope that's what he did on September 11. I hope he just went to sleep and never realized what happened."

Reading this story, I found myself remembering the day nearly two decades earlier when I had to put a price on the last six seconds of the lives of two airplane passengers.

On July 9, 1982, a Pan Am jet carrying 154 passengers and crew clipped a tree just after takeoff from New Orleans International Airport and smashed into the runway. Everyone on board died. Four to six seconds passed between the moment the plane struck the tree and the instant the pilot's desperate efforts to bring the nose up ended on the hard tarmac. In 1986, a jury decided that the children of two of the passengers should receive $20,000 for the mental anguish each of their parents felt during those last four to six seconds. In 1988, the airline appealed this award.

The appeal landed in my inbox. The judge I worked for wanted me to go over the figure the jury had arrived at. He needed a reason to dissent or concur in a draft opinion that was circulating.

In a professional sense, this was a routine assignment. To start with, I had the jury's verdict. And the strong reluctance — going back to medieval English law — to revisit the hard questions the jury had decided. No judge was supposed to fiddle with the jury's numbers unless, as one opinion I read put it, they fell outside "the universe of possible awards" that a "reasonable jury" could assign. So my task settled into a straightforward research job: all I had to do was find every case in the last twenty years or so in which a jury had priced last-minute mental fear and anguish, compare that amount with the one assigned here, and report to my judge whether this jury's number fell within that range.

I set to work. Conveniently, a legal indexing system had a com-puter-searchable category for what I was looking for: "Death," sub-category number 77, "Preimpact Pain and Suffering."

A lawyer doesn't read cases the way he or she reads a novel or a newspaper article. If reading a novel is a stroll along a winding path through a meadow, reading a case is the circling of a hawk hundreds of feet above that meadow, interrupted by a downward swoop to snatch at the barely perceptible scurry of a field mouse. Focused on one question — what is the range of damages that may be awarded for an air crash victim's preimpact pain and suffer-ing? — I skimmed over discussions of weather conditions, control-tower negligence, pilot drug use, mechanical failures, future earn-ings. Not my concern whether the judge should have allowed the jury to read a wind-shear expert's report, whether a nephew could win damages for the loss of an aunt under Illinois law, how much money a medical student would have made over the course of a lopped-off career — or how much to subtract for the cost of fin-ishing medical school and buying stethoscopes and eye charts. But despite my narrow lens, despite the deliberate impersonality of the opinion writers' language, details from one opinion, and then an-other, broke through:

The woman's body found with every inch of its skin charred by the fire that swept the cabin, but with internal organs and bones intact; this showed she did not die when the plane hit the runway, but survived for several seconds afterward. The two minutes a pilot spent desperately trying to right a bucking plane after a wing clipped a baggage truck, while the passengers rattled like dice in a cup. The businessman sucked out of a hole punched in the plane's skin by a bomb, dropping for three conscious seconds to the ground. The elderly couple who sat in the back of the vintage plane they had rented for a wedding-anniversary flight over the Caribbean, listening while their pilot (who, it seemed, had misread the gas gauge) desperately radioed for an airport within gliding distance. The helpless ground witnesses who heard screams coming from inside a burning fuselage.

And, because judges will hunt out analogies when they can't find enough cases directly "on point": the oil worker who put his foot on empty air near the top of an offshore oil platform and took a long two seconds to descend to the platform's deck. The woman struck by a train who bled to death for seventeen minutes on the tracks while a panicked stationmaster tried to get an ambulance. The crewmen seen through fog clinging for long minutes to the upturned hulk of their wrecked ship.

I read only the passage in each case that described the victims' last moments. When I learned how the judge and jury dealt with damages in that case, I moved on to the next. One anecdote of terror and delayed death trod on the heels of another. Suddenly it was too much. I had to break off research and find an errand that would take me out of the office.

Returning to my notes, I realized that in order to make comparisons among cases, I'd have to convert the damages I found into per-second figures. Luckily, the figures slotted into a rough chart:

$138.89 per second (twelve minutes for $100,000)
$208 per second (two minutes for $25,000)
$333.34 per second (thirty seconds for $10,000)
$833 per second (six seconds for $5,000)
$1,250 per second (six seconds for $7,500)
$2,500 per second (six seconds for $15,000)
$5,000 per second (two seconds for $10,000)
$7,955 per second (eleven seconds for $87,500)
$10,625 per second (eight seconds for $85,000)
$15,000 per second ("death was almost instantaneous")

All right, I thought, let's assume that the two passengers in the case I was working on had each lived six seconds, the longest time possible. If so, the jury had priced their fear at $3,334 per second. Since this was within the range that other juries had awarded —

and there was no other objection to that part of the verdict — my job was done. I summarized the research and explained my conclusion to the judge. He sent in his concurrence. I moved on to another assignment.

Everyone working on this case — the lawyers, the judges, myself — assumed that the unlucky couple who died on the runway in New Orleans had been wronged when they were forced to stare at their own deaths for six seconds, more wronged than if they had died without warning. But it could have been otherwise.

In the Middle Ages, books on the *ars moriendi* — the art of dying — instructed the faithful on how to achieve a "good death" and exhorted them to imagine their own deaths in detail as a spur to resist sin and practice for the always-too-soon. Holbein, Dürer, and dozens of lesser-known artists painted "Dances of Death," showing Death prancing bawdily through palaces and marketplaces. Hamlet was almost as angry with his uncle for killing his father during an afternoon nap — "grossly, full of bread; with all his crimes broad blown, as flush as May" — as for the murder itself. That's why Hamlet let pass the opportunity to kill Claudius at prayer; such a death would be too good for him.

The Victorians carefully photographed dead children nested like wax dolls in satin-lined coffins and displayed the pictures in their parlors. Thousands rushed newsstands to buy the last installment of *The Old Curiosity Shop* and join worldwide weeping over the drawn-out final minutes of Dickens's Little Nell. A man's last seconds gave him a chance to apologize to God, to reconcile with loved ones, to balance a life's books.

Even the law grants special status to last moments. Evidently codes recognize an exception to the hearsay rule for a "dying declaration." It's a strangely medieval provision. If Hamlet tells Horatio, "It was Claudius who poisoned the King," and then gallops off to Heidelberg, Horatio cannot testify about Hamlet's statement in court. That would be hearsay. But Horatio can repeat Hamlet's same speech in court if it's a dying declaration, panted out as Hamlet expires in Horatio's arms from the thrust of that poisoned sword tip in the fifth act. The official commentary to the rule in the federal code notes coyly that "the original religious justification for the exception"–no man wants to meet his Creator with a lie on his lips — "may have lost its conviction for some persons over the years." But, the commentary continues, "it can scarcely be doubted that powerful psychological pressures are present."

What exactly are those "powerful psychological pressures"? Do we still believe that people who are about to die are less likely to lie than the rest of us? Do we want to hope that they stand on the threshold of a realm of eternal truth above the sphere of lies and deceit where the rest of us live?

And why, then, is it an injury — compensated in countable cash — for an airline passenger to be forced to watch (and, yes, feel) the last seconds of his life hurtle into the past? Whereas a medieval man might have been grateful for the chance to pray, and a Victorian might have choked out a last word for his family, we sue.

An easy answer, and not necessarily a false one, is that we live in the final triumph of the market economy and that everything, including fear of death, has a price in such an economy. We are materialist to our core, buying and selling our last breaths and heartbeats.

Or perhaps we're just humble. Medieval man thought he could ingratiate himself with the power that rules the universe if he said the right words and thought the right thoughts for a few minutes at the end of his life. Nineteenth-century man thought he could fix lifelong hatreds and misunderstandings with heartfelt words and hands clasped across death-sweated sheets.

We have lower hopes, more reasonable goals. A life's mistakes can't be set right in a few moments, we tell ourselves. But money is undoubtedly useful to a family that has lost a father, a daughter, a brother, a wife. With money, they can pay for therapists, college tuition, fresh flowers in the dining room. Salvation or reconciliation are not in our power to give. We can, however, give $3,334 a second. And so we do.

I have given up trying to decide whether the society I live and earn my living in is wise or shallow in its approach to death. I have only tentative conclusions, subject to revision and applicable only to myself. One is that I'd like to look my death in the face when and however it comes. If I get my wish, I hope my family won't ask to be paid for it. Although I'd prefer to postpone the meeting.

BERT O. STATES

Skill Display in Birding Groups

FROM THE NORTH AMERICAN REVIEW

The adder hisses where the sweet birds sing.
— Shakespeare

BENEATH ITS INNOCENT PLUMAGE, birding is a highly competitive sport. As a small proof of the point, think of an offhand remark to be found in the classic essay of the great Norwegian biologist Thorlief Heilberg, "Despotism in the Pecking Order of Petrels" (1973): "And when the food supply is low, they bicker flamboyantly over the least crumb. Indeed, they are worse than their human counterparts, the birdwatchers whose quarreling over the nomenclature of a bird often drives the birds from the forest." Even Stephen Potter, in his brief treatment of bird gamesmanship in 1951, was moved to remark, "I have said enough I hope to show that Birdsmen [i.e., birders] are natural Lifemen" — meaning, of course, that they are masters of one-upmanship, at times mercilessly adept at turning bird identification into a cruel, if oblique, kind of warfare. It takes a reasonably alert visitor accompanying a group of seasoned birders into the field for the first time less than a morning to discover that there is more to birding than the birds that meet the eye. To put it bluntly, the best side of our species is often eclipsed in the subtle, and not so subtle, give-and-take of skill display.

We start from the premise that the best possible event that can happen in the field is that you find and identify the bird for the group, and the rarer or more unexpected the bird, the higher the achievement. (Thus each night birders say to their pillows: "Per-

haps I will be the one to identify a Golden-Winged Warbler tomorrow.") The next best thing is to reidentify a bird sighted by someone else, who has misidentified it or just doesn't know what it is.
The next-to-least best moment is to see a bird found and identified
by someone else; the very worst thing is to misidentify a bird
roundly and be corrected by someone else, or by several people
crying "Wrong! Wrong!" in unison. Finally, it is simply embarrassing not to be able to locate a bird that has been found and identified by someone else and shared by the entire party. This is one of
birding's most maddening situations, and nothing can be done
about it. The truth is that fifty percent of a typical birding morning
(by Heilberg's calculation at least) is spent making sure that everyone in the party has seen each "find" (defined as an infrequent to
rare bird). More often than not the exasperation is tempered by
something very like a mourning for the person who, for whatever
reason, has failed to see the bird. Such an episode would create
strong suspicions that you were losing your touch (assuming you
had the touch) or your eyesight; several in a row would virtually
disqualify you, and you would shortly find yourself being edged to
the fringe of the group, among the Lesser to Least Birders, somewhat as the runt of a clutch of nestlings is eventually pushed overboard and eaten by its natural prey in the grass. Indeed, rather
than risk a complete loss of face, it would be far better, in such a
case, simply to *fake* seeing the bird:

You: "Ah, yes. Silly of me. I was looking to the left of the whorl."
And then you might add something like: "You know, its markings
seem a little odd. Perhaps it's a juvenile" — anything to get past
the moment and show that you were still able to carry out routine
discriminations.

One of the most famous stories circulating through the birding
world involves just such a case of misidentification, and it would be
irresponsible not to include it here before turning to some com-
moner forms of skill display as practiced by normal birders. In fact,
this anecdote is to birding history what the Wrong Way Corrigan
episode is to the history of aviation. The version I know was told to
me by a student of the great ornithologist Pedersen ("Pistol Pete")
Anscombe, whose reputation scarcely requires an introduction for
the serious birder. He is the author of more than seventy articles
on avian ecology and precocial development. The eminent behav-

iorist Wesley Sutpen was once moved to say of him, "If it flies, Anscombe will have it in his sights" — as we shall soon see, not an altogether flattering remark. Anscombe is also known far and wide as the Woody Hayes of ornithology, and stories of his fury toward incompetent student identifications are legion. To add to the intimidating effect Anscombe made on simply appearing, he was a tensile man, over six feet tall, with a pencil-thin mustache curled at the tips, a fast-shifting eye, and the look of a riverboat gambler. You would swear he had done time in prison.

One afternoon Anscombe was birding in the Gainesville, Florida, area with two advanced graduate students from his ornithology program. One of them happened to sight what seemed to him an unusual bird. Could it, the student wondered, possibly be a . . . ? Surely not! Still, after further scrutiny he was compelled to identify the bird as a Brown-crested Flycatcher. However, feeling some hesitation about the identification — since the Brown-crested was supposed, by all odds, to be wintering in Mexico at that time of year — he sought a second opinion from a fellow student before taking the news to Anscombe, who was birding just ahead. The friend examined the find, sighed mournfully (realizing they were in trouble, given Anscombe's probable reaction), and finally, tossed between elation and outright fear, concurred. What gave it away as a Brown, as opposed to a Great-crested, with which it is nearly identical, was the paleness of the throat and breast, or so it seemed at this distance. Or was it a trick of the sunlight? Still, it seemed inescapable. So, courageously, they took the news to Anscombe, who of course was in total control of their personal funding as teaching assistants. As expected, Anscombe immediately pronounced them as crazy as kiwis. Yet they persisted politely, and Anscombe had no choice (since there were two of them, and the rule was that verification by two sighters could not be summarily overruled by "the master") but to have a look for himself. Fortunately, the bird was still in the tree as Anscombe lifted the glasses that had gazed upon more than seven thousand life birds from Alaska to Tierra del Fuego, and, after some pause, he coolly announced that they (his students) had plainly fallen off their perch: it was, without the least doubt, a Great-crested, the only flycatcher indigenous to the area in the winter. "All Browns," Anscombe said flatly, "are in Mexico in December if they have any sense." But the young birders politely demurred, egged on perhaps by a certain ambiguity in Anscombe's normally explosive demeanor, and they pointed out, again, the distinctive features that Anscombe either chose to ignore or simply couldn't see. Then too, they had waded into the minefield so far that they had nothing more to lose.

"All right. There's only one way to settle it, then," Anscombe said.

Striding to his car (parked nearby), he opened the trunk and brought out a .22 rifle. Taking careful aim, he popped the bird off its limb, and it dropped to the ground with a dull *thut.* Anscombe strode to the bird, picked it up, and examined it while the students awaited their fate. After an interval Anscombe put on his glasses and looked at the bird further. There was a long silence, then his cheek twitched, his scope eye fluttered, his face went completely white, and in the low husky voice of someone who has just discovered he has six weeks to live, he said, "Christ in Cincinnati!" Then he walked slowly back to the students and, under his breath, said, "Good work."

"Is it a Brown?" one of the students asked, ever so politely.

"It is a Brown," Anscombe said flatly. "I was — wrong. You were right."

It so happens that this incident took place on the same day that Barton Sloane, one of Anscombe's lifelong friends and rivals (all of Anscombe's friends were also his rivals), was in Gainesville and scheduled to have dinner at Anscombe's home. Sloane himself was no piker in the bird world. He was the noted author of two pioneering monographs, *Migratory Restlessness in the Indigo Bunting* and *Egg Dumping in the Female Goldeneye;* moreover, he is credited with the identification of at least three new species (among them, Sloane's Goose). Anscombe loved few things better than a prank, and he was still smarting from the morning episode. Following dinner, over cigars and brandy, Anscombe recounted the day's field trip, beginning in the ultra-casual tone of not-much-really-went-on. Suddenly he appeared to come alert and said, "Oh, I almost forgot. We *did* have a piece of luck today. We got a Brown-crested."

"A Brown-crested what?" Sloane asked, releasing a plume of smoke at the ceiling.

"Why, a Brown-crested Flycatcher."

"Heh heh, that's very good," Sloane muttered.

"You don't believe me?"

Sloane looked vaguely into his brandy. "Anscombe, you old coot. You don't even *expect* me to believe it. There are no Browns here in December."

"Exactly," Anscombe said. "It was an accidental."

"Ha! Get off it. Accidental."

"I tell you. I . . . saw . . . it."

"You're losing it, Pete. You're going daft in that lab of yours." A long pause. "You need more field work."

"I'm certain I saw it."

"Well," Sloane sighed, swirling his glass. "We'll never know, will we?"

This was Anscombe's big moment. He rose, strode into the kitchen, opened the freezer, and withdrew a small plastic bag. This he brought to the table and dropped with a ceremonious clunk onto Sloan's greasy plate. "Here is the *corpus delicti,* and the smoking gun is in my car trunk. Case closed!"

Sloane, sensing, as it were, that his goose was about to be cooked, put on his spectacles and with trembling hands undid the metal twister on the bag as Anscombe chuckled maliciously over his shoulder.

Crass, unfeeling, you will say. But recall that Alexander Wilson (1766–1813), the father of American ornithology, to whom we owe so much of our early taxonomy (Wilson's Warbler, Wilson's Plover, Wilson's Thrush, Wilson's Phalarope), literally shot his way into bird fame with a fowling piece. As Wilson sacrificed his life to bring order to the bird kingdom, so each species sacrificed one of its kind (at least!) so that Wilson's pencil and brush might record its characteristics in accurate detail. Then, of course, there is the case of Audubon himself, whom the American poet Robert Penn Warren referred to as "the greatest slayer of birds that ever lived." When it comes to birds, the old adage is, alas, still infallibly true: a bird in the hand is worth a whole flock in the bush.

Obviously, not all birders become as drastically involved in the drama of skill display as the Anscombes of the world. Still, there is little doubt that one of the great attractions of birding is that it offers an almost unique opportunity to display one's prowess as a devotee of a subtle craft. Consider the difficulties: the world is filled with birds of all sizes, from the California Condor to the Mexican Bumblebee Hummingbird, between eight and nine thousand different species whose genera, families, orders, classes, and phyla are, in many cases, discriminated from one another by marks as slight as the length of an eyelash. Moreover, the problem is further complicated by the fact that immature birds look nothing like their parents, but frequently resemble either the male or female of still another family. The situation is so difficult that identification is a pure judgment call, especially in the fall of the year. "In the fall," as Travis Quay once put it, "you just give up and go fishing." Finally, birds do not stay put, like wildflowers, trees, or (relatively speaking) butterflies, but fall into additional categories such as Common, Local, Casual, Vagrant, and Visitor, each of which further complicates the task. There is no lingering over the identification process, no netting or chloroforming the bird while you debate its characteristics (Anscombe's fowling piece notwithstanding). Most sightings last under twenty seconds, often far less, and the bird is constantly on the move, either flitting in and out of dense foliage or streaking through the sky. So getting your bird is more often than not a matter of bringing all your training and memory of birds into sharp, instantaneous focus. And this is one of the great lures and challenges of birding.

In the following observations, I make no claim to having exhausted the strategies of birder competition. We are, after all, an endlessly inventive species. I have simply taken from my field notes instances that demonstrate the range and typicality of certain verbal and postural practices that occur on the scale between, say, Envy and Revenge. Let it be said again: *all birders are not of this sort; most are not, some are;* but it may not be exaggerating the case to say that all birders — like all people — indulge in such stratagems at least *some* of the time in this world where ego and security are constantly compromised by the achievements of others.

Compromising Another's Find

Suppose A has found and identified a comparatively rare species of warbler. As a bystander, perhaps even one who should have made the identification, B is — well, let us admit it — envious. How does

B maintain at least some of his/her skill status when someone else has "scored" first? Assuming B recognizes the species as correctly identified:

B: *(raising his/her glasses to the eyes)* Good work! And there is the telltale marking! *(wing bar, bill color, eye liner, etc.)*

This is really a tepid way of getting your oar into the stream, though it does reduce B's deficiency simply to not having seen the bird as fast as A has seen it, a misfortune one could score entirely to the luck of one's field position. So B might want to try a subtler, if riskier, version (not to be used within earshot of Greater Birders):

B: Ah! And so it is. You'll usually find them in places like this.
A: What do you mean?
B: Near a whorl in the trunk. They fare better with insects there. They prefer a particular kind of mealworm that feeds on the whorls.
A: Ah. I didn't know that.

This tactic is technically referred to as Trumping the Find, and there are almost as many variations and degrees of trumping aggressiveness as there are bird species. For example, on A's sighting a Coues's Flycatcher:

B: Very good! And of course the crest gives it away. Now if we could only get it to give its *ho-say mari-a* song.

Or:

B: If it weren't June, I'd be skeptical, but . . . it *is* June.

Both of these options, of course, give B a certain intellectual edge in bird knowledge, and if carried out properly may even suggest that A was actually damned lucky in getting the bird before B saw it. And finally, the Fail-Safe Position:

B: I *thought* I heard a Coues's back there. And there it is. I was right.
Well, good for you, Sarah. It's your bird now.

Obviously, it *isn't* actually Sarah's bird now: it belongs to both of them. B hasn't given it to Sarah, he/she lent it through an act of generosity (B saw, or heard, it *first*) that will be noted as such by anyone within earshot, even though Sarah gets official credit.

Or as a safe and even subtler variant: "Ah! So it's *still* here."

Which suggests, of course, that you've already seen the bird and, presumably (there being nobody around to confirm it), have gone on to other pursuits.

Bird Lore to the Rescue

Trumping the Find is an especially versatile tactic if you do a little pre-trail reading about such background topics as mating practices, foot and toe differences, food gathering, clutch size, maintenance behavior, bill clattering, nest furnishing, and the like. The list is endless, and the truth is that most birders *do not read about birds* unless they are also naturalists, and naturalists do not regularly mix with plain birders, any more than warblers mix with crows. So a little extra knowledge can go a long way. Such information must be slipped in casually and relevantly, and *not overdone*. Think of the usefulness, for instance, of B's knowing Ashmole's hypothesis concerning the size of clutches should someone innocently wonder how many eggs a bird lays, or knowing that it is the extreme versatility of the shoulder joints that makes it possible for hummingbirds literally to stand still in midair, or that Whitethroated Swifts are one of the few birds that copulate on the wing. Think, finally, what a brilliant trump it might be if B had occasion to mention that female raptors are typically larger than males, *which is not the case with most bird groups*. B wouldn't simply blurt out that fact but would weave it delicately into the identification process, as a bird weaves glitter into its nest. Something like this:

B: That's the thing about telling the sexes of raptors. For most other birds, the males are larger than the females.
A: *(who hasn't thought about this)* Oh? Not so with raptors?
C: *(standing nearby)* Why is that?
B: Well, there are various theories. The most accepted one seems to be that the added size allows the female to avoid wife abuse.

B might then trump his own trump: "Of course, I'm very rusty on the actual size differential, or what they call sexual dimorphism." Even this, however, is flirting with pretentiousness if not offered with the right degree of self-deprecation.

Newton Tabori's Dialect Gambit

Few have perfected the trumping gambit of the odd fact better than Newton Tabori, an Idaho birder with extremely slender credits otherwise. Tabori would not simply refer to "birdsong" but to "dialect," the assumption being that the word "song" was much too sloppy to be of any use to the discriminating ear. And although he didn't know very much *about* bird dialect (or bird*song*, for that matter) and had no ear for it himself, he had perfected a way of using the word — along with such relevant backup vocabulary as "natal territory," "genetic vocal marks," "positive mating promotion," "vowel-to-consonant ratio," and so on — that he could convince you he knew a great deal more than was meeting your ear, when in fact he knew far less. For example, on hearing the song of a Say's Phoebe — or whatever bird one could virtually count on seeing on the day's trip — Tabori might break the group's silence, while all were regarding it through glasses, with something like: "I've just timed the interval between variations. That's a more complex rendition than we usually hear. Did anyone else notice?" Or: "Somehow that dialect sounds odd. Do you notice? It's a shade lower today. I wonder — hmm, could it be foreign? No, surely not." Note particularly the deferential use of "Did anyone else notice?" which gives Tabori's highly aggressive move an aspect of self-doubt and willingness to be "corrected" by fellow birders. Of course, Tabori had read up on the Say's only that morning, but he was circumspect enough to deliver the thought as if it were just occurring to him. Moreover, he never made such comments in the presence of a really good birder, for obvious reasons. In fact, his gambit had a risky side. Eventually people began to assume that he was a dialect specialist, or at least knew more about the topic than the rest of the group, and they began addressing questions to him relating to birdsong for which he had no advance opportunity to prepare. Here, too, he was not without skill. Tabori would simply jut out his lower lip, look off thoughtfully into what seemed to be a vast encyclopedic memory, and say: "Yes and no. It could go either way, depending on gender or age — and species, naturally. For juvenile warblers, no; for adults, yes — most of the time. We know so little." And most of the time he managed to escape safely, like a tomato seed squirting from under the finger of definition.

Countering a Mistaken Identification

Suppose B has mistakenly identified as a Tennessee Warbler a bird that turns out to be something quite different, and C, B's companion, calls B on it.

c: I . . . *think* that's a Warbling Vireo.
b: Oh?
c: Look at the bill.

This is perhaps the most humiliating moment a birder can experience; it is to birding what misidentifying a malignant limb might be to a surgeon who has just performed an amputation. There is no completely successful response. You simply live with the error and try to get on as best you can. You can only make an attempt to cut your losses by some remark that might not impinge on your overall skill. A pitifully weak response might be something like —

b: Damn! I cannot get these glasses to *work* this morning!

— followed by a general posture of despair, together with some fussing with the glasses (wiping the lens, etc.); and, moreover, continuing to fuss with them throughout the morning in C's presence.

Or, in the same vein, B might allow his/her shoulders to sag dramatically, turn and walk away three steps, then turn back and say, to no one in particular, "Where is my eyesight? I swear I'm blind!" This is somewhat better if masterfully enacted and carried off with enough intensity of self-concern to at least divert the focus from your skill as a birder, much as the killdeer leads foes away from its nest. Again, as always, subtlety is the key: in the business of both Trumping and Countering, ostentation is the kiss of disgrace.

A much better response, however, might be to put the blame squarely where it belongs. Thus a sudden bolt of candor, correctly framed, might actually rescue B's reputation by putting it in a halo of his/her humility:

b: *(a shocked pause)* I have no excuse for that one. None.
c: Oh, now, come on. It's just a bird.
b: No. I'm embarrassed. That's not like me. I'm not myself today.
c: No. It's a common . . .
b: I — well, the less said the better.

It goes without saying that this will work only once. Two times, and C is likely to think that this not only *is* like B, but that B's humility was little more than a distraction display.

Being Skeptical of Someone Else's Find

If you're very sure that A has misidentified a find, there is no problem, and it is only a matter of how you point out the error. However, there are various ways of doing this, depending on one's relationship to A and one's mood. A simple and benevolent response might be something like: "I see why you might think it is a Coues's [Flycatcher]. The head and bill *are* similar, but don't you think the breast is more like the Olive-sided? Hmm. Well, maybe, but — ." A less delicate response might be: "Well, you've got the right genus. It is a *Contopus,* all right, but I'm afraid the mandible gives it away. It's a pewee." And finally the real putdown, reserved only for unsubtle rivalries and bitchy moods: "If that's a Coues's I'm a Black-whiskered Vireo. I've never seen a Coues's sit down like *that.* Have you?" (turning to a companion — not A).

A skeptical variation of the Tabori gambit — really more of a simple ploy than a gambit — is especially adaptable to a two-birder situation, and especially two birders who are not close friends but more like rivals. If A and B happen to be birding away from the group, and A finds and identifies a warbler correctly, B might gain a small advantage, or at least a soupçon of dignity, by remaining silent after the call, then exhaling almost (but not quite) inaudibly or emitting a low guttural sound suggesting doubt or polite reserve. This must be done very unaggressively, with a trace of open-mindedness accompanying the sound. And A will probably react with something like:

A: You don't agree?
B: *(another sound escapes)* Well . . .
A: I mean, it certainly has the Black-throat's streaky crown, right?
B: *(pauses, puts glasses at rest position, looks at bird, perhaps tilting head, then takes a step away)* It's close enough.

On Finding a Bird of Your Own

Finding a bird of your own, of course, is the moment for which all birders live. It is the equivalent of the eagle in golf, the fifty-yard touchdown in football, and the million-dollar home sale in real estate. So fortune has given you the reward of actually sighting a bird that, if not rare in these parts, is at least unusual, and not yet sighted on this particular outing. The question is how to announce the find in such a manner that you will receive maximum credit. All the finesse of the master birder is called for in this situation. And, as usual, there are several options.

One is the Melrose gambit, so called because it was practiced to perfection by Melissa (the Dowacher) Melrose, the great Australian birder whose edition of *Eighteenth-Century Bird Calls in the Midlands* is by now the classic of its genre. Melrose is said to have learned the technique on safari with Sidney Putnam, the infamous African guide, later her lover and the source of a scandalous affair (and three little Melroses). The technique is simple but unimprovable. When you have identified the bird *beyond all possible doubt,* you simply raise your arm slowly and point at the tree or bush without comment, much as Clint Eastwood might, at most looking back over your shoulder at the group, if the group happens to be several yards away.

"What is it?" someone is bound to ask.

"A Bohemian," you say, leaving off the "Waxwing" as if it were redundant, or you were too lost in your find to complete the communication, and/or that there were bound to be other varieties of waxwing in the area and you are ticking them off as they appear.

"Agnes has a Bohemian Waxwing!" the other will cry out to the group.

"A Bohemian Waxwing!" ripples through the group. "Ohhh. Where?"

And without pointing, you say, "The dead tree. Top branch. About three-fifteen." And you move on, as if, having seen one Bohemian, you've seen them all.

Horace Hartle: A Greater Birder Portrait

But let us conclude with a portrait of a true master, who was so skillful that it probably never occurred to him that he was displaying his skill. Still, who is to say?

The most secure birder of the modern era, hands down, was Horace ("Hawk Ear") Hartle (1921–1994), so named because of his amazing ear-sight: he could identify the calls of more birds than appear on the average master birder's life list. Hartle led, as it were, two lives: his own and the life of birds, whom he seemed to understand as perfectly as Indian guides in the movies can tell a Kiowa's footprint from a Ute's. Hartle continued to bird well after his unfortunate blindness, with no apparent loss of pleasure or diminution of talent. And he was directly responsible for the passage of "Hartle's Rule" by the American Birding Association, which, simply stated, allows life-list status to the hearing of a bird, provided it is verified by a sighted birder or is heard by a birder of Hartle's stature.

Hartle was invariably accompanied by his devoted wife, Ethyl, who didn't know a hawk from a warbler but certainly deserves more than a passing footnote in the history of the art. In conversation Hartle was impossible, although friendly to a fault. While you were telling him something you thought interesting, his gaze would repeatedly drift into mid-infinity, just to the right of your left ear, and he would mutter "Vireo," or "Bewick's," or "Cassin's" under his breath (one couldn't always tell), then suddenly, as if awakening, he would say, "I'm sorry. I was listening. Can't help it — ah, Cooper's! — an old habit." And of course you had heard . . . nothing, except the sound of your own voice growing ever more strident with frustration. But for Hartle the field was a continuous symphony of birdcalls, and he could extract and exactly identify each instrument, from flute to percussion. Indeed, when Hartle took the field he seemed to wander indolently, sometimes in circles, gazing at the ground or off in the distance, the farthest thing from the alert intensity that marks the good birder's demeanor. Often he would lower his head and chuckle, as if the birds were telling him a story. Or he would raise his hands in a scallop motion, as if he were conducting an orchestra; then he would stand and tap his foot, neck craned toward some distant source of audible wonder, as if he were coaxing a poignant cadenza from the first cello. The choir of birds seemed almost to be following his baton, rather than his arms following the song of the birds. Meanwhile, birds might be flitting all about, ransacking the bushes and trees. If Hartle saw them, he paid no notice. There is even a story that on a weeklong trip to the Texas coast he remained in his tent on inclement mornings while others in the party braved the rain, in slickers and Wellingtons, looking for birds. Hartle simply listened, hands cupped behind his ears, in the comfort of his sleeping bag.

When the others returned, soaked to the skin but bragging of seeing more than thirty species, including a Le Conte's Sparrow, Hartle is said to have said, "Very good. I counted fifty-three. Did you get the Botteri's [Sparrow] and the Bachman's? Very rare just now."

Hartle understood, above all, the courtesy of silence. When a bird was misidentified in his presence, he would simply smile, somewhat as Christ must have smiled at children. But all eyes were on Hartle when some daring soul pointed treeward and cried, "Lichtenstein's Oriole!"

"Is it?" someone would whisper to Hartle. And a hush would fall over the group, like the people in the E. F. Hutton commercial waiting for the answer.

"I'm afraid it's just a Bullock's," Hartle would say gently, out of hearing of the unfortunate misfinder. "The wing bars do throw you off." Then he would add, "The truth is, I cheated. I heard it first, and its song is much too flutelike for a Lichtenstein's."

And so it went with Hartle. A kindly man, one never to raise his voice or utter a criticism or correction. Was he thus within the confines of his own mind, or did he in some way (like the rest of us) relish the quiet use of his impeccable authority?

Not the least of Ethyl Hartle's contributions was her careful carrying out of Hartle's instructions for the conduct of his funeral service. HIs memorial departure from our scene was absolutely prayerless and without eulogy of any kind; it consisted entirely of birdsongs playing softly in the background and seemingly emanating from a loudspeaker concealed in his coffin. "Nothing that has been said or heard on this planet," Hartle is said to have said, "could better the song of the wood thrush." So, to the end of singing him to his rest, he had gathered on one tape a full hour of endemic birdcalls of Madagascar from his vast and probably definitive collection. Many felt it a touching and altogether fitting tribute to the man; others saw in it a final and ironic version of Hartle's Cheshire smile, for it is doubtful that any of the mourners recognized anything they were hearing, and, short of the sound of fingernails on a blackboard, nothing is as frustrating to a birder as being faced with how much she or he doesn't know about the species. In fact, Hartle's chief rival, Shulman Enders, approaching Hartle's casket to pay his respects, was moved to say, well under his breath, "Hartle, you sonofabitch! You rub it in to the end."

ROBERT STONE

The Prince of Possibility

FROM THE NEW YORKER

In 1964, Ken Kesey was working in a cabin so deep in the redwoods south of San Francisco that its indifferently painted interior
walls seemed to grow seaweed instead of mold. Despite its glass
doors, the cabin held the winter light for little more than a midday
hour, and the place had the cast of an old-fashioned ale bottle. It
smelled of ale too, or at least of beer, and dope. Those were the
days of seeded marijuana: castaway seeds sprouted in the spongy
rot of what had been the carpet, and plants thrived in the lamp-
light and the green air. Witchy fingers of morning glory vine
wound through every shelf and corner of that cabin like illuminations in some hoary manuscript.

Across the highway, on the far bank of La Honda Creek, there
were more morning glory vines. They were there, Kesey said, because he had filled the magazines of his shotgun with morning
glory seeds and fired them into the hillside. The morning glory, as
few then understood, is a close relative of the magical *ololiuqui*
vine, which was said to be used by Chibcha shamans in necro-
mancy and augury. Once ingested, the morning glory's poisonous-
tasting seeds produced hours of startling visions and insights. The
commercial distributors of the seeds, officially unaware of this,
gave the varieties names like Heavenly Blue and Pearly Gates. (A
warning: Don't try this at home! The morning glory seeds sold
these days are advertised as being toxic to the point of deadliness.)

La Honda was a strange place, a spot on the road that descended
from the western slope of the Santa Cruz Mountains toward the ar-
tichoke fields on the coast. Situated mostly within the redwood for-

est, it had the quality of a raw northwestern logging town, transported to suburban San Francisco. In spirit, it was a world away from the woodsy gentility of the other peninsula towns nearby. Its winters were like Seattle's, and its summers pretty much the same. Kesey and his wife, Faye, had moved there in 1963, after their house on Perry Lane, in Menlo Park, was torn down by developers. Perry Lane was one of the small leafy streets that meandered around the Stanford campus then, lined with inexpensive bungalows and inhabited by junior faculty and graduate students. (The Keseys had lived there while Ken did his graduate work at the university and afterward.) The area had a bohemian tradition that extended back to the time of the economist and sociologist Thorstein Veblen, who lived there at the beginning of the twentieth century.

Kesey, as master of the revels sixty years later, did a great deal to advance that tradition. There were stoned poetry readings and lion hunts in the midnight-dark on the golf course, where chanting hunters danced to bogus veldt rhythms pounded out on kitchenware. One party on Perry Lane involved the construction of a human cat's cradle. Drugs played a role, including the then legal LSD and other substances in experimental use at the VA hospital in Menlo Park, where Ken worked as an orderly. The night before the houses on the lane were to be demolished, the residents threw a demented block party at which they trashed one another's houses with sledgehammers and axes in weird psychedelic light. Terrified townies watched from the shadows.

I first met Kesey at one of his world-historical tableaux — a reenactment of the battle of Lake Peipus with broom lances and saucepan helmets. (The Keseys' kitchenware often took a beating in those days, though I can't say I remember ever eating much on Perry Lane.) I was a Wallace Stegner Fellow at Stanford's Writing Program and a Teutonic Knight. Ken, who was Alexander Nevsky, was working on his second novel, *Sometimes a Great Notion.*

When the Keseys moved to La Honda, it became necessary to drive about fifteen miles up the hill to see them. Somehow the sun-starved, fern-and-moss-covered quality of their new place affected the mood of the partying. There was the main house, where Ken and Faye lived with their three children, Shannon, Zane, and Jed, and several outbuildings, including the studio cabin where Kesey worked. There were also several acres of dark redwood, which Kesey and his friends transformed little by little, placing sculptures and stringing batteries of colored lights. Speakers broadcast Rahsaan Roland Kirk, Ravi Shankar, and the late Beethoven quartets. The house in the redwoods increasingly became a kind of auxiliary residence, clubhouse, cookout — a semi-permanent encampment of people passing through, sleeping off the previous night's party, hoping for more of whatever there had been or might be. It was a halfway house on the edge of possibility, or so it appeared at the time. Between novels, Ken had forged a cadre in search of itself, the core of which — in addition to Kesey's close friend Ken Babbs, who had just returned from Vietnam, where he had flown a helicopter as one of the few thousand uniformed Americans there — consisted at first of people who had lived on or near Perry Lane. Many of them had some connection with Stanford. Others were friends from Ken's youth in Oregon. Old beatniks, like Neal Cassady, the model for Jack Kerouac's Dean Moriarty, in *On the Road,* also came around. Some of the locals, less used to deconstructed living than the academic sophisticates in the valley below, saw and heard things that troubled them. As the poet wrote, it was good to be alive and to be young was even better.

More than the inhabitants of any other decade before us, we believed ourselves in a time of our own making. The dim winter day in 1964 when I first drove up to the La Honda house, truant from my attempts at writing a novel, I knew that the future lay before us and I was certain that we owned it. When Kesey came out, we sat on the little bridge over the creek in the last of the light and smoked what was left of the day's clean weed. Ken said something runic about books never being finished and tales remaining forever untold, a Keseyesque ramble for fiddle and banjo, and I realized that he was trying to tell me that he had now finished *Sometimes a Great Notion.* Christ, I thought, there is no competing with this guy.

In 1962, he had published *One Flew Over the Cuckoo's Nest,* a libertarian fable to suit the changing times. It had been a bestseller on publication, and has never been out of print. The book had also been adapted for a Broadway stage production starring Kirk Douglas, who then proposed to do it as a movie. Ken and Faye had gone to the opening night, in that era of formal first nights, with gowns and black tie. Now, a few months later, he had another thicket of epic novel clutched in his mitt, and for all I knew there'd be another one after that.

He really seemed capable of making anything happen. It was beyond writing — although, to me, writing was just about all there was. We sat and smoked and possibility came down on us.

Kesey was, more than anyone I knew, in the grip of all that the sixties seemed to promise. Born in 1935 in a town called La Junta, Colorado, on the road west from the Dust Bowl, he had grown up in Oregon, where his father became a successful dairyman. At school, Kesey was a wrestling champion, and champion was still the word for him; it was impossible for his friends to imagine him *losing*, at wrestling or anything else. Leaving the dairy business to his brother Chuck, Kesey had become an academic champion as well, a Woodrow Wilson Fellow at Stanford.

Ken's endorsement, at the age of twenty-six, by Malcolm Cowley, who oversaw his publication at Viking Press, seemed to connect him to a line of "heavyweight" novelists, the hitters, as Norman Mailer put it, of long balls, the wearers of mantles that by then seemed ready to be passed along to the next heroic generation. If American literature ever had a favorite son, distilled from the native grain, it was Kesey. In a way, he personally embodied the winning side in every historical struggle that had served to create the colossus that was 1960s America; an Anglo-Saxon Protestant western white male, an Olympic-caliber athlete with an advanced academic degree, he had inherited the progressive empowerment of centuries. There was not an effective migration or social improvement of which he was not, in some near or remote sense, the beneficiary. That he had been born to a family of sodbusters only served to complete the legend. It gave him the extra advantage of not being bound to privilege.

Some years before *Cuckoo's Nest,* Ken had written an unpublished Nathanael West–like Hollywood story based on Kesey's unsuccessful attempt to break into the picture business as an actor. All his life, Ken had a certain fascination with Hollywood, as any American fabulist might. He saw it in semi-mythological terms — as almost an autonomous natural phenomenon rather than as a billion-dollar industry. (This touch of naive fascination embittered

his later conflicts over the adaptation of his novels into films.)
However, it was as a rising novelist and not as an actor or screen-
writer that he faced the spring of 1964. There was no question of
his limitless energy. But in the long run, some people thought, the
practice of novel-writing would prove to be too sedentary an occu-
pation for so quick an athlete — lonely, and incorporating long silent periods between strokes. Most writers who were not Heming-
way spent more time staying awake in quiet rooms than shooting
lions in Arusha.

Kesey was listening for some inner voice to tell him precisely
what role history and fortune were offering him. Like his old
teacher Wallace Stegner, like his friend Larry McMurtry, he had
the western artist's respect for legend. He felt his own power and
he knew that others did, too. Certainly his work cast its spell. But
beyond the world of words, he possessed the thing itself, in its
ancient mysterious sense. "His charisma was transactional," Vic
Lovell, the psychologist to whom Kesey dedicated *Cuckoo's Nest,*
said to me when we spoke after Ken's death. He meant that Kesey's
extraordinary energy did not exist in isolation — it acted on and
changed those who experienced it. His ability to offer other people a variety of satisfactions ranging from fun to transcendence was
not especially verbal, which is why it remained independent of
Kesey's fiction, and it was ineffable, impossible to describe exactly
or to encapsulate in a quotation. I imagine that Fitzgerald en-
dowed Jay Gatsby with a similar charisma — enigmatic and elusive,
exciting the dreams, envy, and frustration of those who were drawn
to him. Charisma is a gift of the gods, the Greeks believed, but like
all divine gifts, it has its cost. (Kesey once composed an insightful
bit of doggerel about his own promise to the seekers around him.
"Of offering more than what I can deliver," it went, "I have a bad
habit, it is true. But I have to offer more than I can deliver to be
able to deliver what I do.")

Kesey felt that the world was his own creature and, at the same
time — paradoxically, inevitably — that he was an outsider in it, in
danger of being cheated out of his own achievement. His forebears
had feared and hated the railroads and the eastern banks. In their
place Kesey saw New York, the academic establishment, Hollywood. When he was growing up in Oregon, I imagine, all power
must have seemed to come from somewhere else. Big paper com-

panies and unions, the FBI and the local sheriff's department —
he distrusted them all.

While in New York for the opening night of *Cuckoo's Nest,* Kesey
had caught a glimpse of the preparations for the 1964 World's
Fair. It didn't take him long to dream up the idea of riding a bus to
the fair, arriving sometime before the scheduled publication date
for *Sometimes a Great Notion.* Somehow he and his friends the sports
car driver George Walker and the photographer Mike Hagen managed to buy a 1939 International Harvester school bus and refash-
ion it into a kind of disarmed personnel carrier, with welded com-
partments inside and an observation platform that looked like a U-
boat's conning tower on top. It was wired to play and record tapes,
capable of belching forth a cacophony of psychic disconnects and
registering the reactions at the same time. There were movie cameras everywhere. Everyone had a hand in the painting of the bus,
principally the San Francisco artist Roy Sebern. A sign above the
windshield, where the destination would normally be announced,
proclaimed, "FURTHUR."

By then, there were a number of footloose wanderers loitering
around Kesey's spread in La Honda, ready to ride as soon as the
paint was dry — just waiting, really, for Kesey to tell them what to
do next. It was said later that one was either on the bus or off the
bus — no vain remark, mind you, but an insight of staggering pro-
fundity. It meant, perhaps, that some who were physically on the
bus were not actually on the bus in spirit. It meant that millions
were off the bus, but the bus was coming for them. If you were
willing to entertain Kerouac's notion that the blind jazz pianist
George Shearing was God, that bus was coming for you.

I was going to New York, too — off the bus, though I expected to
encounter it again. My wife, Janice, was attending City College, in
Manhattan, and home was where she was. And I was at a strange
point in my life. I had gone to the hospital for the treatment of
what, in the days before CAT scans, was thought to be a brain tumor. The doctors, after shaving my head and pumping air into my
cranium, playing my head like a calliope with their monstrous instruments, had decided that there was no tumor. Or, rather, there
was a condition called pseudo-tumor, something that happens
sometimes. I was conscious during the operation, on some kind of

skull deadener, so I remember snatches of medical conversation. "When you cut, cut *away* from the brain," one of the surgeons suggested. Another asked me if he could sing while he worked. Anyway, they sent me home alive and cured, and I was happy, albeit bald and with crashing headaches. I would forgo the bus trip.

California, the Menlo Park area around Stanford, was no longer home, but it had once been just short of paradise for me. In the cottages clustered among the live oaks, along the quiet streams that watered Herefords grazing on the yellow tule grass, the happiest time of my life had come and gone. Moving there from the wintry Lower East Side of New York, circa 1960, was like switching from black-and-white to color. One evening, Janice and I went to the Jazz Workshop, in San Francisco, to hear John Coltrane with some friends. We had boiled down peyote, poured the extract into pharmaceutical capsules, and ingested as much of the stuff as we could bear. I swallowed twelve. After sixty seconds of 'Trane, the percussion was undulating in great white waves of jagged frost, the serrated edges as symmetrical as if they had been drawn by an artist's hand. The brass erupted in bands of bright color, streaming out of the brazen instruments like a magician's silk. The entire Jazz Workshop was taken up by a wind from the edge of the earth. Synesthesia, I believe it's called, and I fled it. Janice and a friend of ours came after me. Outside was Chinatown. Its exotic effects were never as potent as they were for me that night.

Like everything that was essential to the sixties, the Kesey cross-country trip has been mythologized. If you can remember it, the old saw goes, you weren't there. But the ride in Ken's multicolored International Harvester school bus was a journey of such holiness that being there — mere vulgar location — was instantly beside the point. From the moment the first demented teenager waved a naked farewell as Neal Cassady threw the clutch, everything entered the numinous.

Who rode the bus, who rode it all the way to the World's Fair and all the way back, has become a matter of conjecture. The number has expanded like the opening-night audience for *Le Sacre du Printemps,* a memorial multiplication in which a theater seating eight hundred has come, over time, to accommodate several thousand eyewitnesses.

Who was actually on the bus? I, who waited, with the wine-stained manuscript of my first novel, for the rendezvous in New York, have a count. Tom Wolfe, who did not see the bus back then at all but is extremely accurate with facts, has a similar one. Cassady drove — the world's greatest driver, who could roll a joint while backing a 1937 Packard onto the lip of the Grand Canyon. Kesey went, of course. And Ken Babbs, fresh from Nam, full of radio nomenclature and with a command voice that put cops to flight. Jane Burton, a pregnant young philosophy professor who declined no challenges. Also George Walker; Sandy Lehmann-Haupt, whose electronic genius was responsible for the sound system. There was Mike Hagen, who shot most of the expedition's film footage. A former infantry officer, Ron Bevirt, whom everybody called Hassler, a clean-cut guy from Missouri, took photographs. There were two relatives of Kesey's — his brother Chuck and his cousin Dale — and Ken Babbs's brother John. Kesey's lawyer's brother-in-law Steve Lambrecht was along as well. And the beautiful Paula Sundsten.

To Ken, to America in 1964, World's Fairs were still a hot number. As for polychrome buses, one loses perspective; the Day-Glo vehicle full of hipsters is now such a spectral archetype of the American road. I'm not sure what it looked like then. With Cassady at the throttle, the bus perfected an uncanny reverse homage to *On the Road,* traveling *east* over Eisenhower's interstates. Like *On the Road,* the bus trip exalted velocity. Similarly, it scorned limits: this land was your land, this land was my land — the bus could turn up anywhere. It celebrated sunsets in four time zones, music on the tinny radio, tears in the rain. If the roadside grub was not as tasty as it had been in Kerouac's day, at least the highway grades were better.

Ken had an instinctive distaste for the metropolis and its pretensions. He was not the only out-of-town writer who thought it a shame that so many publishers were based in New York, and he looked forward to a time when the book business would regionally diversify, supposedly bringing our literature closer to its roots in American soil. But the raising of a World's Fair in the seething city was to Kesey both a breath of assurance and a challenge. Fairs and carnivals, exhibitional wonders of all sorts, were his very meat. He wondered whether the big town would trip over its own grandiose

chic when faced with such a homespun concept. Millions were supposed to be coming, a horde of visitors foreign and domestic, all
expecting the moon.

The bus set off sometime in June. Nineteen sixty-four was an
election year. To baffle the rubes along their route, Kesey and
Cassady had painted a motto over the psychedelia on the side of
the bus — "A Vote for Barry Is a Vote for Fun" — hoping to pass
for psychotic Republicans hyping Goldwater. The country cops of
the highways and byways, however, took them for gypsies and
waved them through one town after another. Presumably, the
vaguely troubled America that was subjected to this drive-by re-
pressed its passing image as meaningless, a hallucination. Sometime around then, someone offered a lame joke in the tradition
of Major Hoople, something about "merry pranksters." (Major
Hoople — a droll comic-strip character at the time, the idler husband of a boarding-house proprietress — was one of Cassady's pa-
tron gods.) The witless remark was carried too far, along with everything else, and for forty years thereafter people checked for the
clownish fringe at our cuffs or imagined us with red rubber noses.

Eventually, the bus pulled up in front of the apartment building
on West Ninety-seventh Street, in New York, where Janice and I
were living with our two children. Our apartment was notorious
among our friends for its ugliness and brick-wall views. Suddenly,
the place was filled with people painted all colors. The bus waited
outside, unguarded, broadcasting Ray Charles, attracting hostile
attention with its demented Goldwater slogan. We and the kids
took our places on top of the bus, ducking trees on our way
through Central Park. Downtown, a well-fed button man came out
of Vincent's clam bar to study the bus and the tooting oddballs on
its roof. He paused thoughtfully for a moment and finally said,
"Get offa there!" That seemed to be the general sentiment. Other
citizens offered the finger and limp-wristed "Heil Hitler"'s. Later,
the gang drove the bus to 125th Street. The street was going to
burn in a few weeks, and, but for the mercy of time, some pranksters would have burned with it.

There was the after-bus party, where Kerouac, out of rage at our
health and youth and mindlessness — but mainly out of jealousy at
Kesey for hijacking his beloved sidekick, Cassady — despised us,
and wouldn't speak to Cassady, who, with the trip behind him,
looked about seventy years old. A man attended who claimed to be

Terry Southern but wasn't. I asked Kerouac for a cigarette and was refused. If I hadn't seen him around in the past I would have thought that this Kerouac was an impostor, too — I couldn't believe how miserable he was, how much he hated all the people who were in awe of him. You should buy your own smokes, said drunk, angry Kerouac. He was still dramatically handsome then; the next time I saw him he would be a red-faced baby, sick and swollen. He was a published, admired writer, I thought. How could he be so unhappy? But we, the people he called "surfers," were happy. We left the party and drove to a bacchanal and snooze in Millbrook, New York, where death and transfiguration had replaced tournament polo as a ride on the edge.

The bus riders visited the fair in a spirit of decent out-of-town respect for the power and glory of plutocracy. They filmed everything in sight and recorded everything in earshot. Like most young Americans in 1964, they were committed to the idea of a World's Fair as groovy, which in retrospect can only be called sweet. Sweet but just the least bit defiant. Also not a little ripped, since driver and passengers had consumed mind-altering drugs in a quantity and variety unrivaled until the prison pharmacy at the New Mexico state penitentiary fell to rioting cons.

And, of course, the fair was a mistake for everyone. Now we know that World's Fairs are always bad news. In 1939, the staff of a few national pavilions in New York had nothing to tell the world except that their countries no longer existed. The hardware of national gewgaws and exhibits went as scrap metal to the war effort. In 1964, the fair produced nothing but sinister urban legends in unsettling numbers, grisly stories of abduction, murder, and cover-ups. Children were said to have disappeared. Body parts were allegedly concealed in the sleek aluminum spheres and silos. It was the hottest summer in many years. Some of the passengers were so long at the fair that they went home without their souls. Jane, the philosophy professor, insists to this day that she made it to the fair only because she had lost her purse on the first day of the trip. Back in California, she became a mother and went to law school. Kesey and Cassady went home, too. Fame awaited them, along with the same fascinated loathing that Kerouac and Ginsberg had endured. We couldn't imagine it at the time, but we were on the losing side of the culture war.

It was a war that got meaner as the world got smaller. Ginsberg and Kerouac, in the fifties, had been set upon by illiterate feature writers concocting insulting lies about their personal hygiene and reporting the clever wisecracks that famous people were supposed to have delivered at their expense. Now the drug thing was being used to make the wrongos feel the fire. At the end of the fifties, Cassady, who was not exactly the Napoleon of crime, had done two years in San Quentin for supposedly selling a few joints. Sometime after Kesey's return to California, in 1965, his house in La Honda was raided during a party. The native country he had just visited in such state was biting back. Ken and some friends were charged with possession of narcotics. Then, on a San Francisco rooftop one foggy night, while watching the Alcatraz searchlight probe the bay's radius, he was arrested again on the same charge. At this, he and his friends composed a giggly, overwrought suicide note addressed to the ocean. ("O Ocean," it began, grimly omitting the "h" to indicate high seriousness and despair.) Fleeing south, Kesey made it to the same area in Mexico where Ram Dass and other prototypical acid cranks had conducted their early séances.

In New York, I got a telegram that declared "Everything Is Beginning Again," an Edenic prospect I had no power to resist. I had finally finished my novel, but it would not be published for months, and I was at the time employed by what our lawyers called "a weekly tabloid with a heavy emphasis on sex." I had not published anything much beyond "SKYDIVER DEVOURED BY STARVING BIRDS" and "WEDDING NIGHT TRICK BREAKS BRIDE'S BACK" — fables of misadventure and desperate desire for the distraction of the supermarket browser. Nevertheless, I was the only person *Esquire* could find who knew where Kesey was. By then, his work and his drug-laced adventures in a transforming San Francisco were well known. *Esquire* paid my way south.

It was the autumn of 1966, and Ken, Faye, their children, and some of their friends were staying near Manzanillo. In 1966, the Pacific Coast between Zihuatanejo and Puerto Vallarta did not look the way it looks today. The road ran for many miles along the foot of the Sierra Madre, bordering an enormous jungle crowned by the Colima volcano itself. The peak thrust its fires nearly four thousand meters into the clouds. At the edge of the mountains, the black-and-white sand beach was so empty that you could walk for hours without passing a town or even the simplest dwelling. The waves were deafening, patrolled by laughing gulls and pelicans.

Today Manzanillo is Mexico's biggest Pacific port and the center of an upscale tourist area. In those days, it seemed like the edge of the world, poor and beautiful beyond belief. One of the hotels in town advertised its elevator on a sandwich board outside. Manzanillo's commanding establishment was a naval base that supported a couple of gunboats.

The Keseys' home was a few miles beyond the bay in a complex of three concrete buildings with crumbling roofs, partly enclosed by a broken concrete wall. We called one of the buildings Casa Purina. Despite its chaste evocations, the name derived from the place's having once housed some operation of the Purina company, worldwide producers of animal feed and aids to husbandry. In the sheltered rooms, we stashed our gear and slung our hammocks. We occupied our time seeking oracular guidance in the *I Ching* and pursuing now vanished folk arts, like cleaning the seeds from our marijuana. (Older heads will remember how the seeds were removed from bud clusters by shaking them loose onto the inverted top of a shoebox. Since the introduction of seedless dope, this homely craft has gone the way of great-grandma's butter churn.)

Our landlord was a Chinese-Mexican grocer, who referred to us as *existencialistas,* which we thought was a good one. He provided electricity, which enabled us to take warm showers and listen to Wolfman Jack and the Texaco opera broadcasts on Saturday. No trace remained, fortunately, of whatever the Purina people had been up to between those whitewashed walls.

We were an unstable gathering, difficult to define. The California drug police, whatever they were called at that time, professed to believe that we were a gang of narcotics smugglers and criminals, our headquarters hard to locate, perhaps protected by the local crime lords. In fact, we were a cross between a Stanford fraternity party and an underfunded libertine writers' conference.

We had no nearby neighbors except the grocery store, and most people along the coast hardly knew we were there, at first. The Casa was far from town, and there was little traffic along the intermittently paved highway that wound over the Sierra toward

Guadalajara. It consisted mainly of the local buses, whose passengers might spot our laundry hanging in the salt breeze or glimpse our puppy pack of golden-haired kiddies racing over black sand toward the breakers. Several times a day, the gleaming first-class coaches of the Flecha Amarilla company would hurtle past, a streak of bright silver and gold, all curves and tinted glass. With their crushed air corps caps and stylish sunglasses, the Flecha Amarilla drivers were gods, eyeball to eyeball with fate. Everything and everyone along the modest road gave way to them.

In appreciation of the spectacle they offered, these buses sometimes drew a salute from Cassady. He would stand on a ruined wall and present arms to the bus with a hammer, which for some reason he carried everywhere in a leather holster on his hip. How the middle-class Mexican coach passengers reacted to the random instant of Neal against the landscape I can only imagine. Sometimes he brought his parrot, Rubiaco, in its cage, holding it up so that Rubiaco and the Flecha Amarilla passengers could inspect each other, as though he were offering the parrot for sale. Cassady in Manzanillo was extending his career as a character in other people's work — Kerouac had used him, as would Kesey, Tom Wolfe, and I. The persistent calling forth and reinventing of his existence was an exhausting process even for such an extraordinary mortal as Neal. Maybe it has earned him the immortality he yearned for. It certainly seems to have shortened his life.

People who live in the tropics sometimes claim to have seen a gorgeous green flash spreading out from the horizon just after sunset on certain clear evenings. Maybe they have. Not me. What I will never forget is the greening of the day at first light on the shores north of Manzanillo Bay. I imagine that color so vividly that I know, by ontology, that I must have seen it. In the moments after dawn, before the sun had reached the peaks of the Sierra, the slopes and valleys of the rain forest would explode in green light, erupting inside a silence that seemed barely to contain it. When the sun's rays spilled over the ridge, they discovered dozens of silvery waterspouts and dissolved them into smoky rainbows. Then the silence would give way and the jungle noises rose to blue heaven. Those mornings, day after day, made nonsense of the examined life, but they made everyone smile. All of us, stoned or otherwise, caught in the vortex of dawn, would freeze in our tracks and stand to, squinting in the pain of the light, sweating, grinning. We called that light Prime Green; it was primal, primary, *primo*.

The high-intensity presence of Mexico was inescapable. Even in the *barrancas* of the wilderness, you felt the country's immanence. Poverty, formality, fatalism, and violence seemed to charge even uninhabited landscapes. I was young enough to rejoice in this. On certain mornings, when the tide was low and the wind came from the necessary quarter, you could stand on the beach and hear the bugle call from the naval base in the city. Although it had a brief section that suggested Tchaikovsky's *Capriccio Italien,* the notes of the Mexican call to colors were pure heartbreak. They always suggested to me the triumphalism of the vanquished, the heroic, engaged in disastrous sacrifice. Those were the notes that had called thousands of lancers against the handful of Texans at the Alamo, that had called wave after wave of Juárez's soldiers against the few dozen Foreign Legionnaires at Camerone. Had the same strains echoed off the rock of Chapultepec when the young cadets wrapped themselves in the flag and leaped from the Halls of Montezuma to defy the Marines?

Does any other army figure so large in the romantic institutional memories of its enemies? All those peasant soldiers, underequipped in everything but the courage for Pyrrhic victories and gorgeous suicidal gestures. Naifs led by Quixotes against grim nameless professionals with nothing to lose, loyal to their masters' greed.

So our exile provided more than a hugely spectacular scenic backdrop. The human setting, never altogether out of view, was ongoing conflict. Quite selfishly, we loved the color of history there, the high drama — man at his fiercest. We imagined it all flat out, as presented by Rivera, Orozco, and the rest, the dark and light, La Adelita, El Grito, Malinche. Hard-riding *rebeldes,* leering *calaveras,* honor, betrayal, the songs of revolution. We had ourselves an opera. Or, as someone remarked, a Marvel comic. All this naturally gave our own lives a quality of fatefulness and melodrama. We were fugitives, after all — at least Kesey was.

One thing we failed to grasp in 1966 was that Mexico was a nation at a turning point. Time and geography had caused it to require many things of the United States, but a band of pot-smoking, im-

poverished *existencialistas* who danced naked on the beach and
frightened away the respectable tourists was simply not one of
them. Gradually, as our presence made itself manifest, it drew
crowds of the curious. Young people, especially, were fascinated by
the anarchy, by the lights and the music. The local authorities
became watchful. At that time, marijuana was disapproved of in
Mexico, associated with a low element locally and with the kind of
unnecessary gringos who lived on mangoes and whose antics en-
crimsoned the jowls of free-spending trophy fishermen from Orange County. From the start, I think, the authorities in the state of
Colima understood that there was more hemp than Heidegger at
the root of our cerebration, and that many of us had trouble distin-
guishing Being from Nothingness by three in the afternoon. At the
same time, a sort of fix was in: Ken was paying *mordida* through his
lawyers, enough to deter initiatives on the part of law enforcement.

We were bearing witness, unwittingly, to a worldwide development that had begun in the United States. The original laws for-
bidding classified substances had been conceived in the language
of therapy, emphasizing the discouragement of such addictive nos-
trums as "temperance cola" and cocaine tonics. From the fright
tabloid to the police blotter the matter went, providing the founding documents of a police underworld, featuring informers, jail
time, and the third degree. The resulting damage to American and
foreign jurisprudence, the outlaw fortunes made, the destroyed
children, and the gangsterism are all well known. What had been a
way for Indian workmen to reinforce the pulque they drank and
sweated out by sundown, a disagreeable practice of the hoi polloi,
became, once it was established as a police matter, Chicago-style
prohibition on a global scale. Nothing on earth was more serious
than people getting loaded, America was told. Nothing, travelers
found, so preoccupied stone-faced cops from Mauretania to Luzon
as the possibility of a joint in a sock, hash in a compact.

In Mexico, we failed to interpret the developments on the drug
front to such a degree that when a plainclothes Mexican police-
man — Agent Number 1, as he described himself — appeared to
make awkward probing conversation with us in the local cantina,
we were more amused by his stereotypical overbearing manner
than alarmed. We should have seen the deadly future he represented.

Some twenty years earlier, Cassady had brought Kerouac down to Mexico and revealed it to him as the happy end of the rainbow. In *On the Road,* Kerouac records the dreamy observations of Cassady's character, Dean Moriarty, as he provides his *compañero* — Jack, in the role of Sal Paradise — with lyrical insights into a Land That Care Forgot, Mexico as a garden without so much as the shadow of a snake. "Oh this is too great to be true," Dean exults, from the moment their jalopy clears Nuevo Laredo. "Damn" and "What kicks!" and "Oh, what a land!" Like his model, he goes on at length:

> Sal, I am digging the interiors of these homes as we pass them — these gone doorways and you look inside and see beds of straw and little brown kids sleeping and stirring to wake, their thoughts congealing from the empty mind of sleep, their selves rising and the mothers cooking up breakfast in iron pots, and dig them shutters they have for windows and the old men, the *old men* are so cool and grand and not bothered by anything. There's no *suspicion* here, nothing like that. Everybody's cool, everybody looks at you with such straight brown eyes and they don't say anything, just *look,* and in that look all of the human qualities are soft and subdued and still there.

In 1957, I had sat in the radio shack of the USS *Arneb,* a young sailor with my earphones tuned to Johnson and Winding, reading all this in the copy of *On the Road* that my mother had sent me. If it seems strange that my copy of this hipster testament came from my mother, it would have seemed far more improbable — at least to me — that I would one day be sharing the mercies of Mexico with some of the characters from the book. Nor would I have believed that anyone, anywhere, ever, talked like Dean Moriarty. I was twice wrong, and, as they say, be careful what you wish for.

As we sat in the cantina, watching Agent Number 1 grow more drunk and less convivial with every round, I began to see that Dean Moriarty and his author had been mistaken in some respects. In the bent brown eyes of the agent, I beheld grave suspicion, and my own thoughts began to congeal around the prospect of waking up to breakfast in a Mexican jail.

There are working-class taverns in Mexico (and some pretty fancy ones, too) where the drinking atmosphere seems to change over the course of a few hours in a manner that is somewhat the re-

verse of similar establishments in other countries. For example, a
customer might arrive in the early evening to find the place loud
with laughter and conversations about baseball or local politics
and gossip, the jukebox blaring, the bartender all smiles. Then, as
time progressed and the patrons advanced more deeply into their
liquor, things would seem to quiet down. By a late hour, the joint,
just as crowded, would grow so subdued that the rattle of a coin on
the wooden bar might attract the attention of the whole room.
Men who had been exchanging jokes a short time before would
stand unsteadily and look around with an unfocused caution, as
though reassessing the place and their drinking buddies. These re-
assessments sometimes seemed unfavorable, at which point it was
time to leave.

Thus it went with Agent Number 1. He showed us his badge, and
indeed it was embossed with the number 1, and he assured us that,
as cops went, he was *número uno* as well. He told stories about Elizabeth Taylor in Puerto Vallarta — how her stolen jewelry was returned at the very whisper of his name in the criminal hangouts of
P.V. His mood kept deteriorating. He got drunker and would not
go away. He told us that Mexico's attitude toward marijuana was
very liberal. His private attitude was too, though he never used
drugs himself, no, no, no. Did we know that we were entitled to
keep some marijuana for our own personal use? Quite a generous
amount. I have come to recognize the phrase "your own personal
use" employed in a tone of good-natured tolerance as a standard
police trap around the world; whatever you admit to possessing is
likely to get you put away.

While I let the *federale* buy me drinks, my two companions teased
him as though we were all players in *A Touch of Evil*. Ken Babbs's
Vietnam post-traumatic stress took the form of a dreadful fearless-
ness, which, though terrifying to timid adventurers like myself,
would come in handy more than once. George Walker had a similar spirit. For my part, I went for the persona of one polite but
dumb, an attitude that annoyed the agent even more than Babbs's
and Walker's transparent mockery. For some inexplicable reason, I
thought I could mollify him by talking politics. The agent was an
anti-Communist and excitable on the topic. I have come to realize
that in the context of Mexico in 1966 this portended no good.
Eventually, having bought every round and rather fumbled his ex-

ploratory probe, Agent Number 1 climbed into his Buick and drove off toward Guadalajara. His hateful parting glance told us that this was *hasta luego,* not *adiós.*

We reported our encounter to Kesey, who was philosophical; he had been brooding, wandering the beach at night. In the morning, he would come back to sleep, exhausted, looking for Faye to lead him to cool and darkness, shelter from the green blaze and the reenactment of Creation that could explode at any moment. What was happening to Kesey? He didn't seem to be writing much. It was impossible to tell if we were witnessing a stage of literary development, a personal Gethsemane, or an apotheosis. Some fundamental change seemed to be taking place in the world, and as he smoked the good local herb on the slope of the Sierra and watched the lightning flashes and the fires of the volcano he pondered what his role in it might be. Before his flight to Mexico, he had attended a Unitarian conference at Asilomar, on the California coast, during the course of which a number of people had come to believe that he was God. He had spun their minds with unanswerable gnomic challenges and imaginary paradoxes. Still, it was an especially heady compliment, coming from the Unitarians. Kesey referred to the Unitarian elders, patrician world citizens in sailor caps and fishermen's sweaters, as "the pipes," because they took their tobacco in hawthorn- and maple-scented meerschaums and used the instruments to punctuate their thoughtful, humane fireside remarks. "If you've got it all together," Kesey asked one confounded elder, "what's that all around it?"

Local adolescents took to hanging out at the Casa. Some of them were musicians. On the anniversary of Mexican independence, we decided to hold what someone called an acid test. People appeared on the beach with rum and firecrackers. We put tricolor Mexican bunting up. By this point, Cassady had found it liberating to restrict his diet to methamphetamine. He went everywhere with Rubiaco, the parrot. So constant was their companionship, so exact was Rubiaco's rendering of Cassady's speech, that without looking it was impossible to tell which of them had come into a room. As for Cassady on amphetamine — he never ate, never slept, and never shut up. He also thought it a merry prank to slip several hundred micrograms of LSD into anything anyone happened to be ingesting. No one dared eat or drink without secure refuge from Neal. To cap off our Independence Day celebration, a number of us went into the village market and bought a suckling pig for roasting. Nothing roasted ever smelled lovelier to me than that substance-free pig as we settled under the palms with our paper plates and bottles of Pacifico. We were, unfortunately, deceived. Cassady had shot the creature in vivo with a hypo full of LSD, topped off with his choicest methedrine. After two forkfuls of *lechón*, we were bug-eyed, watching the Dance of the Diablitos, every one of us deep in delusion.

How the parrot survived its friendship with Cassady is beyond me; as far as I remember, neither he nor anyone else fed the bird. Twenty-five years later, on Kesey's farm, Janice and I woke to Neal's voice from the beyond. (The man himself had died by the railroad tracks outside San Miguel de Allende in 1968.) "Fuckin' Denver cops," he muttered bitterly. "They got a grand theft auto. I tell them that ain't my beef." We rose bolt upright and found ourselves staring into Rubiaco's unkindly green eye. If, as some say, parrots live preternaturally long lives, it must be time for some literary zoologist to cop that bird for the University of Texas Library Zoo.

The expatriation had to come to an end; Kesey would have to go back and answer to the State of California. In fact, his spell on the lam had been excellently timed. In 1966, the world, and especially California, was changing fast. The change was actually visible on the streets of San Francisco, at places like the Fillmore and the Avalon Ballroom. Political and social institutions were so lacking in humor and self-confidence that they crumbled at a wisecrack. The *Esquire* consciousness, however, held firm — they declined my copy. "For Christ's sake," an editor kept telling me, "tell it to a neutral reader." They thought I had gone native on the story, and of course I had been pretty native to begin with.

A few months later, Kesey crossed the border and went home. He was able to make a deal for six months at the San Mateo County sheriff's honor farm. No man can call another's prison time easy, but Kesey's was less bitter medicine than Cassady's two years at San Quentin. It was also an improvement on five years to life, a standard sentence on the books for a high-profile defendant at the time of Kesey's arrest.

Over the years, my friend Ken became a libertarian shaman. Above all, he loved performing; he loved preaching and teaching. He was a wonderful father, a fearless and generous friend, who always took back far less than he gave. All his life, he was searching for the philosopher's stone that could return the world to the pure story from which it was made, bypassing syntax and those damn New York publishers. He kept trying to find the message beyond the words, to see the words that God had written in fire. He traveled around sometimes, in successors to the old bus, telling stories and putting on improvised shows for crowds of children and adults. If he had chosen to work through his progressively revealed mythology in novels, rather than trying to live it out all at once, he might have become a writer for the age.

Life had given Americans so much by the mid-sixties that we were all a little drunk on possibility. Things were speeding out of control before we could define them. Those who cared most deeply about the changes, those who gave their lives to them, were, I think, the most deceived. While we were playing shadow tag in the San Francisco suburbs, other revolutions were counting their chips. Curved, finned, corporate Tomorrowland, as presented at the 1964 World's Fair, was over before it began, and we were borne along with it into a future that no one would have recognized, a world that no one could have wanted. Sex, drugs, and death were demystified. The LSD we took as a tonic of psychic liberation turned out to have been developed by CIA researchers as a weapon of the Cold War. We had gone to a party in La Honda in 1963 that followed us out the door and into the street and filled the world with funny colors. But the prank was on us.

ELLEN ULLMAN

Dining with Robots

FROM THE AMERICAN SCHOLAR

ON THE FIRST DAY of the first programming course I ever took, the instructor compared computer programming to creating a recipe. I remember he used the example of baking a cake. First you list the ingredients you'll need — flour, eggs, sugar, butter, yeast — and these, he said, are like the machine resources the program will need in order to run. Then you describe, in sequence, in clear declarative language, the steps you have to perform to turn those ingredients into a cake. Step one: preheat the oven. Two: sift together dry ingredients. Three: beat the eggs. Along the way were decisions he likened to the if/then/else branches of a program: if using a countertop electric mixer, then beat three minutes; else if using a hand electric mixer, then beat four; else beat five. And there was a reference he described as a sort of subroutine: go to page 117 for details about varieties of yeast (with "return here" implied). He even drew a flow chart that took the recipe all the way through to the end: let cool, slice, serve.

I remember nothing, however, about the particulars of the cake itself. Was it angel food? Chocolate? Layered? Frosted? At the time, 1979 or 1980, I had been working as a programmer for more than a year, self-taught, and had yet to cook anything more complicated than poached eggs. So I knew a great deal more about coding than about cakes. It didn't occur to me to question the usefulness of comparing something humans absolutely must do to something machines never do: that is, eat.

In fact, I didn't think seriously about the analogy for another twenty-five years, not until a blustery fall day in San Francisco, when I was confronted with a certain filet of beef. By then I had learned to cook. (It was that or a life of programmer food: pizza, takeout, whatever's stocked in the vending machines.) And the person responsible for the beef encounter was a man named Joe, of Potter Family Farms, who was selling "home-raised and butchered" meat out of a stall in the newly renovated Ferry Building food hall.

The hall, with its soaring, arched windows, is a veritable church of food. The sellers are small, local producers; everything is organic, natural, free-range; the "baby lettuces" are so young one should perhaps call them "fetal" — it's that sort of place. Before shopping, it helps to have a glass of wine, as I had, to prepare yourself for the gasping shock of the prices. Sitting at a counter overlooking the bay, watching ships and ferries ply the choppy waters, I'd sipped down a nice Pinot Grigio, which had left me with lowered sales resistance by the time I wandered over to the Potter Farms meat stall. There Joe greeted me and held out for inspection a large filet — "a beauty," he said. He was not at all moved by my remonstrations that I eat meat but rarely cook it. He stood there as a man who had — personally — fed, slaughtered, and butchered this cow, and all for me, it seemed. I took home the beef.

I don't know what to do with red meat. There is something appalling about meat's sheer corporeality — meat meals are called *fleishidich* in Yiddish, a word that doesn't let you forget that what you are eating is *flesh*. So for help I turned to *The Art of French Cooking*, volume 1, the cookbook Julia Child wrote with Louisette Bertholle and Simone Beck. I had bought this book when I first decided I would learn to cook. But I hadn't been ready for it then. I was scared off by the drawings of steer sides lanced for sirloins, porterhouses, and T-bones. And then there was all that talk of blanching, deglazing, and making a roux. But I had stayed with it, spurred on by my childhood memories of coming across Julia on her TV cooking show, when I'd be zooming around the dial early on weekend mornings and be stopped short at the sight of this big woman taking whacks at red lumps of meat. It was the physicality of her cooking that caught me, something animal and finger-painting-gleeful in her engagement with food.

And now, as rain hatched the windows, I came upon a recipe that Julia and her coauthors introduced as follows:

SAUTÉ DE BOEUF À LA PARISIENNE
[Beef Sauté with Cream and Mushroom Sauce]

This sauté of beef is good to know about if you have to entertain important guests in a hurry. It consists of small pieces of filet sautéed quickly
to a nice brown outside and a rosy center, and served in a sauce. In the
variations at the end of the recipe, all the sauce ingredients may be prepared in advance. If the whole dish is cooked ahead of time, be very
careful indeed in its reheating that the beef does not overcook. The
cream and mushroom sauce here is a French version of beef Stroganoff,
but less tricky as it uses fresh rather than sour cream, so you will not run
into the problem of curdled sauce.

Serve the beef in a casserole, or on a platter surrounded with steamed
rice, *risotto,* or potato balls sautéed in butter. Buttered green peas or
beans could accompany it, and a good red Bordeaux wine.

And it was right then, just after reading the words "a good red Bordeaux wine," that the programming class came back to me: the instructor at the board with his flow chart, his orderly procedural
steps, the if/then decision branches, the subroutines, all leading to
the final "let cool, slice, serve." And I knew in that moment that my
long-ago instructor, like my young self, had been laughably clue-
less about the whole subject of cooking food.

If you have to entertain important guests.

A nice brown outside.

Rosy center.

Stroganoff.

Curdled.

Risotto.

Potato balls in butter.

A good red Bordeaux.

I tried to imagine the program one might write for this recipe.
And immediately each of these phrases exploded in my mind. How
to tell a computer what "important guests" are? And how would
you explain what it means to "have to" serve them dinner (never
mind the yawning depths of "entertain")? A "nice brown," a "rosy
center": you'd have to have a mouth and eyes to know what these
mean, no matter how well you might translate them into temperatures. And what to do about "Stroganoff," which is not just a sauce
but a noble family, a name that opens a chain of association that
catapults the human mind across seven centuries of Russian his-

tory? I forced myself to abandon that line of thought and stay in the smaller realm of sauces made with cream, but this inadvertently opened up the entire subject of the chemistry of lactic proteins, and why milk curdles. Then I wondered how to explain "risotto": the special short-grained rice, the select regions on earth where it grows, opening up endlessly into questions of agriculture, its arrival among humans, the way it changed the earth. Next came the story of potatoes, that Inca food, the brutalities through which it arrives on a particular plate before a particular woman in Europe, before our eponymous Parisienne: how it is converted into a little round ball, and then, of course, buttered. (Then, Lord help me, this brought up the whole subject of the French and butter, and how can they possibly get away with eating so much of it?)

But all of this was nothing compared to the cataclysm created by "a good red Bordeaux."

The program of this recipe expanded infinitely. Subroutine opened from subroutine, association led to exploding association. It seemed absurd even to think of describing all this to a machine. The filet, a beauty, was waiting for me.

Right around the time my programming teacher was comparing coding to cake-making, computer scientists were finding themselves stymied in their quest to create intelligent machines. Almost from the moment computers came into existence, researchers believed that the machines could be made to think. And for the next thirty or so years, their work proceeded with great hope and enthusiasm. In 1967, the influential MIT computer scientist Marvin Minsky declared, "Within a generation the problem of creating 'artificial intelligence' will be substantially solved." But by 1982, he was less sanguine about the prospects, saying, "The AI problem is one of the hardest science has ever undertaken."

Computer scientists had been trying to teach the computer what human beings know about themselves and the world. They wanted to create inside the machine a sort of mirror of our existence, but in a form a computer could manipulate: abstract, symbolic, organized according to one theory or another of how human knowledge is structured in the brain. Variously called "micro worlds," "problem spaces," "knowledge representations," "classes," and "frames," these abstract universes contained systematized arrangements of facts, along with rules for operating upon those — theoretically all that a machine would need to become intelligent. Although it wasn't characterized as such at the time, this quest for a symbolic representation of reality was oddly Platonic in motive, a computer scientist's idea of the pure, unchanging forms that lie behind the jumble of the physical world.

But researchers eventually found themselves in a position like mine when trying to imagine the computer program for my *boeuf à la Parisienne:* the network of associations between one thing and the next simply exploded. The world, the actual world we inhabit, showed itself to be too marvelously varied, too ragged, too linked and interconnected, to be sorted into any set of frames or classes or problem spaces. What we hold in our minds is not abstract, it turned out, not an ideal reflection of existence, but something inseparable from our embodied experience of moving about in a complicated world.

Hubert L. Dreyfus, a philosopher and early critic of artificial intelligence research, explained the problem with the example of a simple object like a chair. He pointed out the futility of trying to create a symbolic representation of a chair to a computer, which had neither a body to sit in it nor a social context in which to use it. "Chairs would not be equipment for sitting if our knees bent backwards like those of flamingoes, or if we had no tables, as in traditional Japan or the Australian bush," he wrote in his 1979 book *What Computers Can't Do.* Letting flow the myriad associations that radiate from the word "chair," Dreyfus went on:

> Anyone in our culture understands such things as how to sit on kitchen chairs, swivel chairs, folding chairs; and in arm chairs, rocking chairs, deck chairs, barber's chairs, sedan chairs, dentist's chairs, basket chairs, reclining chairs . . . since there seems to be an indefinitely large variety of chairs and of successful (graceful, comfortable, secure, poised, etc.) ways to sit in them. Moreover, understanding chairs also includes social skills such as being able to sit appropriately (sedately, demurely, naturally, casually, sloppily, provocatively, etc.) at dinners, interviews, desk jobs, lectures, auditions, concerts . . .

At dinners where one has to entertain important guests . . . at the last minute . . . serving them beef in a French version of Stroganoff . . . with buttered potatoes . . . and a good red Bordeaux.

*

Several weeks after making Julia's *boeuf,* I was assembling twelve chairs (dining chairs, folding chairs, desk chair) around the dining table, and I was thinking not of Dreyfus but of my mother. In her younger days, my mother had given lavish dinner parties, and it was she who had insisted, indeed commanded, that I have all the necessary equipment for the sort of sit-down dinner I was giving that night. I surveyed the fancy wedding-gift stainless she had persuaded me to register for ("or else you'll get a lot of junk," she said), the Riedel wine glasses, also gifts, and finally the set of china she had given me after my father's death, when she sold their small summer house — "the country dishes" is how I think of them, each one hand-painted in a simple design, blue cornflowers on white.

It wasn't until I started setting the table, beginning with the forks, that I thought of Dreyfus. Salad forks, fish forks, crab forks, entrée forks, dessert forks — at that moment it occurred to me that the paradigm for an intelligent machine had changed, but what remained was the knotty problem of teaching a computer what it needed to know to achieve sentience. In the years since Dreyfus wrote his book, computer scientists had given up on the idea of intelligence as a purely abstract proposition — a knowledge base and a set of rules to operate upon it — and were now building what are called social robots, machines with faces and facial expressions, who are designed to learn about the world the way human beings do: by interacting with other human beings. Instead of being born with a universe already inscribed inside them, these social machines will start life with only basic knowledge and skills. Armed with cute faces and adorable expressions, like babies, they must inspire humans to teach them about the world. And in the spirit of Dreyfus, I asked myself: If such a robot were coming to dinner, how could I, as a good human hostess and teacher, explain everything I would be placing before it tonight?

Besides the multiple forks, there will be an armory of knives: salad knife, fish knife, bread knife, dessert knife. We'll have soup spoons and little caviar spoons made of bone, teaspoons, tiny demitasse spoons, and finally the shovel-shaped ice cream spoons you can get only in Germany — why is it that only Germans recognize the need for this special ice cream implement? My robot guest could learn in an instant the name and shape and purpose of every piece of silverware, I thought; it would instantly understand the need for bone with caviar because metal reacts chemically with roe. But its mouth isn't functional; the mouth part is there only to make us humans feel more at ease; my robot guest doesn't eat. So how will it understand the complicated interplay of implement, food, and mouth — how each tool is designed to hold, present, complement the intended fish or vegetable, liquid or grain? And the way each forkful or spoonful finds its perfectly dimensioned way into the moist readiness of the mouth, where the experience evanesces (one hopes) into the delight of taste?

And then there will be the wineglasses: the flutes for champagne, the shorter ones for white wine, the pregnant Burgundy glasses, the large ones for Cabernet blends. How could I tell a machine about the reasons for these different glasses, the way they cup the wine, shape the smell, and deliver it to the human nose? And how to explain wine at all? You could spend the rest of your life tasting wine and still not exhaust its variations, each bottle a little ecosystem of grapes and soils and weather, yeast and bacteria, barrels of wood from trees with their own soil and weather, the variables cross-multiplying until each glassful approaches a singularity, a moment in time on earth. Can a creature that does not drink or taste understand this pleasure? A good red Bordeaux!

I went to the hutch to get out the china. I had to move aside some of the pieces I never use: the pedestaled cigarette holders, the little ashtrays, the relish tray for the carrots, celery, and olives it was once de rigueur to put on the table. Then I came to the coffeepot, whose original purpose was not to brew coffee — that would have been done in a percolator — but to serve it. I remembered my mother presiding over the many dinners she had given, the moment when the table was scraped clean of crumbs and set for dessert, the coffee cups and saucers stacked beside her as she poured out each cup and passed it down the line. Women used to serve coffee at table, I thought. But my own guests would walk over and retrieve theirs from the automatic drip pot. My mother is now ninety-one; between her time as a hostess and mine, an enormous change had occurred in the lives of women. And, just then, it seemed to me that all that upheaval was contained in the silly fact of how one served coffee to dinner guests. I knew I would never want to go back to mother's time, but all the same I suddenly missed the world of her dinner parties, the guests waving their cigarettes as they chatted, my mother so dressed up, queenly by the coffeepot, her service a kind of benign rule over the table. I put the pot in the corner of the hutch and thought: It's no good trying to explain all this to my robot guest. The chain of associations from just this one piece of china has led me to regret and nostalgia, feelings I can't explain even to myself.

The real problem with having a robot to dinner is pleasure. What would please my digital guest? Human beings need food to survive, but what drives us to choose one food over another is what I think of as the deliciousness factor. Evolution, that good mother, has seen fit to guide us to the apple instead of the poison berry by our attraction to the happy sweetness of the apple, its fresh crispness, and, in just the right balance, enough tartness to make it complicated in the mouth. There are good and rational reasons why natural selection has made us into creatures with fine taste discernment — we can learn what's good for us and what's not. But this very sensible survival imperative, like the need to have sex to reproduce, works itself out through the not very sensible, wilder part of our nature: desire for pleasure.

Can a robot desire? Can it have pleasure? When trying to decide if we should confer sentience upon another creature, we usually cite the question first posed by the philosopher Jeremy Bentham: Can it suffer? We are willing to ascribe a kind of consciousness to a being whose suffering we can intuit. But now I wanted to look at the opposite end of what drives us, not at pain but at rapture: Can it feel pleasure? Will we be able to look into the face of a robot and understand that some deep, inherent need has driven it to seek a particular delight?

According to Cynthia Breazeal, who teaches at MIT and is perhaps the best known of the new social-robot researchers, future digital creatures will have drives that are analogous to human desires but that will have nothing to do with the biological imperatives of food and sex. Robots will want the sort of things that machines need: to stay in good running order, to maintain physical homeostasis, to get the attention of human beings, upon whom they must rely, at least until they learn to take care of themselves. They will be intelligent and happy the way dolphins are: in their own form, in their own way.

Breazeal is very smart and articulate, and her defense of the eventual beingness of robotic creatures is a deep challenge to the human idea of sentience. She insists that robots will eventually become so lifelike that we will one day have to face the question of their inherent rights and dignity. "We have personhood because it's granted to us by society," she told me. "It's a status granted to one another. It's not innately tied to being a carbon-based life form."

So challenged, I spent a long time thinking about the interior life of a robot. I tried to imagine it: the delicious swallowing of electric current, the connoisseurship of voltages, exquisite sensibilities sensing tiny spikes on the line, the pleasure of a clean, steady flow. Perhaps the current might taste of wires and transistors, capacitors and rheostats, some components better than others, the way soil and water make up the *terroir* of wine, the difference between a good Bordeaux and a middling one. I think robots will delight in discerning patterns, finding mathematical regularities, seeing a world that is not mysterious but beautifully self-organized. What pleasure they will take in being fast and efficient — to run without cease! — humming along by their picosecond clocks, their algorithms compact, elegant, error-free. They will want the interfaces between one part of themselves and another to be defined, standardized, and modular, so that an old part can be unplugged, upgraded, and plugged back in their bodies forever renewed. Fast, efficient, untiring, correct, standardized, organized: the virtues we humans strive for but forever fail to achieve, the reasons we invented our helpmate, the machine.

The dinner party, which of course proceeded without a single robot guest, turned out to be a fine, raucous affair, everyone talking and laughing, eating and drinking to just the right degree of excess. And when each guest rose to pour his or her own cup of coffee, I knew it was one of those nights that had to be topped off with a good brandy. By the time the last friend had left, it was nearly two A.M., the tablecloth was covered with stains, dirty dishes were everywhere, the empty crab shells were beginning to stink, and the kitchen was a mess. Perfect.

Two days later I was wheeling a cart through the aisles at Safeway — food shopping can't always be about fetal lettuces — and I was thinking how neat and regular the food looked. All the packaged, prepared dinners lined up in boxes on the shelves. The meat in plastic-wrapped trays, in standard cuts, arranged in orderly rows. Even the vegetables looked cloned, identical bunches of spinach and broccoli, perfectly green, without an apparent speck of dirt. Despite the influence of Julia Child and California-cuisine guru Alice Waters, despite the movement toward organic, local produce, here it all still was: manufactured, efficient, standardized food.

But of course it was still here, I thought. Not everyone can afford the precious offerings of the food hall. And even if you could, who really has the time to stroll through the market and cook a meal based on what looks fresh that day? I have friends who would love to spend rainy afternoons turning a nice filet into *boeuf à la Parisienne*. But even they find their schedules too pressed these days; it's easier just to pick something up, grab a sauce out of a jar. Working long hours, our work life invading home life through e-mail and mobile phones, we all need our food-gathering trips to be brief and organized, our time in the kitchen efficiently spent, our meals downed in a hurry.

As I picked out six limes, not a bruise or blemish on them, it occurred to me that I was not really worried about robots becoming sentient, human, indistinguishable from us. That long-standing fear — robots who fool us into taking them for humans — suddenly seemed a comic-book peril, born of another age, as obsolete as a twenty-five-year-old computer.

What scared me now were the perfect limes, the five varieties of apples that seemed to have disappeared from the shelves, the dinner I'd make and eat that night in thirty minutes, the increasing rarity of those feasts that turn the dining room into a wreck of sated desire. The lines at the checkout stands were long; neat packages rode along on the conveyor belts; the air was filled with the beep of scanners as the food, labeled and bar-coded, identified itself to the machines. Life is pressuring us to live by the robots' pleasures, I thought. Our appetites have given way to theirs. Robots aren't becoming us, I feared; we are becoming them.

In memory of Julia Child

DAVID FOSTER WALLACE

Consider the Lobster

FROM GOURMET

THE ENORMOUS, pungent, and extremely well-marketed Maine
Lobster Festival is held every late July in the state's midcoast region, meaning the western side of Penobscot Bay, the nerve stem
of Maine's lobster industry. What's called the midcoast runs from
Owl's Head and Thomaston in the south to Belfast in the north.
(Actually, it might extend all the way up to Bucksport, but we were
never able to get farther north than Belfast on Route 1, whose
summer traffic is, as you can imagine, unimaginable.) The region's
two main communities are Camden, with its very old money and
yachty harbor and five-star restaurants and phenomenal B&Bs, and
Rockland, a serious old fishing town that hosts the Festival every
summer in historic Harbor Park, right along the water.*

Tourism and lobster are the midcoast region's two main industries, and they're both warm-weather enterprises, and the Maine
Lobster Festival represents less an intersection of the industries
than a deliberate collision, joyful and lucrative and loud. The assigned subject of this *Gourmet* article is the Fifty-sixth Annual MLF,
30 July–3 August 2003, whose official theme this year was "Light-
houses, Laughter, and Lobster." Total paid attendance was over
one hundred thousand, due partly to a national CNN spot in June
during which a senior editor of *Food & Wine* magazine hailed the
MLF as one of the best food-themed festivals in the world. The
2003 Festival highlights: concerts by Lee Ann Womack and Orleans, annual Maine Sea Goddess beauty pageant, Saturday's big

* There's a comprehensive native apothegm: "Camden by the sea, Rockland by the
smell."

parade, Sunday's William G. Atwood Memorial Crate Race, annual Amateur Cooking Competition, carnival rides and midway attractions and food booths, and the MLF's Main Eating Tent, where something over twenty-five thousand pounds of fresh-caught Maine lobster is consumed after preparation in the World's Largest Lobster Cooker near the grounds' north entrance. Also available are lobster rolls, lobster turnovers, lobster sauté, Down East lobster salad, lobster bisque, lobster ravioli, and deep-fried lobster dumplings. Lobster Thermidor is obtainable at a sit-down restaurant called the Black Pearl, on Harbor Park's northwest wharf. A large all-pine booth sponsored by the Maine Lobster Promotion Council has free pamphlets with recipes, eating tips, and Lobster Fun Facts. The winner of Friday's Amateur Cooking Competition prepares Saffron Lobster Ramekins, the recipe for which is now available for public downloading at www.mainelobsterfestival.com. There are lobster T-shirts and lobster bobblehead dolls and inflatable lobster pool toys and clamp-on lobster hats with big scarlet claws that wobble on springs. Your assigned correspondent saw it all, accompanied by one girlfriend and both his own parents — one of which parents was actually born and raised in Maine, albeit in the extreme northern inland part, which is potato country and a world away from the touristic midcoast.*

For practical purposes, everyone knows what a lobster is. As usual, though, there's much more to know than most of us care about — it's all a matter of what your interests are. Taxonomically speaking, a lobster is a marine crustacean of the family Homaridae, characterized by five pairs of jointed legs, the first pair terminating in large pincerish claws used for subduing prey. Like many other species of benthic carnivore, lobsters are both hunters and scavengers. They have stalked eyes, gills on their legs, and antennae. There are a dozen or so different kinds worldwide, of which the relevant species here is the Maine lobster, *Homarus americanus.* The name "lobster" comes from the Old English *loppestre,* which is thought to be a corrupt form of the Latin word for locust combined with the Old English *loppe,* which meant spider.

Moreover, a crustacean is an aquatic arthropod of the class

* N.B. All personally connected parties have made it clear from the start that they do not want to be talked about in this article.

Crustacea, which comprises crabs, shrimp, barnacles, lobsters, and freshwater crayfish. All this is right there in the encyclopedia. And an arthropod is an invertebrate member of the phylum Arthropoda, which phylum covers insects, spiders, crustaceans, and centipedes/millipedes, all of whose main commonality, besides the absence of a centralized brain-spine assembly, is a chitinous exoskeleton composed of segments, to which appendages are articulated in pairs.

The point is that lobsters are basically giant sea-insects.* Like most arthropods, they date from the Jurassic period, biologically so much older than mammalia that they might as well be from another planet. And they are — particularly in their natural brown-green state, brandishing their claws like weapons and with thick antennae awhip — not nice to look at. And it's true that they are garbagemen of the sea, eaters of dead stuff,† although they'll also eat some live shellfish, certain kinds of injured fish, and sometimes each other.

But they are themselves good eating. Or so we think now. Up until sometime in the 1800s, though, lobster was literally low-class food, eaten only by the poor and institutionalized. Even in the harsh penal environment of early America, some colonies had laws against feeding lobsters to inmates more than once a week because it was thought to be cruel and unusual, like making people eat rats. One reason for their low status was how plentiful lobsters were in old New England. "Unbelievable abundance" is how one source describes the situation, including accounts of Plymouth pilgrims wading out and capturing all they wanted by hand, and of early Boston's seashore being littered with lobsters after hard storms — these latter were treated as a smelly nuisance and ground up for fertilizer. There is also the fact that premodern lobster was cooked dead and then preserved, usually packed in salt or crude hermetic containers. Maine's earliest lobster industry was based around a dozen such seaside canneries in the 1840s, from which lobster was shipped as far away as California, in demand only because it was cheap and high in protein, basically chewable fuel.

* Midcoasters' native term for a lobster is, in fact, "bug," as in "Come around on Sunday and we'll cook up some bugs."
† Factoid: Lobster traps are usually baited with dead herring.

Now, of course, lobster is posh, a delicacy, only a step or two down from caviar. The meat is richer and more substantial than most fish, its taste subtle compared to the marine gaminess of mussels and clams. In the U.S. pop-food imagination, lobster is now the seafood analogue to steak, with which it's so often twinned as Surf 'n' Turf on the really expensive part of the chain steakhouse menu.

In fact, one obvious project of the MLF, and of its omnipresently sponsorial Maine Lobster Promotion Council, is to counter the idea that lobster is unusually luxe or unhealthy or expensive, suitable only for effete palates or the occasional blow-the-diet treat. It is emphasized over and over in presentations and pamphlets at the Festival that lobster meat has fewer calories, less cholesterol, and less saturated fat than chicken.* And in the Main Eating Tent, you can get a "quarter" (industry shorthand for a 1¼-pound lobster), a 4-ounce cup of melted butter, a bag of chips, and a soft roll w/butter-pat for around twelve dollars, which is only slightly more expensive than supper at McDonald's.

Be apprised, though, that the Maine Lobster Festival's democratization of lobster comes with all the massed inconvenience and aesthetic compromise of true democracy. See, for example, the prenominate Main Eating Tent, for which there is a constant Disneyland-grade queue, and which turns out to be a square quarter-mile of awning-shaded cafeteria lines and rows of long institutional tables at which friend and stranger alike sit cheek to jowl, cracking and chewing and dribbling. It's hot, and the sagged roof traps the steam and the smells, which latter are strong and only partly food-related. It is also loud, and a good percentage of the total noise is masticatory. The suppers come in Styrofoam trays, and the soft drinks are iceless and flat, and the coffee is convenience-store coffee in more Styrofoam, and the utensils are plastic (there are none of the special long skinny forks for pushing out the tail meat, though a few savvy diners bring their own). Nor do they give you near enough napkins considering how messy lobster is to eat, especially when you're squeezed onto benches alongside children of

---

* Of course, the common practice of dipping the lobster meat in melted butter torpedoes all these happy fat-specs, which none of the council's promotional stuff ever mentions, any more than potato industry PR talks about sour cream and bacon bits.

various ages and vastly different levels of fine-motor development — not to mention the people who've somehow smuggled in their own beer in enormous aisle-blocking coolers, or who all of a sudden produce their own plastic tablecloths and try to spread them over large portions of tables to try to reserve them (the tables) for their own little groups. And so on. Any one example is no more than a petty inconvenience, of course, but the MLF turns out to be full of irksome little downers like this — see, for instance, the Main Stage's headliner shows, where it turns out that you have to pay twenty dollars extra for a folding chair if you want to sit down; or the North Tent's mad scramble for the Nyquil-cup-sized samples of finalists' entries handed out after the cooking competition; or the much-touted Maine Sea Goddess pageant finals, which turn out to be excruciatingly long and to consist mainly of endless thanks and tributes to local sponsors. Let's not even talk about the grossly inadequate Port-A-San facilities or the fact that there's no place to wash your hands before or after eating. What the Maine Lobster Festival really is is a midlevel county fair with a culinary hook, and in this respect it's not unlike Tidewater crab festivals, Midwest corn festivals, Texas chili festivals, etc., and shares with these venues the core paradox of all teeming commercial demotic events: it's not for everyone.* Nothing against the euphoric senior editor of *Food*

---

* In truth, there's a great deal to be said about the differences between working-class Rockland and the heavily populist flavor of its Festival versus comfortable and elitist Camden with its expensive view and shops given entirely over to two-hundred-dollar sweaters and great rows of Victorian homes converted to upscale B&Bs. And about these differences as two sides of the great coin that is U.S. tourism. Very little of which will be said here, except to amplify the above-mentioned paradox and to reveal your assigned correspondent's own preferences. I confess that I have never understood why so many people's idea of a fun vacation is to don flip-flops and sunglasses and crawl through maddening traffic to loud, hot, crowded tourist venues in order to sample a "local flavor" that is by definition ruined by the presence of tourists. This may (as my Festival companions keep pointing out) all be a matter of personality and hard-wired taste: the fact that I do not like tourist venues means that I'll never understand their appeal and so am probably not the one to talk about it (the supposed appeal). But, since this FN will almost surely not survive magazine-editing anyway, here goes:

  As I see it, it probably really is good for the soul to be a tourist, even if it's only once in a while. Not good for the soul in a refreshing or enlivening way, though, but rather in a grim, steely-eyed, let's-look-honestly-at-the-facts-and-find-some-way-to-deal-with-them way. My personal experience has not been that traveling around the country is broadening or relaxing, or that radical changes in place and context have a salutary effect, but rather that intranational tourism is radically constricting,

& Wine, but I'd be surprised if she'd ever actually been here, in Harbor Park, watching people slap canal-zone mosquitoes as they eat deep-fried Twinkies and watch Professor Paddywhack, on six-foot stilts in a raincoat with plastic lobsters protruding from all directions on springs, terrify their children.

Lobster is essentially a summer food. This is because we now prefer our lobsters fresh, which means they have to be recently caught, which for both tactical and economic reasons takes place at depths less than 25 fathoms. Lobsters tend to be hungriest and most active (i.e., most trappable) at summer water temperatures of 45 to 50 degrees. In the autumn, most Maine lobsters migrate out into deeper water, either for warmth or to avoid the heavy waves that pound New England's coast all winter. Some burrow into the bottom. They might hibernate; nobody's sure. Summer is also lobsters' molting season — specifically, early to mid-July. Chitinous arthropods grow by molting, rather the way people have to buy bigger clothes as they age and gain weight. Since lobsters can live to be over a hundred, they can also get to be quite large, as in 25 pounds or more — though truly senior lobsters are rare now, because New England's waters are so heavily trapped.* Anyway, hence the culinary distinction between hard- and soft-shell lobsters, the latter sometimes a.k.a. shedders. A soft-shell lobster is one that has recently molted. In midcoast restaurants, the summer menu often offers both kinds, with shedders being slightly cheaper even though they're easier to dismantle and the meat is allegedly sweeter. The reason for the discount is that a molting lobster uses a layer of seawater for insulation while its new shell is hardening, so

---

and humbling in the hardest way — hostile to my fantasy of being a true individual, of living somehow outside and above it all. (Coming up is the part that my companions find especially unhappy and repellent, a sure way to spoil the fun of vacation travel:) To be a mass tourist, for me, is to become a pure late-date American: alien, ignorant, greedy for something you cannot ever have, disappointed in a way you can never admit. It is to spoil, by way of sheer ontology, the very unspoiledness you are there to experience. It is to impose yourself on places that in all noneconomic ways would be better, realer, without you. It is, in lines and gridlock and transaction after transaction, to confront a dimension of yourself that is as inescapable as it is painful: as a tourist, you become economically significant but existentially loathsome, an insect on a dead thing.

* Datum: In a good year, the U.S. industry produces around eighty million pounds of lobster, and Maine accounts for more than half that total.

there's slightly less actual meat when you crack open a shedder, plus a redolent gout of water that gets all over everything and can sometimes jet out lemonlike and catch a tablemate right in the eye. If it's winter or you're buying lobster someplace far from New England, on the other hand, you can almost bet that the lobster is a hard-shell, which for obvious reasons travel better.

As an à la carte entrée, lobster can be baked, broiled, steamed, grilled, sautéed, stir-fried, or microwaved. The most common method, though, is boiling. If you're someone who enjoys having lobster at home, this is probably the way you do it, since boiling is so easy. You need a large kettle w/cover, which you fill about half full with water (the standard advice is that you want 2.5 quarts of water per lobster). Seawater is optimal, or you can add two tbsp salt per quart from the tap. It also helps to know how much your lobsters weigh. You get the water boiling, put in the lobsters one at a time, cover the kettle, and bring it back to a boil. Then you bank the heat and let the kettle simmer — ten minutes for the first pound of lobster, then three minutes for each pound after that. (This is assuming you've got hard-shell lobsters, which, again, if you don't live between Boston and Halifax is probably what you've got. For shedders, you're supposed to subtract three minutes from the total.) The reason the kettle's lobsters turn scarlet is that boiling somehow suppresses every pigment in their chitin but one. If you want an easy test of whether the lobsters are done, you try pulling on one of their antennae — if it comes out of the head with minimal effort, you're ready to eat.

A detail so obvious that most recipes don't even bother to mention it is that each lobster is supposed to be alive when you put it in the kettle. This is part of lobster's modern appeal: it's the freshest food there is. There's no decomposition between harvesting and eating. And not only do lobsters require no cleaning or dressing or plucking, but they're relatively easy for vendors to keep alive. They come up alive in the traps, are placed in containers of seawater, and can — so long as the water's aerated and the animals' claws are pegged or banded to keep them from tearing one another up under the stresses of captivity* — survive right up until they're

---

* N.B. Similar reasoning underlies the practice of what's termed "debeaking" broiler chickens and brood hens in modern factory farms. Maximum commercial

boiled. Most of us have been in supermarkets or restaurants that feature tanks of live lobster, from which you can pick out your supper while it watches you point. And part of the overall spectacle of the Maine Lobster Festival is that you can see actual lobstermen's vessels docking at the wharves along the northeast grounds and unloading fresh-caught product, which is transferred by hand or cart 150 yards to the great clear tanks stacked up around the Festival's cooker — which is, as mentioned, billed as the World's Largest Lobster Cooker and can process over one hundred lobsters at a time for the Main Eating Tent.

So then here is a question that's all but unavoidable at the World's Largest Lobster Cooker, and may arise in kitchens across the United States: Is it all right to boil a sentient creature alive just for our gustatory pleasure? A related set of concerns: Is the previous question irksomely PC or sentimental? What does "all right" even mean in this context? Is it all just a matter of personal choice?

As you may or may not know, a certain well-known group called People for the Ethical Treatment of Animals thinks that the morality of lobster-boiling is not just a matter of individual conscience. In fact, one of the very first things we hear about the MLF . . . well, to set the scene: We're coming in by cab from the almost indescribably odd and rustic Knox County Airport* very late on the night before the Festival opens, sharing the cab with a wealthy political consultant who lives on Vinalhaven Island in the bay half the year (he's headed for the island ferry in Rockland). The consultant and cabdriver are responding to informal journalistic probes about how people who live in the midcoast region actually view the MLF, as in, Is the Festival just a big-dollar tourist thing, or is it something local residents look forward to attending, take genuine civic pride

---

efficiency requires that enormous poultry populations be confined in unnaturally close quarters, under which conditions many birds go crazy and peck one another to death. As a purely observational side note, be apprised that debeaking is usually an automated process and that the chickens receive no anesthetic. It's not clear to me whether most *Gourmet* readers know about debeaking, or about related practices like dehorning cattle in commercial feed lots, cropping swine's tails in factory hog farms to keep psychotically bored neighbors from chewing them off, and so forth. It so happens that your assigned correspondent knew almost nothing about standard meat-industry operations before starting work on this article.

* The terminal used to be somebody's house, for example, and the lost-luggage-reporting room was clearly once a pantry.

in, etc.? The cabdriver (who's in his seventies, one of apparently a whole platoon of retirees the cab company puts on to help with the summer rush, and wears a U.S.-flag lapel pin, and drives in what can only be called a very deliberate way) assures us that locals do endorse and enjoy the MLF, although he himself hasn't gone in years, and now come to think of it no one he and his wife know has, either. However, the demi-local consultant's been to recent Festivals a couple times (one gets the impression it was at his wife's behest), of which his most vivid impression was that "you have to line up for an ungodly long time to get your lobsters, and meanwhile there are all these ex–flower children coming up and down along the line handing out pamphlets that say the lobsters die in terrible pain and you shouldn't eat them."

And it turns out that the post-hippies of the consultant's recollection were activists from PETA. There were no PETA people in obvious view at the 2003 MLF,* but they've been conspicuous at many of the recent Festivals. Since at least the mid-1990s, articles in everything from the *Camden Herald* to the *New York Times* have described PETA urging boycotts of the Maine Lobster Festival, often deploying celebrity spokesmen like Mary Tyler Moore for open letters and ads saying stuff like "Lobsters are extraordinarily sensitive" and "To me, eating a lobster is out of the question." More concrete is the oral testimony of Dick, our florid and extremely gregarious rental-car liaison,† to the effect that PETA's been

* It turned out that one Mr. William R. Rivas-Rivas, a high-ranking PETA official out of the group's Virginia headquarters, was indeed there this year, albeit solo, working the Festival's main and side entrances on Saturday, 2 August, handing out pamphlets and adhesive stickers emblazoned with "Being Boiled Hurts," which is the tagline in most of PETA's published material about lobster. I learned that he'd been there only later, when speaking with Mr. Rivas-Rivas on the phone. I'm not sure how we missed seeing him in situ at the Festival, and I can't see much to do except apologize for the oversight — although it's also true that Saturday was the day of the big MLF parade through Rockland, which basic journalistic responsibility seemed to require going to (and which, with all due respect, meant that Saturday was maybe not the best day for PETA to work the Harbor Park grounds, especially if it was going to be just one person for one day, since a lot of diehard MLF partisans were off-site watching the parade [which, again with no offense intended, was in truth kind of cheesy and boring, consisting mostly of slow homemade floats and various midcoast people waving at one another, and with an extremely annoying man dressed as Blackbeard ranging up and down the length of the crowd saying "Arrr" over and over and brandishing a plastic sword at people, etc.; plus it rained]).

† By profession, Dick is actually a car salesman; the midcoast region's National Car Rental franchise operates out of a Chevy dealership in Thomaston.

around so much during recent years that a kind of brittlely toler-ant homeostasis now obtains between the activists and the Festi-val's locals, e.g.: "We had some incidents a couple years ago. One lady took most of her clothes off and painted herself like a lobster, almost got herself arrested. But for the most part they're let alone. [Rapid series of small ambiguous laughs, which with Dick happens a lot.] They do their thing and we do our thing."

This whole interchange takes place on Route 1, 30 July, during a four-mile, fifty-minute ride from the airport* to the dealership to sign car-rental papers. Several irreproducible segues down the road from the PETA anecdotes, Dick — whose son-in-law happens to be a professional lobsterman and one of the Main Eating Tent's regular suppliers — articulates what he and his family feel is the crucial mitigating factor in the whole morality-of-boiling-lobsters-alive issue: "There's a part of the brain in people and animals that lets us feel pain, and lobsters' brains don't have this part."

Besides the fact that it's incorrect in about eleven different ways, the main reason Dick's statement is interesting is that its thesis is more or less echoed by the Festival's own pronouncement on lob-sters and pain, which is part of a Test Your Lobster IQ quiz that ap-pears in the 2003 MLF program, courtesy of the Maine Lobster Promotion Council:

> The nervous system of a lobster is very simple, and is in fact most similar to the nervous system of the grasshopper. It is decentralized with no brain. There is no cerebral cortex, which in humans is the area of the brain that gives the experience of pain.

Though it sounds more sophisticated, a lot of the neurology in this latter claim is still either false or fuzzy. The human cerebral cortex is the brain part that deals with higher faculties like reason, meta-physical self-awareness, language, etc. Pain reception is known to be part of a much older and more primitive system of nociceptors and prostaglandins that are managed by the brain stem and thala-

---

* The short version regarding why we were back at the airport after already arriving the previous night involves lost luggage and a miscommunication about where and what the midcoast's National franchise was — Dick came out personally to the air-port and got us, out of no evident motive but kindness. (He also talked nonstop the entire way, with a very distinctive speaking style that can be described only as mani-cally laconic; the truth is that I now know more about this man than I do about some members of my own family.)

mus.* On the other hand, it is true that the cerebral cortex is involved in what's variously called suffering, distress, or the emotional experience of pain — i.e., experiencing painful stimuli as unpleasant, very unpleasant, unbearable, and so on.

Before we go any further, let's acknowledge that the questions of whether and how different kinds of animals feel pain, and of whether and why it might be justifiable to inflict pain on them in order to eat them, turn out to be extremely complex and difficult. And comparative neuroanatomy is only part of the problem. Since pain is a totally subjective mental experience, we do not have direct access to anyone or anything's pain but our own; and even just the principles by which we can infer that other people experience pain and have a legitimate interest in not feeling pain involve hardcore philosophy — metaphysics, epistemology, value theory, ethics. The fact that even the most highly evolved nonhuman mammals can't use language to communicate with us about their subjective mental experience is only the first layer of additional complication in trying to extend our reasoning about pain and morality to animals. And everything gets progressively more abstract and convoluted as we move farther and farther out from the higher-type mammals into cattle and swine and dogs and cats and rodents, and then birds and fish, and finally invertebrates like lobster.

The more important point here, though, is that the whole animal-cruelty-and-eating issue is not just complex, it's also uncomfortable. It is, at any rate, uncomfortable for me, and for just about everyone I know who enjoys a variety of foods and yet does not want to see herself as cruel or unfeeling. As far as I can tell, my own main way of dealing with this conflict has been to avoid thinking about the whole unpleasant thing. I should add that it appears to me unlikely that many readers of *Gourmet* wish to think hard about it, either, or to be queried about the morality of their eating habits in the pages of a culinary monthly. Since, however, the assigned

* To elaborate by way of example: The common experience of accidentally touching a hot stove and yanking your hand back before you're even aware that anything's going on is explained by the fact that many of the processes by which we detect and avoid painful stimuli do not involve the cortex. In the case of the hand and stove, the brain is bypassed altogether; all the important neurochemical action takes place in the spine.

subject of this article is what it was like to attend the 2003 MLF, and thus to spend several days in the midst of a great mass of Americans all eating lobster, and thus to be more or less impelled to think hard about lobster and the experience of buying and eating lobster, it turns out that there is no honest way to avoid certain moral questions.

There are several reasons for this. For one thing, it's not just that lobsters get boiled alive, it's that you do it yourself — or at least it's done specifically for you, on-site.* As mentioned, the World's Largest Lobster Cooker, which is highlighted as an attraction in the Festival's program, is right out there on the MLF's north grounds for everyone to see. Try to imagine a Nebraska Beef Festival† at which part of the festivities is watching trucks pull up and the live cattle get driven down the ramp and slaughtered right there on the World's Largest Killing Floor or something — there's no way.

The intimacy of the whole thing is maximized at home, which of course is where most lobster gets prepared and eaten (although note already the semi-conscious euphemism "prepared," which in the case of lobsters really means killing them right there in our kitchens). The basic scenario is that we come in from the store and make our little preparations like getting the kettle filled and boiling, and then we lift the lobsters out of the bag or whatever retail

---

* Morality-wise, let's concede that this cuts both ways. Lobster-eating is at least not abetted by the system of corporate factory farms that produces most beef, pork, and chicken. Because, if nothing else, of the way they're marketed and packaged for sale, we eat these latter meats without having to consider that they were once conscious, sentient creatures to whom horrible things were done. (N.B. "Horrible" here meaning really, really horrible. Write off to PETA or peta.org for their free "Meet Your Meat" video, narrated by Mr. Alec Baldwin, if you want to see just about everything meat-related you don't want to see or think about. [N.B.$_2$ Not that PETA's any sort of font of unspun truth. Like many partisans in complex moral disputes, the PETA people are fanatics, and a lot of their rhetoric seems simplistic and self-righteous. But this particular video, replete with actual factory-farm and corporate-slaughterhouse footage, is both credible and excruciating.])

† Is it significant that "lobster," "fish," and "chicken" are our culture's words for both the animal and the meat, whereas most mammals seem to require euphemisms like "beef" and "pork" that help us separate the meat we eat from the living creature the meat once was? Is this evidence that some kind of deep unease about eating higher animals is endemic enough to show up in English usage, but that the unease diminishes as we move out of the mammalian order? (And is "lamb"/"lamb" the counterexample that sinks the whole theory, or are there special, biblico-historical reasons for that equivalence?)

container they came home in . . . whereupon some uncomfortable things start to happen. However stuporous the lobster is from the trip home, for instance, it tends to come alarmingly to life when placed in boiling water. If you're tilting it from a container into the steaming kettle, the lobster will sometimes try to cling to the container's sides or even to hook its claws over the kettle's rim like a person trying to keep from going over the edge of a roof. And worse is when the lobster's fully immersed. Even if you cover the kettle and turn away, you can usually hear the cover rattling and clanking as the lobster tries to push it off. Or the creature's claws scraping the sides of the kettle as it thrashes around. The lobster, in other words, behaves very much as you or I would behave if we were plunged into boiling water (with the obvious exception of screaming).* A blunter way to say this is that the lobster acts as if it's in terrible pain, causing some cooks to leave the kitchen altogether and to take one of those little lightweight plastic oven timers with them into another room and wait until the whole process is over.

There happen to be two main criteria that most ethicists agree on for determining whether a living creature has the capacity to suffer and so has genuine interests that it may or may not be our moral duty to consider.† One is how much of the neurological hardware required for pain experience the animal comes equipped with —

---

* There's a relevant populist myth about the high-pitched whistling sound that sometimes issues from a pot of boiling lobster. The sound is really vented steam from the layer of seawater between the lobster's flesh and its carapace (this is why shedders whistle more than hard-shells), but the pop version has it that the sound is the lobster's rabbitlike death scream. Lobsters communicate via pheromones in their urine and don't have anything close to the vocal equipment for screaming, but the myth's very persistent — which might, once again, point to a low-level cultural unease about the boiling thing.

† "Interests" basically means strong and legitimate preferences, which obviously require some degree of consciousness, responsiveness to stimuli, etc. See, for instance, the utilitarian philosopher Peter Singer, whose 1974 *Animal Liberation* is more or less the bible of the modern animal-rights movement:

> It would be nonsense to say that it was not in the interests of a stone to be kicked along the road by a schoolboy. A stone does not have interests because it cannot suffer. Nothing that we can do to it could possibly make any difference to its welfare. A mouse, on the other hand, does have an interest in not being kicked along the road, because it will suffer if it is.

nociceptors, prostaglandins, neuronal opioid receptors, etc. The
other criterion is whether the animal demonstrates behavior associated with pain. And it takes a lot of intellectual gymnastics and
behaviorist hairsplitting not to see struggling, thrashing, and lid-
clattering as just such pain behavior. According to marine zoolo-
gists, it usually takes lobsters between thirty-five and forty-five seconds to die in boiling water. (No source I could find talked about
how long it takes them to die in superheated steam; one rather
hopes it's faster.)

There are, of course, other ways to kill your lobster on-site and
so achieve maximum freshness. Some cooks' practice is to drive a
sharp heavy knife point-first into a spot just above the midpoint between the lobster's eyestalks (more or less where the Third Eye is
in human foreheads). This is alleged either to kill the lobster instantly or to render it insensate, and is said at least to eliminate
some of the cowardice involved in throwing a creature into boiling
water and then fleeing the room. As far as I can tell from talking to
proponents of the knife-in-the-head method, the idea is that it's
more violent but ultimately more merciful, plus that a willingness
to exert personal agency and accept responsibility for stabbing the
lobster's head honors the lobster somehow and entitles one to eat
it. (There's often a vague sort of Native American spirituality-of-
the-hunt flavor to pro-knife arguments.) But the problem with the
knife method is basic biology: lobsters' nervous systems operate off
not one but several ganglia, a.k.a. nerve bundles, which are sort of
wired in series and distributed all along the lobster's underside,
from stem to stern. And disabling only the frontal ganglion does
not normally result in quick death or unconsciousness.

Another alternative is to put the lobster in cold saltwater and
then very slowly bring it up to a full boil. Cooks who advocate this
method are going on the analogy to a frog, which can supposedly
be kept from jumping out of a boiling pot by heating the water
incrementally. In order to save a lot of research-summarizing, I'll
simply assure you that the analogy between frogs and lobsters turns
out not to hold — plus, if the kettle's water isn't aerated seawater,
the immersed lobster suffers from slow suffocation, although usually not decisive enough suffocation to keep it from still thrashing
and clattering when the water gets hot enough to kill it. In fact,
lobsters boiled incrementally often display a whole bonus set of

gruesome, convulsionlike reactions that you don't see in regular boiling.

Ultimately, the only certain virtues of the home-lobotomy and slow-heating methods are comparative, because there are even worse/crueler ways people prepare lobster. Time-thrifty cooks sometimes microwave them alive (usually after poking several extra vent holes in the carapace, which is a precaution most shellfish-microwavers learn about the hard way). Live dismemberment, on the other hand, is big in Europe: some chefs cut the lobster in half before cooking; others like to tear off the claws and tail and toss only these parts into the pot.

And there's more unhappy news respecting suffering-criterion number one. Lobsters don't have much in the way of eyesight or hearing, but they do have an exquisite tactile sense, one facilitated by hundreds of thousands of tiny hairs that protrude through its carapace. "Thus," in the words of T. M. Prudden's industry classic *About Lobster,* "it is that although encased in what seems a solid, impenetrable armor, the lobster can receive stimuli and impressions from without as readily as if it possessed a soft and delicate skin." And lobsters do have nociceptors,* as well as invertebrate versions of the prostaglandins and major neurotransmitters via which our own brains register pain.

Lobsters do not, on the other hand, appear to have the equipment for making or absorbing natural opioids like endorphins and enkephalins, which are what more advanced nervous systems use to try to handle intense pain. From this fact, though, one could conclude either that lobsters are maybe even *more* vulnerable to pain, since they lack mammalian nervous systems' built-in analgesia, or, instead, that the absence of natural opioids implies an absence of the really intense pain sensations that natural opioids are designed to mitigate. I for one can detect a marked upswing in mood as I contemplate this latter possibility. It could be that their lack of endorphin/enkephalin hardware means that lobsters' raw subjective experience of pain is so radically different from mammals' that it may not even deserve the term "pain." Perhaps lob-

---

* This is the neurological term for special pain receptors that are "sensitive to potentially damaging extremes of temperature, to mechanical forces, and to chemical substances which are released when body tissues are damaged." (The quoted phrase is from a textbook.)

sters are more like those frontal-lobotomy patients one reads about
who report experiencing pain in a totally different way from you
and I. These patients evidently do feel physical pain, neurologi-
cally speaking, but don't dislike it — though neither do they like it;
it's more that they feel it but don't feel anything *about* it — the
point being that the pain is not distressing to them or something
they want to get away from. Maybe lobsters, who are also without
frontal lobes, are detached from the neurological-registration-of-
injury-or-hazard we call pain in just the same way. There is, after
all, a difference between (1) pain as a purely neurological event,
and (2) actual suffering, which seems crucially to involve an emotional component, an awareness of pain as unpleasant, as something to fear/dislike/want to avoid.

Still, after all the abstract intellection, there remain the facts of
the frantically clanking lid, the pathetic clinging to the edge of the
pot. Standing at the stove, it is hard to deny in any meaningful way
that this is a living creature experiencing pain and wishing to
avoid/escape the painful experience. To my lay mind, the lobster's
behavior in the kettle appears to be the expression of a *preference;*
and it may well be that an ability to form preferences is the decisive
criterion for real suffering.* The logic of this (preference → suffering) relation may be easiest to see in the negative case. If you cut
certain kinds of worms in half, the halves will often keep crawling
around and going about their vermiform business as if nothing
had happened. When we assert, based on their post-op behavior,
that these worms appear not to be suffering, what we're really saying is that there's no sign that the worms know anything bad has
happened or would *prefer* not to have gotten cut in half.

Lobsters, though, are known to exhibit preferences. Experiments have shown that they can detect changes of only a degree or
two in water temperature; one reason for their complex migratory
cycles (which can often cover one-hundred-plus miles a year) is
to pursue the temperatures they like best.† And, as mentioned,

---

* "Preference" is maybe roughly synonymous with "interests," but it is a better term
for our purposes because it's less abstractly philosophical — "preference" seems
more personal, and it's the whole idea of a living creature's personal experience
that's at issue.
† Of course, the most common sort of counterargument here would begin by ob-
jecting that "like best" is really just a metaphor, and a misleadingly anthropomor-

they're bottom dwellers, and do not like bright light: if a tank of food-lobsters is out in the sunlight or a store's fluorescence, the lobsters will always congregate in whatever part is darkest. Fairly solitary in the ocean, they also clearly dislike the crowding that's part of their captivity in tanks, since (as also mentioned) one reason why lobsters' claws are banded on capture is to keep them from attacking one another under the stress of close-quarter storage.

In any event, at the Festival, standing by the bubbling tanks outside the World's Largest Lobster Cooker, watching the fresh-caught lobsters pile over one another, wave their hobbled claws impotently, huddle in the rear corners, or scrabble frantically back from the glass as you approach, it is difficult not to sense that they're unhappy, or frightened, even if it's some rudimentary version of these feelings . . . and, again, why does rudimentariness even enter into it? Why is a primitive, inarticulate form of suffering less urgent or uncomfortable for the person who's helping to inflict it by paying for the food it results in? I'm not trying to give you a PETA-like screed here — at least I don't think so. I'm trying, rather, to work out and articulate some of the troubling questions that arise amid all the laughter and saltation and community pride of the Maine Lobster Festival. The truth is that if you, the Festival attendee, permit yourself to think that lobsters can suffer and would rather not,

---

phic one at that. The counterarguer would posit that the lobster seeks to maintain a certain optimal ambient temperature out of nothing but unconscious instinct (with a similar explanation for the low-light affinities upcoming in the main text). The thrust of such a counterargument will be that the lobster's thrashings and clankings in the kettle express not unpreferred pain but involuntary reflexes, like your leg shooting out when the doctor hits your knee. Be advised that there are professional scientists, including many researchers who use animals in experiments, who hold to the view that nonhuman creatures have no real feelings at all, merely "behaviors." Be further advised that this view has a long history that goes all the way back to Descartes, although its modern support comes mostly from behaviorist psychology.

To these what-look-like-pain-are-really-just-reflexes counterarguments, however, there happen to be all sorts of scientific and pro–animal rights counter-counterarguments. And then further attempted rebuttals and redirects, and so on. Suffice to say that both the scientific and the philosophical arguments on either side of the animal-suffering issue are involved, abstruse, technical, often informed by self-interest or ideology, and in the end so totally inconclusive that as a practical matter, in the kitchen or restaurant, it all still seems to come down to individual conscience, going with (no pun) your gut.

the MLF begins to take on the aspect of something like a Roman circus or medieval torture-fest.

Does that comparison seem a bit much? If so, exactly why? Or what about this one: Is it possible that future generations will regard our own present agribusiness and eating practices in much the same way we now view Nero's entertainments or Aztec sacrifices? My own initial reaction is that such a comparison is hysterical, extreme — and yet the reason it seems extreme to me appears to be that I believe animals are less morally important than human beings*; and when it comes to defending such a belief, even to myself, I have to acknowledge that (a) I have an obvious selfish interest in this belief, since I like to eat certain kinds of animals and want to be able to keep doing it, and (b) I haven't succeeded in working out any sort of personal ethical system in which the belief is truly defensible instead of just selfishly convenient.

Given this article's venue and my own lack of culinary sophistication, I'm curious about whether the reader can identify with any of these reactions and acknowledgments and discomforts. I am also concerned not to come off as shrill or preachy when what I really am is more like confused, uneasy. For those *Gourmet* readers who enjoy well-prepared and -presented meals involving beef, veal, lamb, pork, chicken, lobster, etc.: How much do you think about the (possible) moral status and (probable) physical suffering of the animals involved? If so, what ethical convictions have you worked out that permit you not just to eat but to savor and enjoy flesh-based viands (since of course refined *enjoyment,* rather than just ingestion, is the whole point of gastronomy)? If, on the other hand, you'll have no truck with confusions or convictions and regard stuff like the previous paragraph as just so much fatuous navel-gazing, what makes it feel OK, inside, to just dismiss the whole thing out of hand? That is, is your refusal to think about any of this the product of actual thought, or is it just that you don't want to think about it? And if the latter, then why not? Do you ever think, even idly, about the possible reasons for your reluctance to think

---

* Meaning *a lot* less important, apparently, since the moral comparison here is not the value of one human's life versus the value of one animal's life, but rather the value of one animal's life versus the value of one human's taste for a particular kind of protein. Even the most diehard carniphile will acknowledge that it's possible to live and eat well without consuming animals.

about it? I am not trying to bait anyone here — I'm genuinely curious. After all, isn't being extra aware and attentive and thoughtful about one's food and its overall context part of what distinguishes a real gourmet? Or is all the gourmet's extra attention and sensibility just supposed to be sensuous? Is it really all just a matter of taste and presentation?

These last few queries, though, while sincere, obviously involve much larger and more abstract questions about the connections (if any) between aesthetics and morality — about what the adjective in a phrase like "The Magazine of Good Living" is really supposed to mean — and these questions lead straightaway into such deep and treacherous waters that it's probably best to stop the public discussion right here. There are limits to what even interested persons can ask of each other.

HOLLY WELKER

Satin Worship

FROM PMS

A NOTION is "a small useful item, such as needles, buttons or thread." Thread is a notion; destiny is a thread.

Clotho spins it, Lachesis measures it, and Atropos cuts it off. They were the Fates, or the *Moirai,* of Greek mythology. Not only is necessity the mother of invention; some say that Themis, goddess of necessity, was also the mother of the Fates. You can find depictions of Clotho ("the spinster") holding a distaff, Lachesis ("disposer of lots") with a scroll, and Atropos ("the inexorable one") with a pair of scissors. Sometimes in these depictions all three of them are hideous hags who share a single eye between them (they pass it around when they need it); in some depictions Clotho is young, Lachesis is middle-aged, and Atropos is a crone. But there are also depictions of all three as gorgeous, graceful, divine women.

That's the depiction I like best. Embedded in it is the idea of life as raw material to be shaped into something beautiful and useful according to a woman's fancy, as well as the idea of death, not as a scary old guy with a scythe, but as a pretty goddess with a pair of very sharp scissors.

Scissors, a mundane object to which we are introduced in kindergarten (if not earlier), are a sophisticated tool requiring opposable thumbs and some dexterity. Sharp scissors are potentially a weapon; hence the instruction never to run with scissors. I imagine few homes in modern America are without at least one pair of scissors, but I also imagine that few homes are as well stocked with scissors as mine. I have kitchen scissors, several pairs of paper scissors, embroidery scissors, dressmaker shears, and pinking shears.

To "pink" means to cut something with a decorative border; a saw-toothed zigzag edge is standard in sewing, and a way to prevent fabric from raveling. Because they have so many cutting edges, pinking shears must be kept well oiled and protected. They are also heavier than normal scissors, and not something you use every day.

My favorite scissors are my dressmaker shears; each time I use them, I admire not only their usefulness but how well made and aesthetically satisfying they are. They have a pleasing heft, and despite that heft, the handles never pinch my thumb. The blades open smoothly and the cuts they make are even and crisp. The scissors are also visually appealing, made as they are from high-quality chrome (says so right on them) and very shiny. I keep them in a case so that the blades are protected; I have used them for over twenty years, and they have never required sharpening — they could be a weapon easily enough. They were a Christmas gift from my mother when I was in high school; at the time I received them, they seemed to me an acknowledgment that I was a pretty good seamstress, good enough to have my own shears. I still feel a trace of pride whenever I take them out of their case. But it occurs to me now that my mother might also have tired of letting me borrow her good scissors every time I wanted to cut some fabric.

Ecclesiastes 3:7 says that there is "a time to rend, and a time to sew." I think about this every time I lay fabric on the floor and cut out a dress. I suppose it is something of a risk — something whole is rent — but it rarely feels like one; it feels like a necessary step, part of a making, not an unmaking.

I love how sewing makes me feel capable and efficient. People often ask me to mend things. "Sew this button on for me, fix this hem, repair this ripped seam," they plead, as if these were difficult tasks.

I would guess that needles are one of the oldest tools humanity has invented, and there are myths to support this. In Genesis we are told that Adam and Eve are commanded to tend the Garden of Eden; maybe that means that they had to fashion hoes and rakes; maybe they just used their hands. But the next activity in which they engage is sewing aprons out of fig leaves; that would require needles.

I've also found a book to support the antiquity of needles: *Women's Work: The First 20,000 Years: Women, Cloth, and Society in Early Times* by Elizabeth Wayland Barber. But Barber also talks about the antiquity of string. It had not occurred to me that someone had to invent string, had to figure out that if you twisted shorter, weaker filaments together, plying in new strands as needed, you'd end up with a longer, stronger length of cord. Seventeen-thousand-year-old string has been found embedded in the walls of ancient cave dwellings in southern France. The theory is that some Paleolithic Ariadne figured out that by running a cord from cave to cave, the inhabitants could make their way through that dark labyrinth of the past.

If the Fates saw fit to cut that string, how many lives would drop away with it?

My sewing machine is a sturdy brown electric Singer, a heavy piece of cast iron. My grandmother gave it, brand-new, to my mother as a high school graduation gift in 1955. I inherited it because I was the only one of my mother's four daughters with the patience to learn to read a pattern, to rip out seams when I sewed the pieces together wrong, to spend two hours pinning and hemming a dress by hand. I was the only one with fabric lust.

Calico, flannel, gabardine, corduroy, velveteen, lace, silk, satin. I've seen a bumper sticker that reads, "Whoever dies with the most fabric wins," and I think I'm in the running. There are two components to my fabric lust. One is pragmatic, a sense of fabric as raw material for that practical necessity, clothing. The other is admiration for something both sensual and beautiful: the smoothness of finely woven cotton or silk, the fuzzy nap of something like velvet or brushed flannel, the vividness of certain prints. I have four big bins of fabrics in various lengths, as well as a giant crate of scraps, which I sew together for quilts.

In my final year of work on a Ph.D. in English literature, I found myself in need of both extra cash and a break from my dissertation, so I took a part-time job at a fabric store, where I could get paid to fondle the fabric. The job paid barely more than minimum wage, and most of the employees were part-time; hiring women who considered the job a hobby was one of the ways the company kept costs down. There were a few teachers as well as several well-to-do grandmothers, women with financial security who wanted to get out of the house for ten hours a week and be around fabric. The store was actually a fabric and craft store, but I never understood the craft aspect, why people felt compelled to buy Styrofoam balls of various sizes and meld them into new objects, why someone would want to paint preprinted designs on cheap wooden boxes, especially when there was all that fabric to be had on the other side of the store.

I liked cutting fabric for patrons well enough; it meant I could spread the fabric out, rub it between my fingers, and admire the color and design, but it also meant I had to talk to the customer. Preferable was the solitary activity of putting things away. I liked stocking the notions wall. It was a truly awesome sight: a thousand square feet covered with gadgets to assist in an array of fabric-related tasks such as measuring, cutting, ironing. It was the usefulness of the notions that captivated me, and the human ingenuity that had led to their invention. Surveying that wall, it seemed to me that one could never have enough notions.

But my favorite task was reshelving the bolts of fabric after a customer had bought whatever length she needed. I would load up a shopping cart, then wander the store, looking for each bolt's place among its companion fabrics, comparing colors and wasting a moment coveting the fabrics I couldn't afford: thirty or forty or eighty dollars for a yard of full-nap, one-hundred-percent-cotton velvet or genuine Thai silk.

The job had one primary perk: a hefty discount. More than once I spent my entire check on fabric that went straight into a storage box. I rarely had plans for the fabric I bought; it was simply beautiful, and while I did imagine that someday I would find something worthwhile to do with it, there was the more pressing imperative to *own it immediately*, five yards of that charcoal flannel, six yards of this teal and gold paisley calico.

When it came to anything but fabric I was a lousy salesperson. I could help someone locate the aisle for beads or embroidery floss, but I became testy with customers who expected me to demonstrate a thorough knowledge of the details of stenciling or doll-making. I especially hated working the cash register, where I was supposed to engage in pleasant banter with people who often were buying crap that I felt shouldn't exist in the first place, and I absolutely couldn't bear that much of that crap was wrapped in excessive packaging that would end up in some landfill. The line to my register was always long, a fact the people in it always resented. "All I wanted was to buy some buttons, and I have to wait in a line like this. Can't you have a few more cashiers?" they'd ask.

"Listen, lady, I'd love it if there were a few more cashiers. But this is corporate America you're dealing with. The people in charge of decisions like that want to make money, not spend it," I'd think — sometimes I'd say it aloud. And despite the fact that I was clearly a terrible cashier, the manager seemed to think it wise to put me on cash-register duty and leave me there. Once it became clear that I would be handling the cash register more than I handled fabric, I quit.

In the 1970s, when I was growing up, all Mormon girls were required to study certain homemaking skills, including the fundamentals of childcare; we then had to scare up babysitting gigs so we could implement that knowledge. We also had to study needlework. It was part of the official church curriculum to teach eleven-year-old girls to embroider and crochet; twelve-year-olds learned to knit. I never cared for embroidery; the stitches were too small and the results too purely ornamental, not at all utilitarian. I did like knitting, however. One day my grandmother saw me knitting the way I had been taught to knit at church, with a superfluous step where the yarn is wrapped by hand around the needle for the upcoming stitch, and after she recovered from her outrage, she sat me down and taught me how to do it *correctly*, by using the needles themselves to pick up a new stitch.

Knitting is a skill that has come in handy throughout my life, mostly because I am so afflicted by the Protestant work ethic that I can't bear to watch television unless I am doing something productive with my hands. I suppose in this way I am somewhat like Madame Defarge, the enigmatic matron in *A Tale of Two Cities* who sits beside the guillotine, knitting to pass the time and making a mark in her stitches for each head that is chopped off. I am a competent but not a superior knitter. My stitches, while even and smooth, are fairly tight; this makes it hard for me to do fancy stitches (not

enough room to maneuver the needles inside the old stitches), but
I do well with easy projects like pillows or dish towels or baby
afghans. If I'm working with a simple pattern, I don't even need to
look at my stitches; my hands can tell what they should be doing,
and the repetitive nature of the work makes it as restful and soothing as fingering prayer beads.

Knitting is a very old activity. There was a time in European history when all peasant children learned to knit; they knit their own
very scratchy underwear out of wool as well as items to sell at market. Despite its historical position as a craft of the lower classes,
knitting is now rather a bourgeois activity: good yarn is anything
but cheap, and the time necessary to complete something like a
sweater means that you must be blessed not only with leisure but
with resolve.

I prefer to sew with cotton fabric, but I would rather knit with
wool; it's stretchy and forgiving. You can undo your stitches and
the yarn will spring back and look smooth when you knit it again.
When I bother to make something as time-intensive as a sweater, I
always use wool. Cotton yarn isn't nearly so forgiving; the less expensive varieties of cotton yarn can feel like rope.

The sweaters I've made aren't impressive specimens, but they've
taught me a lot. If it's true that "a stitch in time saves nine," it's
even truer that a stitch not in time can cost hundreds or thousands
of additional stitches. One dropped stitch — a single moment's in-
attention — can throw an entire pattern out of whack. In a knitting class a few years ago I noticed that one of the hardest things
for people to do is to take out stitches after they've made a mistake.
They would rather finish a garment that has a serious flaw than go
back and start over; they just keep hoping that the mistake isn't
that critical, that it won't show. They can't bear to have their time
rendered a waste by dint of a mistake and would rather commit to
continuing a flawed article than to just starting over. And so they
waste more time and more yarn and end up with something they
can't even use.

I make a lot of baby quilts, partly because I know a lot of people
who have babies, and partly because a baby quilt is a gratifyingly
manageable project. You can design the pattern and sew together
all the blocks for the top in a weekend. Furthermore, the sandwich

of fabric backing, batting, and patchwork-quilt top with which you work is small enough that you can easily hold it on your lap and keep it taut with a quilting hoop rather than having to stretch it out on a frame that could fill an entire room.

"Quilting" refers to stitching all the layers together; things can be hand- or machine-quilted, stitched with elaborate patterns or simple lines. I consider quilting one of the most artistic things I do. I'm not much good at drawing, but I have a decent eye for color and shape; I always design my own quilts, and I can tell when a pattern needs a dark block here, a light one there. Someone once asked me to show her all the quilts I've made. "I gave them away," I said, surprised. "I made them as gifts."

"Didn't you take pictures of them first?" she asked. But I didn't, any more than I took pictures of dresses I made before I wore them.

"Spinning a yarn" is a metaphor for telling a story, and stories can be "embroidered." But quilting doesn't seem to be of much use as a way to talk about narrative. Stitching contrasting pieces of fabric into a pattern, stitching that to another piece of fabric with some stuffing in the middle so that heat-trapping pockets of air are formed — that's too elaborate for the way our culture likes to talk about writing. In fact, it's rather an insult to call a story a patchwork, but high praise to call it seamless.

I was commanded to learn a lot of homemaking skills; I acquired the skills but not the home, not in the way I was supposed to, anyway. My skills are not put to use in service of a husband and children of my own. In fact, I am what you might call a spinster aunt. My four siblings have provided me with more than a dozen nieces and nephews. The term "spinster" originally meant one who spins, though it has come to mean an old maid, someone who has womanly attributes but whose womanhood is not fully realized.

I've seen spinning wheels in museums and in photographs, but I've never handled one, and I want to. I want to learn to spin fibers into thread. If nothing else, I think it would help me understand what's going on the next time I encounter a fairy tale in which a maiden is required to spin or is caught at her spinning or is killed because she pricks her finger on a spindle. I've seen a drawing of the *Venus de Milo* with arms — and they're in the right position for spinning. I'm intrigued by the way *spinning* has equaled *women* throughout history, and by the vestiges of that notion in our culture. For instance, while the patrilineal side of a family is known as the "spear side," the matrilineal side is called the "distaff side," a distaff being a wooden board, sometimes plain but often intricately carved, to which the raw material to be spun (flax, wool, cotton) is tied, and from which the spinner draws as she winds the thread or yarn onto a spindle or wheel.

For many, many centuries, the average person would have been familiar with the complex processes by which fiber becomes clothing, having either observed or engaged in the processes herself. First the fiber is carded and spun. It can be dyed before or after it is woven. It can be cut and sewn together in shapes resembling the body, and it can then be embroidered, beaded, pleated, smocked, quilted, painted, sequined, bejeweled.

Fabric stimulates several of our senses. It can be any color, shiny or matte, patterned or plain; its texture can be soft or silky or fuzzy or nubby or fluffy. Fabric can even appeal to the ear: there is the crinkle of a stiff fabric like taffeta or the rough sound of corduroy rubbing against itself. Textiles can be utilitarian, sensual, expressive, beautiful, and extravagant all at once.

For millennia, textiles have served as a metaphor for both an entire gender and an individual life. Even when the myth that spinning women controlled the fate of humanity was abandoned, the idea that *spinning = women* hung on. Spinning is now a task done by machines, not real women, and so spinning is now associated with a form of counterfeit womanhood. Well, I'm not afraid of working with my hands or of old maidenhood. I'm trying to spin and weave the fibers of my life into a tapestry both beautiful and useful, and of my own design.

Biographical Notes

Roger Angell has been a writer for *The New Yorker* since 1944 and a fiction editor since 1956. He has written nine books about baseball, including *Game Time* (2003). A collection of memoirs, *Let Me Finish*, will be published in 2006.

Andrea Barrett is the author of five novels, most recently *The Voyage of the Narwhal*, and two collections of short fiction: *Ship Fever*, which received the 1996 National Book Award, and *Servants of the Map*, a finalist for the Pulitzer Prize. A MacArthur Fellow, she's also received NEA and Guggenheim fellowships, and in 2001–2002 she was a Fellow at the Center for Scholars and Writers at the New York Public Library. She lives in western Massachusetts.

Paul Crenshaw is a graduate of the M.F.A. writing program at the University of North Carolina at Greensboro, where he was a Fred Chappell Fellow. His short stories and essays have appeared in *The North American Review, Southern Humanities Review, Hayden's Ferry Review, South Dakota Review*, and *North Dakota Quarterly*, among other publications. "Storm Country" is the title essay of a recently completed collection. Twice nominated for the Pushcart Prize, he has also completed a novel and a collection of short stories.

Brian Doyle is the editor of *Portland* magazine at the University of Portland, in Oregon. He is the author of five collections of essays, most recently *Spirited Men*, about writers and musicians. The essay here is adapted from his book *The Wet Engine*, about "the magic & muddle & mangle & miracle & music of hearts," which was published in May 2005.

KITTY BURNS FLOREY is the author of nine novels, most recently *Solos* (2004) and *Souvenir of Cold Springs* (2001). Her short stories and essays have been published in the *New York Times, Harper's Magazine, The North American Review, The Greensboro Review,* and *House Beautiful.* "Sister Bernadette's Barking Dog" was originally published on her Web site, www.kittyburnsflorey.com; a version of it also appeared in *The Vocabula Review.* She lives in the Greenpoint section of Brooklyn with her husband and cats.

JONATHAN FRANZEN was educated in the Missouri public schools and at Swarthmore College. He is the author of the novels *The Twenty-Seventh City, Strong Motion,* and *The Corrections,* and a collection of essays, *How to Be Alone.* He lives in New York City.

IAN FRAZIER writes humor, essays, journalism, and other nonfiction. His books include *Dating Your Mom, Great Plains, Coyote v. Acme,* and *On the Rez.* He was guest editor of *The Best American Essays 1997.* He lives in Montclair, New Jersey.

MARK GREIF is a cofounder and an editor of *n+1,* a new journal of literature, politics, and culture. He was a Marshall Scholar at Oxford in 1997, and his writing has appeared in *TLS,* the *New York Times, Harper's Magazine, Dissent, Raritan,* and elsewhere. The essay "Against Exercise" first appeared in the inaugural issue of *n+1* and is part of an ongoing project about the history of morality. Since 2000, he has been a senior correspondent at *The American Prospect.* He lives on Cape Cod.

EDWARD HOAGLAND has published eight collections of essays, most recently *Balancing Acts* and *Tigers & Ice;* five books of fiction, including *Seven Rivers West;* two travel books, *Notes from the Century Before: A Journal from British Columbia* and *African Calliope: A Journey to the Sudan;* and a memoir, *Compass Points* (2001). He also writes criticism and was the editor of the Penguin Nature Classics series. He is a member of the American Academy of Arts and Letters and has taught at ten colleges. He was guest editor of *The Best American Essays 1999.*

TED KOOSER is the Poet Laureate Consultant in Poetry to the Library of Congress and the winner of the 2005 Pulitzer Prize in poetry for *Delights & Shadows* (2004). His two prose books are *Local Wonder: Seasons in the Bohemian Alps,* a book of short essays, and *The Poetry Home Repair Manual.*

JONATHAN LETHEM is the author of *The Fortress of Solitude* and five other novels. His fifth, *Motherless Brooklyn,* won the National Book Critics Circle Award in 2000. His essay collection, *The Disappointment Artist,* which includes a slightly different version of the essay that appears here, was published in March 2005. He lives with his wife in Brooklyn and Maine.

E. J. LEVY earned an M.F.A. in creative writing from Ohio State University in 2002 and holds a B.A. in history from Yale. Her fiction has appeared in *The Paris Review, The Gettysburg Review, Bloom,* and elsewhere; her essays have been published in *Salmagundi, Fourth Genre,* and *Orion.* She has received numerous prizes for her writing, as well as a Lambda Literary Award for her anthology *Tasting Life Twice: Literary Lesbian Fiction by New American Writers.* An assistant professor in the graduate program in creative writing at American University in Washington, D.C., she is completing a memoir set in the Brazilian rain forest, *Amazons: A Kind of Love Story.*

MICHAEL MARTONE is a professor of English and the director of the creative writing program at the University of Alabama, where he has been teaching since 1996. Before that, he taught at Syracuse University, Iowa State University, and Harvard University. He was born and grew up in Fort Wayne, Indiana, studied at Butler University in Indianapolis, and graduated from Indiana University and from the Writing Seminars of Johns Hopkins University. The author of five books of short fiction — *Seeing Eye* (1995), *Pensées: The Thoughts of Dan Quayle* (1994), *Fort Wayne Is Seventh on Hitler's List* (1990), *Safety Patrol* (1988), and *Alive and Dead in Indiana* (1984) — he has also edited two collections of essays about the Midwest, *A Place of Sense: Essays in Search of the Midwest* (1988) and *Townships: Pieces of the Midwest* (1992). He edits Story County Books, and his newest book, *The Flatness and Other Landscapes* (2000), a collection of his essays about the Midwest, won the Association of Writers and Writing Program's award for creative nonfiction in 1998. His next book will be *Michael Martone,* a memoir in contributor's notes.

DAVID MASELLO is the articles editor at *Country Living* and the longtime New York editor of *Art & Antiques.* His essays have appeared in the *New York Times,* the *Boston Globe, Newsweek,* the *San Francisco Chronicle,* and *The Massachusetts Review,* among other periodicals. His work has also been included in several anthologies, including *The Man I Might Become, Wonderlands,* and *New York Stories.* He is the author of two books, *Architecture Without Rules: The Houses of Marcel Breuer and Herbert Beckhard* and *Art in Public Places.* In the coming year, he plans to visit the actual locales of Lodovico and Bronzino.

DANIELLE OFRI, M.D., PH.D., is the author of two collections of essays about life in medicine, *Incidental Findings* and *Singular Intimacies.* She is the cofounder and editor in chief of *The Bellevue Literary Review.* Her writings have appeared in the *New York Times,* the *Los Angeles Times, The Best American Essays, The Best American Science Writing, The New England Journal of Medicine, The Lancet,* and on National Public Radio. She is an attending physician at Bellevue Hospital and assistant professor of medicine at New York University School of Medicine. She lives in New York City with her husband and two children.

SAM PICKERING teaches English at the University of Connecticut. *The Best of Pickering,* a selection of his essays, and *Waltzing the Magpies,* an account of a year he and his family spent in Australia, were published in 2004. That year, *Letters to a Teacher,* his book about teaching, also appeared, and in summer 2005 he publishd a new collection of essays, *Indian Summer.*

OLIVER SACKS, M.D., was born in London in 1933 and educated in London, Oxford, and California. A clinical professor of neurology at the Albert Einstein College of Medicine, he has received numerous honors for his writings, which include *Awakenings, The Man Who Mistook His Wife for a Hat,* and *An Anthropologist on Mars.* His most recent books are *Uncle Tungsten: Memories of a Chemical Boyhood* (2001) and *Oaxaca Journal* (2002). Dr. Sacks practices neurology in New York City, and he is a Fellow of both the American Academy of Arts and Letters and the American Academy of Arts and Sciences.

CATHLEEN SCHINE is the author of six novels, including *Alice in Bed, To the Birdhouse, The Evolution of Jane,* and *She Is Me.* Two of her books, the international bestsellers *Rameau's Niece* and *The Love Letter,* were made into movies. She has written for *The New York Times Magazine* and *The New York Review of Books,* among other publications. Her new novel, *The New Yorkers,* will be published in 2006. She lives in New York City.

DAVID SEDARIS is the author of the collections *Dress Your Family in Corduroy and Denim, Me Talk Pretty One Day, Naked, Holidays on Ice,* and *Barrel Fever.* He is a regular contributor to *The New Yorker, GQ,* and National Public Radio's *This American Life.* "Old Faithful" has also appeared in an anthology, *Committed* (2005), edited by Chris Knutsen and David Kuhn, who commissioned the essay.

PAULA SPECK has published essays in *The Gettysburg Review, The Literary Review,* and *The Massachusetts Review,* among other literary journals. Three of her essays have appeared as notable works in previous editions of *The Best American Essays,* and one of her essays was selected as notable in *The Best American Travel Writing.* Speck is a frequent instructor at the Writer's Center in Bethesda, Maryland. She would like to dedicate this essay to the late Judge Sam D. Johnson, U.S. Court of Appeals for the Fifth Circuit.

BERT O. STATES, who died in October 2003, was the author of eight books on literary theory, drama, and dreaming, including *The Rhetoric of Dreams* (1989), *Dreaming and Storytelling* (1993), and *Seeing in the Dark* (1997). His essays and fiction have appeared in *The Hudson Review, The Georgia Review, The Gettysburg Review, The Kenyon Review, The Yale Review, Salmagundi, The American Scholar, Boulevard,* and elsewhere. His essay "On Being Breathless" was selected for *The Best American Essays 2001.* He had taught at Skidmore College, the University of Pittsburgh, Cornell University, and the University of California, and had recently completed a new book on metaphorical vision, *Seeing Double: Reflections on the Metaphorical Eye.*

ROBERT STONE was born in Brooklyn, New York, in 1937. He is the author of seven novels: *A Hall of Mirrors* (1967), *Dog Soldiers* (1974), *A Flag for Sunrise* (1981), *Children of Light* (1986), *Outerbridge Reach* (1992), *Damascus Gate* (1998), and *Bay of Souls* (2003). He has also written short stories, essays, and screenplays, and he published a short story collection, *Bear and His Daughter,* in 1997. *Dog Soldiers* won a National Book Award in 1975. He lives in Key West, Florida.

ELLEN ULLMAN is the author of *Close to the Machine,* a memoir about her twenty years of experience as a software engineer, and *The Bug,* a novel. Her essays about the emotional and social effects of computing have appeared in *Harper's Magazine, Salon, Wired,* and the *New York Times.* She was a contributing editor of *The American Scholar,* where "Dining with Robots" first appeared. She lives in San Francisco.

DAVID FOSTER WALLACE is from Illinois but now lives — along with what seems like half the entire race — in California. His second volume of collected essays, in which "Consider the Lobster" is included, will be published in 2006.

HOLLY WELKER is an assistant professor of English and creative writing at Penn State Erie, the Behrend College. She holds a Ph.D. in English literature from the University of Iowa. She has published poetry, fiction, and nonfiction in such journals as *Black Warrior Review, Dialogue: A Journal of Mormon Thought, Gulf Coast, Hayden's Ferry Review, The Iowa Review, Other Voices, PMS, Sunstone,* and *TriQuarterly.* She has written a memoir, *The Rib Cage,* about her experiences as a Mormon missionary in Taiwan. Born and raised in southeastern Arizona, she currently lives and writes in northwestern Pennsylvania.

Notable Essays of 2004

SELECTED BY ROBERT ATWAN

MARILYN ABILDSKOV
Every Verb Imagined. *Apalachee Review,* **(TK)**

ANWAR F. ACCAWI
Plastic. *Sewanee Review,* Fall.

ANDRÉ ACIMAN
Remanence. *Harvard Review,* no. 27.

JOAN ACOCELLA
Blocked. *The New Yorker,* June 14/21.

FAITH ADIELE
Black Men. *Indiana Review,* Summer.

JONIS AGEE
The Altitudes of Dreams. *The Iowa Review,* Fall.

MARCIA ALDRICH
Of Snakes. *Puerto del Sol,* Spring.

SAM ANDERSON
Re: Re: Re: Re: Re: Joyce, *The American Scholar,* Summer.

NATALIE ANGIER
My God Problem — and Theirs. *The American Scholar,* Spring.

DONALD ANTRIM
The Kimono. *The New Yorker,* March 15.

CHRIS ARTHUR
Miracle Story. Southern Humanities Review, Winter.

DIANA ATHILL
Alive, Alive-Oh! *Granta,* Spring.

DAVID BAHR
Mothered. *GQ,* August.

FREDERICK BARTON
How the State of Illinois Made Me a Criminal in Louisiana. *The Literary Review,* Fall.

LOUIS BEGLEY
An Orphaned Writer. *The American Scholar,* Summer.

GENE H. BELL-VILLADA
Who Was Ayn Rand? *Salmagundi,* Winter/Spring.

PAULA BELNAP
Trappings. *Raritan,* Spring.

CATHERINE BERGART
Doing It. Bellevue Literary Review, Fall.

BRUCE BERGER
Six Degrees of Connection, *Southwest Review,* vol. 89, no. 1.

SVEN BIRKERTS
Flaubert's Anatomy. *The American Scholar,* Winter.

WILLIAM E. BLUNDELL
My Florida. The American Scholar, Winter.

Notable Special Issues of 2004

The Antioch Review, "All Essay Issue: People, Places, Prose," ed. Robert S. Fogarty, Spring.

Critical Inquiry, "The Future of Criticism," ed. W.J.T. Mitchell, Winter.

Daedalus, "On Happiness," ed. James Miller, Spring.

Denver Quarterly, "Literary Geography," guest ed. Paul Maliszewski, vol. 38, no. 4.

Mānoa, "In the Shadow of Angkor," ed. Frank Stewart and Sharon May, Summer.

The Massachusetts Review, "Food Matters," ed. Anita Mannur, Autumn.

Michigan Quarterly Review, "Viet Nam: Beyond the Frame," ed. Barbara Tran, Fall.

The Mississippi Review, "Politics and Religion," guest ed. Gary Percesepe, Fall.

Notre Dame Magazine, "The Love That Dare Not Speak Its Name," ed. Kerry Temple, Summer.

The Virginia Quarterly Review, "Integrated Education in America," ed. Ted Genoways, Winter.

Witness, "Our Best: 1987–2004," ed. Peter Stine, vol. 18, no. 2.

THE B·E·S·T AMERICAN SERIES®

THE BEST AMERICAN SHORT STORIES® 2005

Michael Chabon, guest editor, Katrina Kenison, series editor. "Story for story, readers can't beat the *Best American Short Stories* series" (*Chicago Tribune*). This year's most beloved short fiction anthology is edited by the Pulitzer Prize–winning novelist Michael Chabon and features stories by Tom Perrotta, Alice Munro, Edward P. Jones, Joyce Carol Oates, and Thomas McGuane, among others.

0-618-42705-8 PA $14.00 / 0-618-42349-4 CL $27.50

THE BEST AMERICAN ESSAYS® 2005

Susan Orlean, guest editor, Robert Atwan, series editor. Since 1986, *The Best American Essays* has gathered the best nonfiction writing of the year and established itself as the premier anthology of its kind. Edited by the best-selling writer Susan Orlean, this year's volume features writing by Roger Angell, Jonathan Franzen, David Sedaris, Andrea Barrett, and others.

0-618-35713-0 PA $14.00 / 0-618-35712-2 CL $27.50

THE BEST AMERICAN MYSTERY STORIES™ 2005

Joyce Carol Oates, guest editor, Otto Penzler, series editor. This perennially popular anthology is sure to appeal to crime fiction fans of all tastes. This year's volume is edited by the National Book Award winner Joyce Carol Oates and offers pieces by Scott Turow, Dennis Lehane, Louise Erdrich, George V. Higgins, and others.

0-618-51745-6 PA $14.00 / 0-618-51744-8 CL $27.50

THE BEST AMERICAN SPORTS WRITING™ 2005

Mike Lupica, guest editor, Glenn Stout, series editor. "An ongoing centerpiece for all sports collections" (*Booklist*), this series has garnered wide acclaim for its extraordinary sports writing and topnotch editors. Mike Lupica, the *New York Daily News* columnist and best-selling author, continues that tradition with pieces by Michael Lewis, Gary Smith, Bill Plaschke, Pat Jordan, L. Jon Wertheim, and others.

0-618-47020-4 PA $14.00 / 0-618-47019-0 CL $27.50

THE BEST AMERICAN TRAVEL WRITING 2005

Jamaica Kincaid, guest editor, Jason Wilson, series editor. Edited by the renowned novelist and travel writer Jamaica Kincaid, *The Best American Travel Writing 2005* captures the traveler's wandering spirit and ever-present quest for adventure. Giving new life to armchair journeys this year are Tom Bissell, Ian Frazier, Simon Winchester, John McPhee, and many others.

0-618-36952-X PA $14.00 / 0-618-36951-1 CL $27.50

THE B·E·S·T AMERICAN SERIES®

THE BEST AMERICAN SCIENCE AND NATURE WRITING 2005

Jonathan Weiner, guest editor, Tim Folger, series editor. This year's edition promises to be another "eclectic, provocative collection" (*Entertainment Weekly*). Edited by Jonathan Weiner, the author of *The Beak of the Finch* and *Time, Love, Memory*, it features work by Oliver Sacks, Natalie Angier, Malcolm Gladwell, Sherwin B. Nuland, and others.

0-618-27343-3 PA $14.00 / 0-618-27341-7 CL $27.50

THE BEST AMERICAN RECIPES 2005–2006

Edited by Fran McCullough and Molly Stevens. "Give this book to any cook who is looking for the newest, latest recipes and the stories behind them" (*Chicago Tribune*). Offering the very best of what America is cooking, as well as the latest trends, time-saving tips, and techniques, this year's edition includes a foreword by the celebrated chef Mario Batali.

0-618-57478-6 CL $26.00

THE BEST AMERICAN NONREQUIRED READING 2005

Edited by Dave Eggers, Introduction by Beck. Edited by the best-selling author Dave Eggers, this genre-busting volume draws the finest, most interesting, and least expected fiction, nonfiction, humor, alternative comics, and more from publications large, small, and on-line. With an introduction by the Grammy Award–winning musician Beck, this year's volume features writing by Jhumpa Lahiri, George Saunders, Aimee Bender, Stephen Elliott, and others.

0-618-57048-9 PA $14.00 / 0-618-57047-0 CL $27.50

THE BEST AMERICAN SPIRITUAL WRITING 2005

Edited by Philip Zaleski, Introduction by Barry Lopez. Featuring an introduction by the National Book Award winner Barry Lopez, *The Best American Spiritual Writing 2005* brings the year's finest writing about faith and spirituality to all readers. This year's volume gathers pieces from diverse faiths and denominations and includes writing by Natalie Goldberg, Harvey Cox, W. S. Merwin, Patricia Hampl, and others.

0-618-58643-1 PA $14.00 / 0-618-58642-3 CL $27.50

HOUGHTON MIFFLIN COMPANY www.houghtonmifflinbooks.com